The Short Road
to Great Presentations

The Short Road to Great Presentations

How to Reach Any Audience Through Focussed Preparation, Inspired Delivery, and Smart Use of Technology

Cheryl Reimold

Peter Reimold

Scarsdale, NY

IEEE Professional Communication Society, *Sponsor*

IEEE Press

A JOHN WILEY & SONS PUBLICATION

Published by John Wiley & Sons, Inc., Hoboken, New Jersey.

For general information on our other products and services please contact our Customer Care Department within the U.S. at 877-762-2974, outside the U.S. at 317-572-3993 or fax 317-572-4002.

Wiley also publishes its books in a variety of electronic formats. Some content that appears in print, however, may not be available in electronic format.

Library of Congress Cataloging-in-Publication Data is available.

ISBN 0-471-28136-0

Printed in the United States of America.

10 9 8 7 6 5 4 3 2 1

To Alfred H. Nissan
For his love, kindness, and support

Contents

Foreword xiii
Preface xv
Acknowledgments xvii

PART 1: AUDIENCE-FOCUSED PREPARATION

1   Knowing Your Audience and Purpose 3
How To Care About the Audience from the Start 5
Playing "Twenty Questions" with Your Audience 6
    The Importance of Being Specific in Your Questions 8
    Asking the Tough Questions — If Necessary, with Help 9
    Example 1-1: Audience and Purpose Analysis 10
    Example 1-2: Audience and Purpose Analysis 13
Exercises 16

2   A Universal Presentation Structure 23
The Basis for the Universal Presentation Structure 23
    The Need for Simple, Linear Order 23
    The Need for Well-Spaced Repetition 24
    The Need to Adapt to the Audience's Natural Attention Curve 24
Discussion 25

3   The *RAMP* Formula for Effective Introductions 27
The Four Functions of the Introduction 27
The Rapport Builder 28
    Title Slides vs. Rapport Builders 29
    Some Turn-Offs 29
Effective Attention Getters 30
    Four Important Reasons for an Attention Getter 31
    Delaying the Attention Getter 32
    Example of Problem or Benefit 32
    Anecdote 33
    Quote 34
    Question 35
    Visual 35
    Statistics 37
    Analogy 37
    Demo Object 38
    Demonstration Event 38
    How About Jokes as Ice-Breakers? 39
The Main Message 39
The Plan 40
Overcoming Common Obstacles to a Strong Start 42
    Obstacle #1: Fear of Being Different 42
    Obstacle #2: Fear of Commitment 43
    Obstacle #3: Fear of Appearing Biased or Unscientific 43
    Obstacle #4: Fear of Losing Suspense 44
    Obstacle #5: The "I Have No Message, Only Information" Fallacy 45
Exercises and Discussion 48

4   The Body 51
Making It Easy To Follow 51
           A Simple, Linear Structure 51
           Helpful Repetition 52
           No Unnecessary or Overly Complex Details **52**
Keeping It Varied 53
Using the Power of Examples 55
           Why Do People Avoid Using Examples? 57
Example 4-3: Poorly Structured Presentation 57
Example 4-4: More Effective Presentation Approach and Structure 59
Exercises and Discussion 63

5   The Summary 65
How To Summarize 65
A Cardinal Error: Outstaying Your Welcome 67
Exercises and Discussion 68

6   Preparing Effective Visuals 69
Being Selective: Know Your Purpose 69
Choosing the Right Chart Type 70
Making Text and Images Big and Bold (The 18-Point Rule) 72
Keeping It Simple and Easy To Process (The Three-Second Rule) 73
           Some Simple Ways To Make Visuals Easier To Process 74
           The Limits of Direct Labeling 78
           Word Charts and the Three-Second Rule 79
Making Key Ideas Memorable Through Graphics 81
           Why Create Memorable Visuals? 81
           Using Symbolic Images As a Layout Element 82
           Using Graphics for (Tasteful and Gentle) Humorous Effect 84
           How To Produce Memorable Visuals 84
           A Caveat 87
Using Color to Advantage 87
           A Balanced Palette: How Your Software Can Help 88
           The Color Wheel 88
           Common Color Schemes Based on the Color Wheel 89
           Psychology of Colors 91
Exercises 92

7   Notes, Rehearsing, and Handouts 97
Preparing Notes and Rehearsing 97
           Right and Wrong Notes 97
           Practicing From Your Notes 98
           Weaning Yourself From Your Notes 99
           Answers to Some Common Questions About Notes 99
Being Prepared for Trouble 101
           Problems with Equipment or Facilities 101
           Problems with Time or Audience Resistance 103
Preparing Handouts 103
Exercise and Discussion 104

PART 2: PERSUASIVE DELIVERY

8   The Magic of Connection   109
     The Triangle of Power: Real You, Real Audience, Real Purpose   109
     Four Aspects of Audience Connection   110

9   The Winning Attitude   113
     The Starting Point: A Caring Attitude   113
          Check Your Preparation   113
          Check the Setup   114
          Learn To Love *Any* Audience   115
     The Power of a Smile
     Beating Stage Fright   115
     Exercises   118

10   Connecting Through Body Talk   121
     Getting Past the "Terror Line" Into Comfortable Contact Zone   121
     Keeping in Touch Through Motivated Movement   123
     Energy—The Language of Success   123
          Finding Your Base: The Athletic Stance   123
          Focusing Energy in Your Upper Body   126
     Developing Natural, Useful Gestures   128
          1. Common Action Verbs   131
          2. Other Common Words and Phrases   132
          3. Abstract Ideas Made Concrete   133
     Understanding and Controlling Body Language   135

     Exercises   135

11   Connecting Through Voice and Language   139
     The Basics: Be Heard and Understood   139
     Improving Your Articulation   139
     The Right Speed   143
     Emotions and Voice   142
          A Simple Exercise To Improve Your Expressiveness   143
          The Heavy Price of Shunning Emotions   144
          Controlling Your Pitch   145
     Using Language That Reaches People   145
          Word Choice and Your Listeners' Learning Styles   147
     Overcoming Distracting Verbal Habits   147
          Getting Rid of "Uhm," "You Know," and Other Verbal Crutches   147
     Exercises   149

12   Staying in Touch Through Eye Contact   151
     The Art of Conversing with Your Eyes   151
     Eye Contact and Fear   152
     How To Achieve Strong Eye Contact   153
     Exercise and Discussion   155

13   Handling Notes 157
Park or Carry? 157
Recovering From an Omission 158
Exercise 159

14   Handling Visuals 161
Reviewing Your Preparation and Setup 161
Keeping in Touch with Your Audience 167
Avoiding Distractions 170
    Pointer Fiddling 170
    Moving Shadows 170
    Demo Objects or Samples 170
Special Issues with Overhead Projectors 171
    The Keystone Effect 171
    Transparencies Sliding Around or Falling Off 173
    Transparencies Curling and Floating Off the Projector 173
Exercises and Discussion 174

15   Handling Questions 175
Reducing Surprises Through Preparation 175
Deciding When To Take Questions 176
Setting and Using Q&A Rules 176
Basic Question-Handling Skills 177
    Controlling Your Body Language While Dealing with Questions 178
    Your Key Skill: "Simple Answer First" 179
    What To Do When You Don't Know the Answer 181
    Handling Multiple Questions 182
    Handling Complex Questions 183
    Postponing Questions 183
    Diverting Off-Track Questions 184
    Stopping People From Monopolizing the Discussion 184
    Closing the Session with Style and Focus 185
Handling Hostile Questions 185
    Problem #1: The Unsettling Effect of a Surprise Attack 186
    Problem #2: The Lingering Effect of the Caustic Question or Remark 186
    Problem #3: The Tendency for the Attack To Continue 187
Exercises 188

16   Dealing with Unpleasant Surprises 195
Equipment Troubles 195
The "Shrinking Time" Problem 196
Bored or Turned-Off Audience 196
Sleepers 198
Side Shows 198
Impromptu Presentations 199
    Prepared "Impromptu" Speeches 199
    Dealing with True Surprises 199
Exercises 201

17   Moderating a Conference Session 203
Common Complaints About Conference Sessions 203
Learning Your ABC — or PQR 204
The Power of Early Preparation 204
            Motivating Speakers To Prepare Well and Early 205
            Getting a Head Start on Your Own Contributions 205
            Laying the Groundwork for Interesting Questions 206
On the Scene: Making Your Contract with the Speakers 207
Getting Off to a Strong Start 207
Keeping the Session Lively But Under Control 208
Closing the Session in Style 209
The Art of Stimulating Discussion Through Good Questions 210
            Using Focused Questions 210
            Specific Use of Focused Questions in Panel Discussions 211
Controlling Uncivilized or Otherwise Out-of-Line Questions 211
Exercises 212

PART 3: MAKING THE MOST OF PRESENTATION TECHNOLOGY

18   Making the Transition to Electronic Slide Shows 219
Scenario 1: Gone with the Wind II 219
Scenario 2: Hot Under the Collar 220
Is It Worth Getting Involved? 222
A Painless Migration Path via Color Transparencies 222
Incorporating Color Photographs 223
Moving to Electronic Slide Shows 224
        Typical Equipment 225
        Audio and Video Integration 225

19   Using Presentation Software Intelligently 227
Making Visuals Easy To See and Understand 227
Achieving Consistency and Balance Through Slide Masters 233
Using Content Templates 234
Using and Customizing Electronic Clip Art 236
Preparing Slide Shows 239
        The Triple Challenge 239
        Transitions 240
        Text Animation, or Build-Up Slides 241
        Animating Graphics 242
        Hidden Slides 243
        Optional Branches to Embedded Presentations 244
        Black Slides 245
        Embedding Video, Sound, and Other Applications in Your Show 245

Exercises 246

20   Practicing and Delivering Slide Shows   255
The Radical Approach to Practicing   255
A Sample Practice Session Without Projector   257
      Practicing Setup   257
      Practicing Troubleshooting Image and Sound Problems   259
      Practicing Slide Show Control   262
Practicing with a Projector   267
Delivering Your Electronic Presentation   267
      Basic Setup   267
      Projector Setup   269
      Troubleshooting   269
Issues with Remote Controls   271
Show Time!   272
Exercise and Discussion   273

21   Web Presentations and Web Meetings   275
What Is an E-Meeting?   275
Why Meet This Way?   276
Getting Started   276
Presentations, the Web, and Multimedia   276
      Visiting the Web During a Presentation   277
      Saving a Presentation for Web Delivery   277
      Adding Animation, Transitions, and Video or Audio Clips   277
      Narrated Presentations   279
Exercises   280

Appendix A   Sample Annotated Presentation Structure   285
Appendix B   Procedure and Worksheet for Analyzing Audience and Purpose   287
Appendix C   General Presentation Outline Form   291
Appendix D   Specific Outlines for Common Presentation Types   293
Appendix E   Checklist for Presentations   305

Solutions to Exercises   307

Index   333

Foreword

When I was asked to review Peter and Cheryl Reimold's manuscript as a potential book for the IEEE Press and Wiley & Sons, I replied immediately:

> You will have a winner if you publish this book. The authors' rationale is "spot on." There are many books on **what** to do to make an effective oral presentation; few books show in depth **how** to do it. This one does just that.

Over one hundred years ago, in 1901, the Society for the Promotion of Engineering Education (SPEE) reported that "The writing skills of Engineering students are deplorable and need to be addressed by engineering colleges." In the ensuing years engineering professors took heed and quietly started introducing technical writing into the curriculum, and subsequently published their ideas in what became the first books on technical communication. In 1908 T. A. Rickard wrote:

> Language is a vehicle of expression designed to convey ideas from one man to another. It was not intended for the soliloquy; civilized man does not live by himself, nor does he talk to himself. *(We have to forgive Rickard for using language that was not gender-neutral: he was not yet aware that women would be entering the engineering profession.)*
>
> Conscientious writers try to improve their mode of expression by precision of terms, by careful choice of words, and by the arrangement of them so that they become efficient carriers of thought from one mind to another.
>
> If you describe a stamp-mill to an experienced mill-man, a mining student, or a bishop, you will vary the manner of telling. The most effective will be that which has a sympathetic appreciation of the other fellow's receptiveness. Do not plant carnations in a clay soil, or rice in a sand-heap.

Rickard was followed in the US by Karl Owen Thompson (1922: *"English is more than a tool, it is a part of life itself in its many activities."*) and J. Raleigh Nelson (1940: *"In report writing, in particular, there is an increasing demand that the first page or two shall provide a comprehensive idea of the whole report."*), and in the UK by Reginald Kapp (1948: *"You must consider carefully the extent of [the reader's] knowledge, his range of interests, his likes and dislikes, his capacity for understanding, his limitations...[and] his receptivity for the information you have to impart."*).

All four authors focused on the need to clearly identify their audience before writing, and Nelson was the first person to draw attention to what we now call the executive summary. Yet none of them mentioned that most of technical professionals' communications are oral, either in person-to-person conversations or in a more formal delivery at a meeting or conference. Or that the guidelines they offer for writing apply equally to oral communications.

In the intervening years, other authors have written books that describe what one needs to do to speak well, but the Reimolds are the first to provide unique prescriptions that demonstrate *how* to do it. And their ideas are just as valuable for the business speaker as they are for the technical speaker.

In the following chapters you will see how, like their counterparts who tell us how to write well, they stress the need to identify one's purpose and focus attention on the audience; how to identify the main message and place it up front; how to capture and hold listeners' attention; and how to use visuals to good effect. They also tell us how to make speakers' notes, how to rehearse, how to speak confidently, and how to use body language to close the gap between speaker and audience. And they convey their message in a style that appeals to readers, because they use a strong "you" approach that is both personable and comfortably readable.

I hope you enjoy reading their book as much as I have.

Ron Blicq
President, RGI International

Preface

Let's keep this short. Preparing for presentations typically takes too long, and the results aren't what people hoped for. This book will help you with these common problems. It shows you how to get to a great presentation in one go, without rework. You'll learn to follow a systematic approach that cuts out the guesswork.

The material has been arranged as a self-teaching course, essentially mirroring intensive presentation skills seminars we have taught for more than two decades. Take the presentation skills self-assessment (Exercise 1-2), which will tell you what parts of the course need your special attention. Then work through the rest of the course, making sure to complete those exercises that fall within your personal improvement areas.

The "Short Road" we're showing you here is the *direct* route, with no unnecessary detours. It ignores all the fussy nonessentials that worry so many presenters and focuses on the real musts:

- A single-minded focus on the audience and their needs and interests
- A clear grasp of what goals you can realistically achieve in a given presentation
- A simple structure that works for you every time
- Visuals and other backup material that supports your message in persuasive and varied ways
- The attitudes and techniques that will keep you connected to the audience all through your talk
- Helpful technology that you should learn to use efficiently

Taking that Short Road is not at all difficult, but it requires a bit of *self-discipline*. In particular, you must avoid the temptation of taking *shortcuts* (such as today's favorite, filling in some Wizard outline template before even thinking about the audience). Those shortcuts usually are anything but short; on the contrary, they cost you lots of time and extra effort. Why? Because you'll end up redoing everything from scratch.

So, get ready to do some good, clear, original thinking within a surefire, systematic framework. The results, we are sure, will please you.

One last point: We always like to hear from people who are interested in improving their communication skills. There are two easy ways to get in touch with us. One, you can reach us by e-mail; the address is **perccom@aol.com**. Two, we invite you to visit our web site at **www.allaboutcommunication.com**, where you will find useful information not only about presenting but all aspects of communication.

Best luck in your efforts, and we hope to hear from you!

Peter Reimold
Cheryl Reimold

Acknowledgments

Many people have been influential and helpful in creating this book. First of all, we would like to thank our editor at the IEEE Press, Chrissy Kuhnen, for encouraging us to take on this project despite our objections that we were too busy with professional and personal commitments. Our anonymous reviewers pointed out many opportunities for improvement, all of which we were delighted to follow. Andrew Prince at Wiley & Sons saw us through the demanding process of production and helped (we hope) to make this an easy-to-read book.

Above all, we want to thank our students over the years, who participated in our workshops and individual coaching programs with good humor and amazing energy. They taught us what works and what doesn't work in learning presentation skills. We hope that you will profit from their collective experience, as distilled by us.

PART 1

AUDIENCE-FOCUSED PREPARATION

1   Knowing Your Audience and Purpose 3

2   A Universal Presentation Structure 23

3   The *RAMP* Formula for Effective Introductions 27

4   The Body 51

5   The Summary 65

6   Preparing Effective Visuals 69

7   Notes, Rehearsing, and Handouts 97

1

Knowing Your Audience and Purpose

When we asked workshop participants once what they most wanted to learn, one of them (let's call him George) replied: "Some tips and techniques on delivery." Of course, we wanted to know what kinds of delivery tips he was interested in. After some hesitation, he admitted that he was looking for things that would make him "more lovable" to the audience.

We thought the request charming in its honesty. Who doesn't feel that way to some extent? Yet who would admit craving affection from the audience? We're all much too cool for that!

Unfortunately, though, the underlying idea, expressed pictorially in Figure 1-1, is all wrong. What works is the reverse, shown in Figure 1-2: the audience wants to know that you care about *them* and *their* interests.

Figure 1-1. The self-directed view of presentation success — a sure recipe for failure.

Figure 1-2. The audience-directed presentation attitude — the only one that leads to success.

Of course, it's tempting to sneak yourself back into the "beneficiary" position, as in Figure 1-3 — a creative combination of the two presentation philosophies. Unfortunately, that also does not work. It's not honest caring at all but just a deceitful form of self-love — and the audience will spot it immediately and detest it. In short, as soon as "please love me!" is in that picture, you'll get the opposite of what you crave.

There is a two-part lesson here:

1. Care honestly about the audience.
2. Do it without any notion of rewards — those will take care of themselves.

There is a second interesting point about our friend George's question. Is all this a matter of *delivery* — say, a good smile, strong eye contact, and enthusiastic inflection? No way! Just think about it. What does the audience most want from you? Something they can *use!* They want *value* from you. But that doesn't come from your smile, your eye contact, or your voice; it comes from the material you've prepared for them. So, if you really care about them, you can't just start loving them when you stand up there; ***care has to be the driving force behind all your preparation.***

This is the secret behind all great presentations: honestly caring about the audience from beginning to end, and going out of your way to tailor everything to their needs and limitations. It's more than technique — it's a basic attitude that requires a deep shift in thinking. This is not achieved at the last minute, as you face the audience, or even at one sitting in presentations training. For example, it took George quite a few workshop sessions and a bit of personal feedback to change his self-centered approach — but he finally did and became a very successful, respected presenter.

Figure 1-3. The manipulator's version of self-directed love — another guarantee of presentation failure.

That's what this book is all about: how to develop that attitude of caring about the audience, and how to *express* it through your material and your delivery. If you can do that, you will become a truly great presenter. So, remember:

> **It all starts with the audience.**
> **Your job is to *care* about them**
> **and to *prove* that you care**
> **by giving them value.**

HOW TO CARE ABOUT THE AUDIENCE FROM THE START

Your starting point is a good understanding of your listeners. Great presentations are radical in their focus on the audience. They address real people with real needs and ask them for a real response. Poor presentations (including many that seem quite polished) play out in thin air, removed from the audience, in an abstract space of ideas. Because they don't address real people, they rarely get a real response, either.

Your first job, then, is to understand clearly

1. Who the audience is
2. What you want them to *do* or *believe*
3. What the important audience *needs* and *interests* are

Thinking about these three things will lead to a strong ***main message*** and possible ***key points*** that matter to the audience. Unfortunately, most presenters totally omit this step —

Tip
To develop audience-focused material, start your preparation by writing down (1) your purpose and (2) as many detailed, realistic audience questions and objections as you can think of. Then let your ideas grow out of your answers to those questions and comments.

and that is the main reason they end up with weak material and awkward delivery. You just can't feel good about a presentation when you haven't done your homework and thought about the people who have to listen to it. And you can't get a proper response when you've never thought about what you want from the audience.

Many books mention the need for an audience analysis — but few make it clear that this is the key to presentation success. What's more, it will rarely be enough to do it once; you have to revisit it several times as you progress with your preparation. Why is this? Because as we get involved in the details of preparation, our self-centered nature reasserts itself and we lose track of our audience. We may still remember our own purpose (although even that usually gets lost once we start wrestling with the visuals), but the audience intrudes only occasionally as a vaguely frightening, faceless mob that we want nothing to do with.

Remember: caring about the audience starts with preparation — and it means thinking seriously about their needs, concerns, limitations, and questions. Any minutes you invest in this thinking will be repaid handsomely in goodwill and affection from your listeners, because they'll recognize that you have done the unusual: gone out of your way to give them something of real value to them.

PLAYING "TWENTY QUESTIONS" WITH YOUR AUDIENCE

Your audience analysis need not be formal; in fact, the messier it is, the better it may be. The key is to make it *real* and *lively*. Have an informal discussion with the audience. As you tell them what to do or believe, let them call in their questions and comments. Let them be direct, tough, even obnoxious; let them verbalize all their private thoughts, fears, misgivings, wishes.

The scheme in Figure 1-4 summarizes the main things to consider in such an analysis. But the analysis can be as simple as a list of twenty questions and objections the people in the audience might have. If you are the kind of person who likes to work with forms, use the one in Appendix B or make up your own. If you hate forms, just jot down the questions and comments. Following a format is less important than being *specific* and *tough*.

Strong presentations grow out of a good understanding of the audience. Here are the main questions you should consider in analyzing the needs of your audience and the purpose of your presentation. In its simplest form, your analysis will be a list of audience questions and objections that you must address, plus a list of things you want to say and achieve.

Questions	*Actions/Answers*
1. YOU AND YOUR PURPOSE	
What do you want to tell them?	Write draft of main message.
What do you want to happen as result of your talk? - immediately - in the long run	List what you want them to - do - believe
What can you realistically achieve in your presentation?	List things they can take in and remember. List things that will need written backup (handout).
2. THE AUDIENCE AND THEIR NEEDS	
Who are they?	List individuals or groups who will attend.
What do they want to know?	List all questions different people or groups might have.
What do they hate or fear? Why might they not accept what you are saying?	List all objections and emotional comments.
What do they like or need?	List likes and needs; translate into benefits that can outweigh objections.
What's unfamiliar to them? What might they have trouble understanding?	List concepts needing an explanation.
What do they already know?	List familiar concepts you can use to explain unfamiliar ones. List "old news" not to belabor.

Main Message
3-5 Key Points
Extra Questions To Be Prepared for

Figure 1-4. General scheme for a thorough Audience & Purpose Analysis.

Tip

By doing a proper audience analysis, you also take care of half the preparation for questions. The important questions should form the core of your presentation; the others are your list of additional questions for which you need to prepare answers.

This early stage of preparation is also the best time to decide the *format* of the presentation. Is interaction essential — say, because you want to reach a consensus at the end? Then you'll want to encourage questions throughout or at the end of each section (unless the audience includes some very disruptive or controlling people). Generally, to engage your audience, *use the least formal and most interactive format.*

The Importance of Being Specific in Your Questions

We said you should write down 20 questions the audience might have. Why so many? (Often, you will have trouble coming up with more than five.) The reason is that the first few questions you write down are apt to be vague, general ones: "How will this work?" or "Will this improve our quality?" Your listeners do want answers to those broad questions — but they will be much more engaged when they hear you verbalizing and answering very *specific* concerns of theirs: "How will departments A, B, and C and operations X and Y be affected while we implement this?" "What kind of training will we need, who will take care of it, and how long will it take?" "How will this lower our rejects rate?" "How will this create new marketing appeal?" "How will this open up the possibility of new product lines?" "How will this affect color uniformity?" "How can we be sure that solving this one set of problems will not cause problems in other areas, such as ...?"

Some of your listeners might be looking forward to nursing all their grudges and private concerns while tuning you out. When they hear you addressing their questions directly, it will draw them in and make them take you seriously. At the least, it will get their attention, because they're not used to dealing with mind readers!

Often, you know the detailed questions different people in the audience have, if you only think about it a little bit. Pushing yourself to come up with question 11, 12, or 13 will set that thinking in motion. So don't stop after five questions; go on until you feel you've really covered all the ground.

But what if you just don't know enough about your audience to think of detailed questions? The temptation is great to stick with generalities — and bore your listeners. The solution is obvious: *ask!* Even if you don't know people well, they will usually not resent a few targeted questions about their concerns. And if you can't ask them directly, or you are really uncomfortable doing it in a given case, you may know somebody who can help you indirectly. It can make all the difference.

For example, we once were invited to give a talk to 50 salespeople on how to give an effective presentation. We do know something about presentations, and we could have just answered a few general questions about effective presenting. However, we had never dealt with any of these people before, and we were not sure what exactly their needs and problems were. So, we started asking some questions.

First, we asked the person who had invited us, and he gave us some ideas of the problems these sales reps faced when giving sales presentations. He also sent us examples of sales "scripts" they had followed in previous years. But we wanted to get a better feel for the different people in our audience. So we talked to three sales reps in different parts of the country — and we got three very different views of presentation problems we should address! For instance, we knew there was interest in specific questions such as: "How do you present information on 20 new products and 10 product improvements without overwhelming the audience?" "How do you reach distributor sales reps who'd rather be out selling than listen to you?" "How do you stand out from five competitors also presenting on the same day?" "What do you do with the 'script' management gives us?"

Those were the questions that formed the core of our interactive presentation — and they turned it into an enjoyable, productive event, with people participating vigorously. They knew the material was relevant to them — because they had told us so beforehand. Answering general questions such as "How do you prepare and deliver a good presentation?" could never have produced the same response.

So, push until you get to the specific questions that reflect what's really on the audience's mind — and if you don't know what those questions are, do the leg work and find out!

Asking the Tough Questions — If Necessary, with Help

One of the things that makes presenters fearful is the dread of tough questions. Well, they will be much easier to handle when you have thought about them beforehand and worked out some convincing answers, perhaps backed up by visuals that show your data, process details, or the like.

Here are some tough questions you should *always* be prepared for:

- Why do we need this?
- How much does it cost?
- How much do we save?
- What are the *real* costs — including all the downtime, extra trials, etc.?
- Will it really work? How do we know?
- Who has done this before? Has it worked?
- How long will this take? (Why not shorter?)
- Why don't we do something else?
- How can we be sure all reasonable alternatives have been considered?
- How reliable are the data? How well do they correspond with other data from previous work or the literature?
- Can we trust you (or others) to *implement* this without problems?
- What troubles can we expect as we go along with this?
- How will other processes, departments, etc. be affected?
- When problems develop, who will take care of them and how?

Some of these are things you really don't want to think about. The trouble is, the audience probably *will* think about them — and then you'll have to answer without proper preparation. If you can't get tough enough with yourself, ask a friendly colleague to do it for you.

Don't forget tough comments or thoughts like "Leave me alone — I'm just here because I *have* to be here. (Wake me up when this is over.)" If you've been involved in mandatory safety talks, you (and everybody in the audience!) will have watched thinkers of these thoughts luxuriously snoozing through your presentation. How are you going to reach them? Are you going to think about that only at delivery time, or are you going to address it from the start? Perhaps you could have a straight talk with such people beforehand and figure out some ways to involve them. The point is, answering these irreverent comments, hurtful as they are, is the best way to lift your talk above the usual boring, repetitive mandatory presentation.

EXAMPLE 1-1: AUDIENCE AND PURPOSE ANALYSIS

In one of our seminars, an engineer gave a presentation on a certain computerized system intended to replace error-prone manual control. The intended audience was a group of operators who were expected to work with the new system. The speaker began with a comprehensive flowchart of the system that showed how all the parts worked together. He then discussed each of the control screens people would see for different parts of the operation. He concluded by inviting suggestions for improving the system.

This presentation seemed built on the assumption that the audience had just one major question: "How does this new system work?" In answer to that question, the speaker had developed a complete "information" talk. But was this appropriate? Or did the audience have some other needs, questions, and objections? And did the speaker have some purpose other than giving his listeners the information they needed?

The answer to both questions was yes. First, the audience could be expected to be hostile, skeptical, and afraid. The speaker had no trouble imagining their questions and objections; in fact, he'd heard the operators say some of them:

- So how many people are going to lose their job because of this new system?
- New stuff never works; this won't either.
- When it doesn't work, who will get the blame? I will!
- When things go wrong in the middle of the night, who will help me? Nobody!
- This newfangled computer stuff is too complicated to understand.
- Even if I understand it, how am I supposed to *remember* all this?
- I liked the old system: I knew what I was doing.
- Keep it simple: What buttons do I push? Then what happens?
- Suppose I do get things to work well. Who'll get credit? Not me!
- I don't want to be here; wake me up when it's over.

Second, the speaker had two urgent goals that had little to do with "giving information." Goal 1 was to overcome the operators' resistance to the new system and make them excited about it. Showing them schematic slides of all the control screens was not going to achieve that. Goal 2 was to get the operators to participate in fine-tuning the system by contributing what they knew about controlling each part of the process. That was why he had asked for suggestions at the end of his talk. The fact was, the new system was not yet really useful: at this point, it was set up to monitor every conceivable variable, regardless of importance. To give efficient control, the system had to be much more selective in the variables and ranges it highlighted at different stages of the production process. And the people who knew best which were the relevant variables and ranges were the operators.

The audience analysis that emerged from this looked something like this:

1. PURPOSE

What do I want to tell them?

The new computerized material control system is a great tool that will make work easier, safer, and more pleasant for you. However, I need your support and input so we can fine-tune it.

What do I want them to DO as a result of this talk?

Immediately:

Give input on appropriate control variables, ranges, etc.

Voice all concerns, objections, questions so we can address them.

In the long run:

Support the new system; get involved in optimizing it.

What do I want them to BELIEVE as a result of this talk?

Nobody will lose his or her job.

I'm on your side and appreciate your support and any information you can give.

The system will make things easier and safer.

Successes will be shared.

You'll get training and help on any problems you may run into.

What can I realistically achieve in this presentation? What can they take in and remember?

Benefits; importance of participating in optimizing system.

General nature of system; rough function of a control screen; major problems to watch out for.

How to get help.

Written support/handouts/follow-up:

Phone numbers and names for help.

Overview of system; system manual with detailed instructions for each control screen.

See them on the job: train, observe, get reactions and more input.

2. AUDIENCE

Who are they?
    Operators.

What do they want to know?
    What's in it for me?
    How does it work, in general terms?
    What do I do if I have questions?
    What do I do if things go wrong?

What do they hate or fear?
    Anything new.
    Complicated things; things that don't work.
    Not getting credit.
    Not being consulted or taken seriously; being treated as stupid.
    Not getting help.
    Getting blamed for failure.
    Losing the option of overtime.

What do they like or need?
    Feeling important, needed, appreciated.
    Getting help promptly.
    Things that are easy, safe.

What benefits could outweigh objections?
    Easier (objection: "new").
    Training; help hotline; clear manual (objection: "complicated computer stuff").
    Challenge; promise of credit and glory (objection: "won't work").

What do they already know? History of system.

What's unfamiliar to them?
    Total integrated computer control for this work area; programming and system detail.
    Theoretical issues in process control.

    Difficult details to skip:
        Details of control screens, theoretical control issues, equations, etc.

    Familiar concepts to use to explain important unfamiliar ones:
        Valves, levels, visual inspection, gauges.

From that kind of analysis, it's easy to choose a main message and a few key points that will get results with this audience. The stress should be on benefits, answers to objections, and the help that will be available; technical details should be presented in small chunks, with immediate chance for questions and discussion so the audience isn't asked to remember complex material for a long time. Here is a possibility:

> ***Main Message:*** *We have a great new system for automatically monitoring all the levels and properties of our process materials. This system will make work easier, safer, and more pleasant for you. However, I need your support and input so we can fine-tune it, and that's what I hope to achieve with you today.*

> ***Key Point 1:*** *The system will save you work, hassle, worry, errors, downtime, and friction with management — and you'll have a good chance for personal credit and glory if we can make it work as well as expected.*

> ***Key Point 2:*** *It poses no threats or costs to you: nobody will lose his job, nobody will have to work harder, there will be no effect on overtime — and if you run into problems, you have access to round-the-clock help.*

> ***Key Point 3:*** *The system is really simple — just like the gauges, visual levels, and valves you're used to. I'll explain it section by section, and at the end of each section I'll stop to get your suggestions and answer any questions. Of course, you'll also get plenty of training and a good manual.*

The analysis also suggests some nice details of approach, such as playing benefits off against objections in order to bring them to life. For instance, the speaker might say:

> *You may be thinking "I liked the old system." But did you really, always? How about in the rain? Did you like climbing up high storage vessels to check the level? What about downtime when you forgot to check? Did you enjoy the yelling, the threats of getting fired and all that? Did you enjoy the "bad press" your whole department got for the poor production or quality records? All these things will disappear with the new system.*

All in all, a few minutes of realistic, caring thinking about the audience would have produced material for a very successful talk to a difficult audience. As a bonus, the speaker would have immediately made good decisions on how and when to handle questions and done half the preparation for question-and-answer. That's what it means to take the short road to a great presentation!

EXAMPLE 1-2: AUDIENCE AND PURPOSE ANALYSIS

A controller addressed a group of engineers with a talk on financials. His chosen main message was: "Controlling costs is *everybody's* job — and you can't do that properly unless you understand financials." After noting that most engineers lacked even the most basic understanding of financial terms and theory, he went on to describe 15 financial measures commonly used to monitor the performance of the company.

Tip

Whenever you have a choice, make your main message positive. The audience will find it easier to like you when you say "I would like to help you with X" than when you tell them "You've been doing everything wrong; here is what you've got to do."

It may not surprise you that this presenter felt stiff and removed from the audience throughout his whole talk. First, he had chosen a *negative message*. Of course, there are situations where you have no choice but deliver a negative message — but this was not one of them. Listeners don't like to be told that they *have* to do things and that they are *incompetent*. They'd rather be told that you can help them do some exciting things, and that they'll benefit from it — and such an approach was perfectly possible in this case.

Second, these engineers probably were not interested in a detailed run-down on 15 financial measures; that was more than they could possibly absorb, let alone remember. On the other hand, they did have some important questions and objections that should have been addressed in this talk. Here are some of them:

- Isn't it *our* job to do outstanding engineering, and *your* job to worry about finance? Why not let everybody do the things they do best?
- I'm tired of cost cutting. What about quality and technical excellence?
- Finance is boring.
- What's in it for me?
- I don't have a head for finance. Isn't this beyond me?
- What's the best way for me to learn these things?
- Would an MBA program give me the right information, or is the company using special methods? (The latter turned out to be true.)

An effective audience/purpose analysis for this presentation might then look as follows:

1. PURPOSE

What do I want to tell them?

You can make a big difference to the company as well as to your career by taking financial factors into account as you do your engineering work.

What do I want them to DO as result of my talk?
Immediately:

Start learning about financials, through books and discussion.

In the long run:

Integrate financial thinking into their work; contribute to cost control.

What do I want them to BELIEVE as result of my talk?

Finance is challenging, not boring.

Finance is a friend and career helper, not an enemy.

Finance is much easier to learn than people assume.

What can I realistically achieve in this presentation?
> Persuade them to keep an open mind about financials; to start learning more about financials and to consider them in their projects and daily work.
> Explain the concepts most important to the company (kick off the learning process).

What will need written or other support?
> Details, equations on most financial factors.
> Basics of financial control (article and references).

2. AUDIENCE

Who are they?
> Mostly young engineers; some older engineers.

What do they want to know?
> What are the benefits to them?
> Where can they get more information — if possible, quickly, easily, cheaply?
> Just how can they apply such knowledge on the job? (Examples)

What do they hate or fear?
> Being restrained by financial people or financial controls.
> Feeling insecure about financial theory and practice.
> Being overwhelmed with lots of numbers, derivations, and equations.
> ANY talk about cutting costs.

What do they like or need?
> Ways to further their career.
> Challenging work.
> Getting credit for achievement.
> Learning new things.
> Doing things well.

What's unfamiliar to them? What might they have trouble understanding?
> Details: equations; relationships between variables.

What do they already know?
> Company wants everybody to cut costs.
> Some basic financial terms: ROI, productivity, cost, sales, inventory, etc. (general idea only).

Looking at that analysis, you would come up with a very different presentation — say:

Main Message: *You can make a big difference to the company as well as to your career by taking financial factors into account as you do your engineering work. My staff and I will be happy to help you with that.*

Key Point 1: Some technical people in the company have been very successful because they treated financial performance as an exciting challenge — and you can do the same.

Key Point 2: It's much easier than you'd think; I'll start the learning process by explaining the three most important concepts.

Key Point 3: Once you get started, there are plenty of resources available to help you deepen your knowledge, including people in the company, books, and some articles and other handouts I'll give you at the end of this talk. [Bulk of original talk to be handled by a handout explaining all the financial measures that routinely appear in company reports]

You would probably also see that an interactive, informal setting would work best, because it would help get the listeners involved and diminish the hostility toward finance. After explaining a key financial factor, you might stop to take questions and discuss some of the listeners' projects, to show them ways to integrate financial control into their work.

EXERCISES

Exercise 1-1. Choose one of the following topics and do an Audience and Purpose Analysis, using Examples 1-1 and 1-2 in this chapter as guidance. That is, define your purpose, note likely audience questions and objections, and use the result to develop a strong main message and 3–5 key points.

Topic	Audience
a. A hobby of yours	A group of retirees
b. Loyalty	Disillusioned employees
c. Loyalty	Managers under continuous performance and cost-cutting pressure
d. The urgent need to deliver more to the customer, at lower cost, in order to stay competitive (You are the manager of a production facility.)	Employees who already feel stretched to the limit and are afraid to lose vacation time, travel budgets, etc.

Exercise 1-2. Self-assessment of presentation skills

Use the following self-assessment to decide which areas of presentation skills you should concentrate on as you work through this book. In the first column, put a number from 0 to 10 to indicate the improvement need. The second column lists some ideas for making progress in each area, including chapters to study in depth. In this column, you can also add notes describing your problem in more detail, plus your own ideas for making progress.

Improvement Areas *(Degree: 0 = OK, 1= minor,…, 10 = big problem)*	Possible Approaches *(Also note details of problem & own ideas for improving)*
PREPARATION ISSUES	
Preparation takes too long __	Follow process outlined in App. B; study all of Part 1 of book, & esp. Chs. 1, 3-4, and 7.
Material scattered, poorly organized__	Study Chs. 1-5.
Material often too complex, high-level__	Do audience analysis (Ch.1); leave some details for Q&A and handout.
Material often too detailed for audience__	Do audience analysis (Ch.1); leave some details for Q&A and handout.
Material often **incomplete:** important points missing__	Do thorough audience analysis (Ch. 1).

Exercise 1-2. Self-assessment of presentation skills *(continued)*

PREPARATION ISSUES *(continued)*	
Material heavy, dry; no relief for audience__	Start with lively introduction (Ch. 3); use *variety* in the body (Ch. 4).
Boring visuals__	See Ch. 6; also, vary between visuals and *other* support.
Unclear visuals (hard to read/understand)__	See Ch. 6.
Too many visuals__	Use *varied* means to support points; see Ch. 6.
Need more imaginative approaches to encourage **interaction** with the audience__	See Ch. 3 (Introduction) and 4 (Body).
Not enough **examples** or other **evidence** to persuade listeners__	See Ch. 4 (Body).
Bad **notes** (small, disorganized, etc.)__	See Ch. 7; also, wean yourself from notes.

Exercise 1-2. Self-assessment of presentation skills *(continued)*

DELIVERY ISSUES	
Losing point__	Use clear visuals & notes; practice as discussed in Ch. 7.
Dependent on notes__	See strategy in Ch. 7 for weaning yourself from notes.
Not much audience contact: tend to stay far away__	Work on attitude (Ch. 9) & body (Ch. 10).
Not enough eye contact__	Study Ch. 12; face people squarely while making eye contact.
Trouble moving around the room__	Study Ch. 10; work on *motivated* movement.
Finding audience interaction hard__	*Prepare* for it (see Chs. 1, 3, 4); work on *connecting* — esp. eye contact (Ch. 12); also see Ch. 15, Handling Questions.
Speaking too softly__	Work on voice projection (Ch. 11); lessen problem by moving into audience (see Ch. 10).
Rushing uncontrollably__	Make strong eye contact to get into "conversational mode"; slow down by *articulating super-clearly.*
Hesitation signals: "uhm," "and…," etc.__	Replace with *silence;* also, slow down by articulating clearly.
Tending toward monotone__	Use eye contact and moving into audience to get into conversational mode; develop strong message to get *enthusiastic* about.

Exercise 1-2. Self-assessment of presentation skills *(continued)*

DELIVERY ISSUES *(continued)*	
Articulation not always clear__	See Chapter 11 for special simple exercises.
Too serious or negative — no smile__	Have lively material, incl. attention getter (Ch. 3); improve attitude (Chs. 8 & 9).
Nervous at start__	Rehearse first minute thoroughly; have simple, lively attention getter.
Nervous throughout__	Put focus on *audience* (Ch. 1); practice strong eye contact; work on general attitude (Ch. 9); have good notes/visuals & practice from them.
Easily thrown off by interruptions__	Prepare thoroughly for questions (Chs. 1 & 7); improve Q&A skills (Ch. 15) and skills for handling surprises & difficult audiences.
Unsure what to do with hands__	Improve body language (Ch. 10); use energized upper body to support & illustrate your points.
Fiddling with hands, pointer, etc.__	Improve body language (Ch. 10).

Exercise 1-2. Self-assessment of presentation skills *(continued)*

HANDLING QUESTIONS	
Uncomfortable handling **any** questions__	Prepare thoroughly for Q&A (Chs. 1, 7); learn to *slow down;* work through Ch. 15.
Trouble answering **concisely**__	See Chapter 15.
Trouble answering **hostile** questions__	See Chapter 15.
Trouble handling **complex** or **multiple** questions__	See Chapter 15.

2

A Universal Presentation Structure

Once you have formulated your message and your key points, you need to fit them into the most effective structure so you can be sure to get the response you want. There is, in our experience, only one structure that works uniformly well for all presentations — technical or nontechnical, informative, or persuasive. This structure is as follows:

Introduction (1-2 minutes)	Body	Summary (1 minute)
• Rapport builder • Attention getter • Main message • Presentation plan (preview of key points)	• Three to five key points • Each key point backed up by varied evidence and examples	• Restatement of main message and key points • Call to action (or other memorable concluding thought)

THE BASIS FOR THE UNIVERSAL PRESENTATION STRUCTURE

We have been involved in revising many presentations and have always found that returning to this simple formula strengthened the final product. The main reason for this is that every audience has severe *limitations,* and the structure works with or around these limitations. Let's take a look at these limitations and the requirements they impose on presenters.

The Need for Simple, Linear Order

First, the audience is *easily confused by any structural complexity.* This is mainly because they can't go back over what you said, as they can when reading a memo. They have to understand everything the first time they hear it. So, your points must be laid out simply and clearly — as they are in the universal structure: preview of only a few key points, followed by discussion in the same order.

Unfortunately, it's very easy to underestimate the complexity of your own presentation. Usually, you go over your material many times as you develop and then rehearse it. After a while, everything seems perfectly clear and obvious — *because you're so familiar with it!* Just remember that the audience is not in that position, and keep the structure simple.

The Need for Well-Spaced Repetition

Second, the audience is apt to **miss or mishear** parts of what you say, because of the intrinsic noise of the situation. The air conditioning may be loud; somebody's view may be blocked; some people may be distracted by other audience members or outside events; and so on.

In fact, a well-known rule of thumb says that the audience takes in only one-third of what you say. That means you should present your important points three times so most listeners will hear you at least once. The universal structure encourages you to do just that: preview your message and key points in the introduction; repeat and expand them in the body; and restate them in the summary.

The Need to Adapt to the Audience's Natural Attention Curve

Third — and most distressing — your listeners tend to take turns **napping or daydreaming.** More precisely, their natural attention curve looks like Figure 2-1.

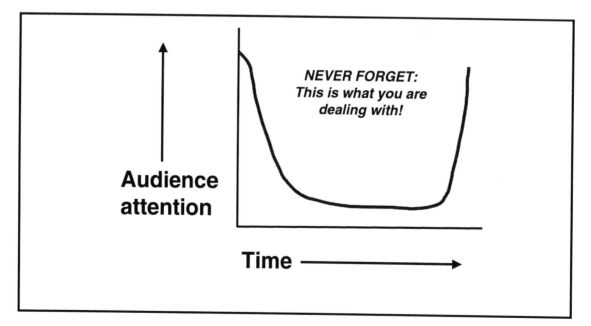

Figure 2-1. The audience's natural attention curve — a major limitation and challenge for any presenter.

They start out quite awake, wondering why you're there and whether this is going to be interesting to them. Then their bodies take over and drag them down. (Don't be fooled by appearances: many of them have learned to nap with their eyes open!) Finally, they wake up again as you say the magical words "In summary..." and try to learn what they missed during their nap.

The point is this: in the middle of your talk, you will have to struggle to keep your listeners conscious. Chances are, they may miss some of the things you say. But in the beginning and end, you have their natural attention without much effort. You would be foolish to waste these natural high points of attention on trivialities; you *must* use them for the most important parts of your talk. Again, the universal structure encourages you to do that.

In the next chapters, we'll look in more detail at the three elements of this structure: (1) the introduction, (2) the body, and (3) the summary. Also, in Appendix A, you will find an annotated presentation outline that illustrates how to apply the structure.

DISCUSSION

Discussion 2-1. Think of presentations you have given or witnessed. Were they structured to take into account the audience's attention curve — that is, main message preview in the introduction, body with change of pace/approach, strong summary, etc.? If not, what view of natural audience attention did these presentations imply? Express this faulty view as a curve (see Figure 2-1 above for the *correct* model of natural audience attention over time).

3

The *RAMP* Formula for Effective Introductions

For most people, the introduction is by far the hardest part. The air feels thick with expectations and unuttered thoughts; you are stiff and nervous; and everybody is waiting for you to break the silence with something good. You know you're setting the tone for the whole presentation — but everything seems to conspire against making a strong first impression.

It's good to *remember* how awkward the beginning of a presentation feels, because it will give you an incentive to prepare the right material — something easy, friendly, and full of strong emotional content that gets you going. You don't have to be an entertainer, or even an experienced speaker, to do it. All you need to do is to follow the surefire recipe we'll give you.

THE FOUR FUNCTIONS OF THE INTRODUCTION

In the introduction, you have to accomplish four important things:

1. Let the audience know that you are delighted to be with them (otherwise, they won't be happy to be with you, either).
2. Motivate them to make an extra effort to pay attention during the body.
3. Give them your main message while they're still naturally attentive.
4. Share your presentation plan so they can digest your points more easily and don't have to worry that they will suffer the usual "torture by chaos."

The *RAMP* formula shown in Figure 3-1 helps you achieve all four goals, and it is simple to remember (just think of a ramp leading up to the body of your presentation).

The whole introduction should never take more than about two minutes. Most important, *you must get to your main message within two minutes.* Remember the treacherous shape of the audience's attention curve (Figure 3-2). Even the best-intentioned listeners soon wander off unless you get them involved in something that really matters to them (your main message, if your thinking was right). So, don't get

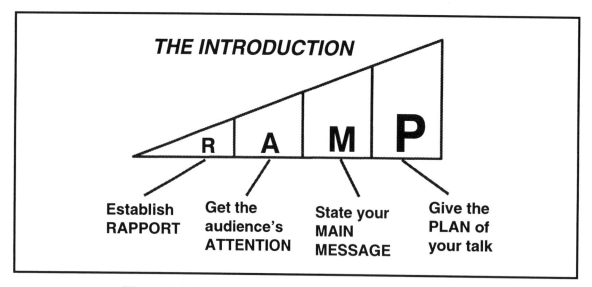

Figure 3-1. The *RAMP* formula for effective introductions.

carried away with your rapport builder ("funny things that happened to me on the way to this presentation") or attention getter. In extreme cases, the audience will begin to assume that you've actually rambled off into the body, and they'll be very confused about the whole presentation.

THE RAPPORT BUILDER

When you meet somebody, you shake hands and say "Hi!" — unless you skipped crucial sessions in kindergarten. It's similar in a presentation. People like establishing human contact and getting a sense that you are excited about talking to them. It makes them feel appreciated. The rapport builder does that. If you don't use one, you are signaling to the audience either that you don't care about them or that you are stiff and nervous.

> ### Tip
>
> Keep your rapport builder as short as possible — but never omit it, even if you use a title slide. A title slide doesn't make human contact — only *you* can do that.

On the other hand, you are not there for chitchat, so you'll want to keep your rapport builder very short — just enough to create a pleasant bond between you and the audience. If some of your listeners don't know you, give them your name and then show them you're happy to be with them: "Good morning! I am Don Barker from the Purchasing Department, and I am glad I have this chance to talk to you about some important changes in our purchasing procedures."

At one company's two-day "technology conference," we saw powerful evidence of the importance of a rapport builder. Most speakers went right into their agenda and from there into background and technical details. After a few hours, the audience seemed not even to notice when one speaker had finished and the next had taken over. They just sat in open-mouthed stupor — except when a presenter acknowledged them as human beings

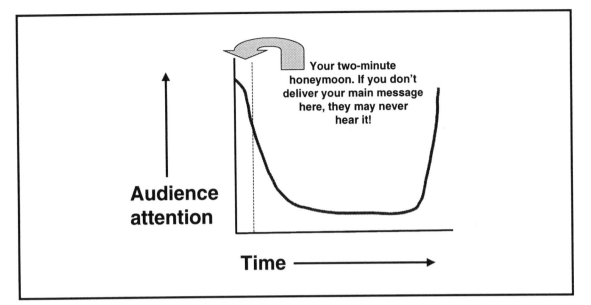

Figure 3-2. A reminder: the audience's natural attention curve with which you need to work.

and greeted them with: "Hi! It's good to be here." Then they woke up and blinked and took a good look at the speaker.

Title Slides vs. Rapport Builders

What if you use a title slide? Doesn't that take the place of the rapport builder? People often ask us if it isn't unprofessional to duplicate what's on the slide. Obviously, the audience can read the name, association, and title on the screen, so isn't it a waste of everybody's time to say it as well?

To answer that question, think about the typical title slide. Do you see many that look like Figure 3-3?

We certainly haven't seen such title slides. They all just state the title and the speaker's name. That leaves the main rapport building job still to you. If your rapport remarks should duplicate the information on the screen, it doesn't matter — the audience is not going to think you immodest or self-centered.

If the culture in which you're presenting allows it, consider omitting the title slide unless you have a foreign accent that makes you hard to understand (in that case, use visuals throughout as an extra help). Without the title slide, you're more likely to start in an enthusiastic, personal way. If the culture demands a title slide, just use it but act as if it weren't there.

Some Turn-Offs

Some rapport builders are intrinsically boring. Thanking 20 people for their existence, presence, or some contribution is an example. It's appropriate only if the main purpose of

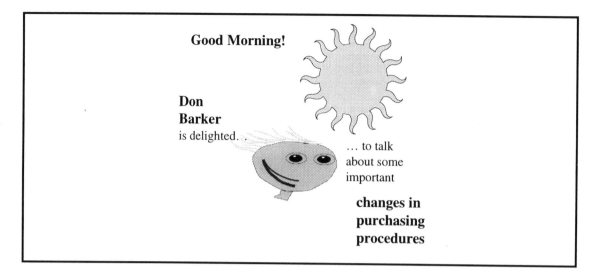

Figure 3-3. Title slides don't create rapport – *you* do! Or how often have you seen a title slide that looks like this?

the speech is to thank or honor people in the audience — and even then you have to keep in mind that they are all suffering through the recital, except for that brief moment when their own sweet name is mentioned.

Another turn-off is a long explanation of why you chose the topic you did, or discarded four others. The audience is just not that interested in the intricate workings of your mind — they just want to know the end product of all that reasoning.

Even worse are self-conscious or apologetic rapport builders: "I didn't have much time to prepare for this, so if you'll just bear with me..." or: "I don't know why they asked *me* to talk on this." Although such remarks may show some honesty and modesty, they make the audience fear for the worst. They certainly don't make them feel that you cared enough about them to prepare something really useful! So forget about apologizing and just do the best you can.

Finally, joking about the town or organization you are visiting will usually build the opposite of rapport with the loyal locals in the audience. You may draw some laughs — but that doesn't make up for the resentment from the silent ones.

EFFECTIVE ATTENTION GETTERS

The second element of the RAMP is the attention getter. (Actually, this is a misnomer: unless you get lost in your rapport builder, you already have the audience's attention at this point. A better word might be *attention reinforcer;* however, since "attention getter" is a universally accepted term, we'll simply stick with it here.) The attention getter should **relate directly to your main message,** in a professional way. For instance, if you are proposing a piece of equipment, the attention getter might be a severe problem that will be solved by it:

In the last two months, we had 19 major customer complaints related to nonuniform color. A conservative estimate of the costs of this problem is $200,000 for just those two months, or $1.2 million per year. This is a major drain on our profitability.... [Leading to the main message: *To solve these and other color problems, once and for all, we have designed a new color control system that is inexpensive and easy to install.*]

Other effective attention getters include examples of major benefits of your proposal or idea, anecdotes, relevant quotes, questions that involve the audience, simple visuals, significant statistics, analogies, and demonstration objects.

Four Important Reasons for an Attention Getter

Why do you need such an attention getter — especially if it's true that the audience is naturally attentive anyway, at this early stage? There are four good reasons:

1. It puts the audience on notice that your talk is going to be interesting and well constructed. (It's like giving them a shot of adrenaline to keep them awake during the most difficult part, the body.)

2. It stretches out your main message so the audience won't miss it altogether. When your message is just one sentence, it usually flashes by without making any impression. The attention getter prepares the ground so the audience anticipates the message and hears it clearly.

3. It helps you sell your main message by illustrating its urgency or relevance and making it memorable.

4. It makes it much easier for you to start your talk with conversational ease. An attention getter is a simple, nontheoretical point that involves both you and the audience and is therefore easy to deliver with enthusiasm.

The attention getter is the part most often omitted in technical presentations. This omission is a big mistake. Even in a technical presentation, all the reasons for an attention getter are still valid: you need to raise the audience's energy level for the body, you need to make your message noticed and accepted, and you need to avoid a slow, awkward start. Without an attention getter, it is usually impossible to achieve these things.

Still, it's understandable that technical presenters should be concerned about being professional and objective. The mere term "attention getter" suggests something brash, so people shy away from it.

Can you have it both ways — professional *and* exciting? Certainly. All you need is a point or example that is interesting, clearly related to your message, and free of exaggerations or gimmicks. Nobody listening to such an attention getter will feel that you're being brash or unprofessional.

For instance, take another look at our sample attention getter (customer complaints related to color problems) at the beginning of this section. Do you find anything inappropriate or unprofessional in it? We have asked that question many times about similar attention getters, and nobody seemed put off by them. On the contrary, everybody appreciated them as interesting and helpful.

Delaying the Attention Getter

We talked about the attention getter as the second element of the introduction (the *A* in the *RAMP*). Occasionally, you may find that this just doesn't come out smoothly. In that case, try putting the attention getter right *after* the main message rather than before it. Generally, this has a more low-key flavor — which will feel more natural in some settings, such as an informal talk to peers or fellow team members. For instance, to review the status of the color control system with team members, you might start as follows:

> [Rapport:] *Good morning! I'm glad everybody could make it to this meeting to discuss the status of our project.* [Main message:] *We've finished our design of the color control system and believe that our solution is inexpensive and very easy to install.* [Attention getter:] *Everybody agrees that there is an urgent need for this system. Just in the last two months, we had 19 major customer complaints related to nonuniform color. A conservative estimate of the costs of this problem is $200,000 for just those two months, or $1.2 million per year. This is a major drain on our profitability. The new color control system will solve these and other color problems, once and for all.*

In most situations, however, you get greater benefits from an attention getter that precedes the main message. For instance, the main message is more easily lost in the low-key version, and it's harder to start the delivery on an enthusiastic note. So don't automatically go for the low-key formula just because you're afraid to come on too strong.

Example of Problem or Benefit

Especially in a technical presentation, highlighting a major problem addressed by your project, system, or idea provides a good, professional attention getter. We had an example of this type at the beginning of this section. A variant of this is a description of a benefit:

> *Imagine being able to run your large graphics, statistics, and word processing programs simultaneously, while staying connected to the Web or intranet — and not having to worry about some program crashing and bringing the operating system down with it. It might make the difference between getting home at five or*

staying all night to finish a big job. Well, these are some of the benefits you'll gain if we upgrade our computers to the Mach 5 operating system.

Tip

Don't spend too much time thinking about an attention getter in the beginning. Instead, firm up your main message and key points and then develop examples and other backup for each key point. At that stage, a strong, professional attention getter, such as an example or a problem, will more easily occur to you.

Many speakers feel that mentioning the amount of money saved or generated by a project or idea will serve as a nice attention getter. Usually, it doesn't work out that way. For instance, there are several problems with an attention getter such as: "How would you like to save $400,000 per year?" First, it's so short that it is easily missed. Second, it doesn't have much *human* interest, so it doesn't help you get started in a natural, enthusiastic way. Third, it just isn't classy — it's like a cheap, loud commercial.

The low-key variant is just as poor:

[Main message:] *The Waste Reduction Team has devised a comprehensive plan for cutting waste in all phases of production, inventory, and maintenance.* [Attention getter:] *This will save us $400,000 per year.*

Here, most listeners will see the savings figure as part of the main message and not at all as an attention getter. As in the other version, the benefit for lively delivery is also zero. The only advantage is that it lacks the cheap flavor.

A better solution is to mention some major examples of waste, with cost figures (that is, focus on the problems rather than the benefits). The savings figure can then be brought into the main message:

[Attention getter:] *Over the last year, our rejects rate has been 4 percent, which translates into a loss of $300,000. Inventory costs have been 2 percent of sales, or $180,000. And the cost of unscheduled downtime was $160,000.* [Main message:] *The Waste Reduction Team has come up with a plan for cutting all such waste in production, inventory, and maintenance. This plan will save us $400,000 per year.*

Anecdote

Anecdotes are intrinsically interesting: we all like to listen to quick stories involving real people. Very often, anecdotes used as attention getters will be related to a problem, as in this example:

Over the past six months, we've had 13 accidents — three of them serious enough to require a hospital visit. In one case, a technician fell off a partially opened step ladder. The reason he hadn't opened the ladder all the way was that there were two chairs in the way, and he was too lazy or rushed to move them. He fell onto one of those chairs and broke most of his front teeth, plus he suffered a concussion. This and all the other accidents could have easily been avoided if people had followed a few common sense rules....

But general anecdotes are also common and effective. For instance, a talk on practical approaches to creativity might start as follows:

[Attention getter:] *The famous chemist Kekule was trying for a long time to solve the puzzle of the structure of benzene. One night, he had a dream about a snake biting its own tail — and the solution to his puzzle came to him: the carbons in benzene were arranged in a ring, just like the snake, so that every one of the six carbons in the benzene molecule had the right number of bonds. The creative solution to a fundamental problem — coming out of a dream. Is that what creativity is all about? Is it just a matter of luck, sudden inspiration? Is it totally out of rational reach?* [Main message:] *Not at all. As I'll try to show you, there are practical, rational aspects of creativity that anybody can learn and continuously strengthen....*

Tip

Spin the attention getter out over a few sentences. Short attention getters are missed just as easily as short main messages without a preceding attention getter.

If you don't have a real anecdote, an imaginary one may be almost as good. For instance, a talk on safety procedures, including maintenance of equipment and training, might start out with an imaginary event:

Imagine you are working on the late shift. Suddenly an alarm is going off indicating there was a release of a hazardous gas. You rush to the nearest respirator on your way to the emergency exit — but that crucial piece of equipment isn't there...

Quote

Quotes can be very effective attention getters, as long as they are well related to your message. They also allow you to introduce humor safely. For instance, a talk on how to use statistics properly might start like this:

[Attention getter:] *According to Mark Twain, there are three kinds of lies: lies, damn lies, and statistics. From what I hear, he wasn't alone in this view: it's a popular perception of statistics. But is it true? Are statistics really just a way of deceiving and manipulating people, of proving just about anything you want to prove?* [Main message:] *What I will try to show you this morning is that there is nothing manipulative about statistics, only about improper USES of statistics. When you use them properly, statistics can help you make reasonable decisions in cases where you have incomplete information.*

A quote from a respected authority (your company chief, a U.S. president, a well-known industry figure, a major writer, a historical figure or philosopher) can increase your credibility or underline the urgency of what you are saying. For instance, a talk on an environmental project might start by quoting the company's president:

Last month, our president announced a new challenging environmental philosophy: "Within two years, we shall be 25% LOWER than the legal limit on all emissions."

A quote from a newspaper, journal, or book can also be authoritative. It's not a bad idea to bring the paper or book as a prop. This gives you something interesting and easy to handle and removes the initial temptation to clutch the pointer. For example, you might hold up your newspaper and announce:

This is the New York Times *from last Tuesday. It has a very interesting article on recent advances in climate research. I'd like to quote just two sentences from the end of that article:...*

Question

Questions can be a good way to draw in the audience and establish a conversational atmosphere, provided you avoid a few pitfalls.

The simplest type is a *challenging question* that you answer yourself. For instance, a talk on the importance of complying with environmental laws might start like this:

How would you like to go to jail? Well, that's what may happen to you if you are not careful about complying with environmental laws on your job. In fact, two managers in this company are facing that very real possibility right now....

The disadvantage of this type of question is that the audience doesn't really get involved; its advantage is that you keep control and avoid surprises.

A *knowledge question* offers real interaction. For instance, you might start a talk on a project to improve inventory control with the question: "Does anybody here know how much we lose each month in damaged or missing inventory?" However, this type of question has its own problems. Above all, it tends to have a school flavor unless you handle it delicately. Asking for "guesses" may help lessen the teacher image. Also, you must be prepared for all possibilities: no response, right answer, only low guesses, only high guesses, and low and high guesses. Whatever the answers, though, don't make a teacher face, and don't say things like "wrong" or "excellent." What you want to achieve is a little easy interaction on an *equal level.*

A related type is the *experience question.* For example, a talk aimed at getting people to comply with purchasing procedures might start with such a question:

Tip

If you use a question as an attention getter, plan what to do if you get no response, or responses that don't lead in the direction you need.

[Rapport:] *Good morning! I am Don Barker from the Purchasing Department, and I am glad I have this chance to talk to you about some important changes in our purchasing procedures.*" [Attention getter:] *How many of you have ever had trouble with a supplier who promised the earth and then found all kinds of excuses not to honor the guarantee when things went wrong?*

With experience questions, there is much less danger of slipping into an offputting teacher role. However, you still have to anticipate all conceivable responses, including deadly silence. What will you do in each case? Too many speakers don't plan this well and end up with lame transitions such as: "Oh, that's surprising. Usually people say..." That kind of remark does a lot less for you than a properly prepared answer like: "Well, consider yourselves lucky, because there are many people in this company who've had some very painful experiences with that."

Visual

Your attention getter can be built around a simple chart, such as Figure 3-4. However, don't discuss the chart at length; just highlight the key idea, then lead over to your main message. You can return to the chart later, in the body, to discuss it in detail.

The visual might even be a single number that is central to your talk. Make it big enough to fill the screen. If the number is truly important, this won't seem overdramatic.

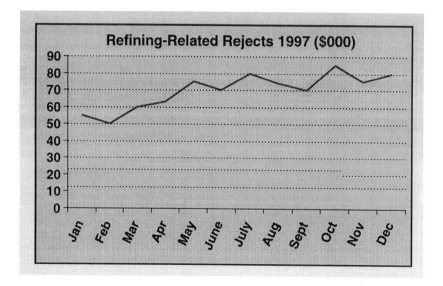

Figure 3-4. A simple chart such as this one can serve as an attention getter — but don't give in to the temptation to discuss details.

Here's an example:

[Visual filling the screen]

Four-and-a-half million dollars — that's our magical monthly sales number. Below that, we're either losing money or keeping profits stagnant. Above it, we're making our contribution to keeping the company growing. [Main message:] *What's been keeping us from getting past that number lately?* **A dangerous shift toward servicing old accounts at the expense of pursuing new customers.** *This is our biggest area of decline, and it's where we need to refocus our energies starting today...*

Statistics

A cogent statistic can support your arguments from the very start. For instance, a talk to employees on preventing car theft might start with something like

Every 20 seconds, a car is stolen somewhere in the United States. There's a pretty good chance that yours will be next — especially if you make it easy for thieves to drive off with it.

Analogy

An analogy works well as an attention getter when you need to explain the significance of technical concepts or numbers. For instance, a speaker for Rockwell International wanted to illustrate the power the company could deliver, as exemplified by the Saturn V rocket that launched Apollo astronauts to the moon. He did it with the following analogy:

If you ran all the rivers and streams of America through steam turbines at the same time, you'd get only half the 160 million horsepower that all five of the Saturn F1 engines generate.

A number like 160 million horsepower is too large and mind-boggling to be an effective attention getter by itself: 1.6 million, 16 million, 160 million — to the audience, it's all just "big." They just can't take it in. The analogy makes the number real and interesting. Similarly, an analogy can serve to explain hard-to-imagine technological or scientific processes, such as the mapping of genes or chip design and manufacturing, to nontechnical audiences.

Demo Object

Demo objects can lend drama to your opening. For instance, a talk on the importance of paying meticulous attention to detail in maintenance work might start with something like this:

> *Take a look at this screw. A little screw just like this killed four people last year when a service technician dropped it into the control system of a cargo plane. That's all that was needed — a small mistake like that.*

In other cases, the object simply conveys information better than words could. For example, you might show an interesting new product or a product with a defect. Or a sales rep talking to retailers might start by showing some promotion pieces to be used in a sales campaign.

The main problem with demo objects is that they are very distracting if you pass them around. It's much better to keep control of them and pass them around only after your talk. In many cases, holding an object up is enough, as in the example above. If that doesn't work, decide if you can spare the time to walk from table to table and show the object to everybody, without letting it out of your hand. Usually, this takes no longer than half a minute and works quite well; however, it's not feasible if chairs are arranged classroom style in several rows.

In some cases, it's best to convert the object into a visual. For instance, you might photograph a small object and show it much magnified on a slide, or you might make a schematic drawing of a product or defect.

Tip

If at all possible, avoid the distraction created by passing demo objects around; instead, walk quickly from table to table with the object while describing its significance.

If you do decide to pass the object around, make sure that those waiting for the object can still understand what you are saying. Generally, that means spelling out the significant aspects of the object *before* you pass it around.

Demonstration Event

Rather than handle a simple object, you may involve one or several audience members in some demonstration. This has the obvious advantage of being lively and fun. For example, when talking about static electricity, you might bring an electrostatic generator and charge a couple of volunteers so people can see how little it takes to generate powerful sparks. This would be a memorable way to lead into your main message: "Static electricity is powerful, destructive stuff — we need to pay great attention to protecting sensitive electronic equipment from it."

If a live demonstration is not feasible, it may be possible to substitute a video clip for it. In either case, keep the demonstration itself short and avoid detailed discussion, or people may think you've jumped right into the body, without main message or plan.

How About Jokes as Ice-Breakers?

Most people we have asked don't enjoy listening to jokes in a presentation. One problem with jokes is that they are usually neither professional nor properly related to your message. Another, perhaps even more severe, drawback is that they are fake and impersonal; a real anecdote, humorous or not, will get a much better response.

The worst choice is a tasteless joke. In one case, we witnessed a keynote speaker warming up with some Polish jokes. There was a collective gasp of disbelief and not much laughter. Remember, even as keynote speaker, you don't *have* to be funny; you just need to give the audience something that is interesting to them.

How about disguising a joke as a personal anecdote — say: "A friend of mine recently went into a hardware store..." [obscure joke follows]? We've seen quite a few speakers trying this. Unfortunately, it often misfires, because some listeners may know the joke. It's amazing how strongly most people react to this innocent little deception: they begin to mistrust everything you have to say, including your main message. That's just too big a risk for too little payback.

THE MAIN MESSAGE

The most important element of your introduction is a clear preview of your main message. For reasons we'll discuss later, this part seems to give people the greatest trouble. They are naturally drawn to weak, incomplete statements, or "promises to pay later."

Here is an example of a proper, complete main message:

Our evaluation of the XYZ energy plant shows that we can save most of the equipment and move it to the new location. The main things that will need to be replaced are the ductwork, the condenser, and the lower section of the stack. However, to ensure uninterrupted energy production during the changeover, the plant should be moved in two stages, even though this is more expensive.

This statement clearly spells out your major conclusions and recommendations — the things you most need to get across to the audience. Because it has meat to it, it's also much easier to deliver with enthusiasm than lame "preparatory noises" or pseudo messages such as

This morning, I'll be pleased to report on our evaluation of the feasibility of moving the XYZ energy plant.

Tip

Always test your main message: If you can ask "What about it?" then you have chosen a pseudo message. Revise it until it is a strong statement of what you want the audience to do or believe.

This is a pseudo message because it *says nothing* about the topic (feasibility of moving the energy plant); it just *announces* it and promises that you'll say something about it later (when people have drifted off into daydreams). Listeners can ask: "What *about* the evaluation? What came out of it?" At this point, they have simply no idea.

If you have problems formulating a strong main message, just think about what you want to put into your conclusions or summary section. (At that point, most speakers do get around to committing themselves to a real message.) Then take that idea and put it up front in succinct form as your main message. Table 3-1 shows more examples of real and pseudo messages.

TABLE 3-1. Pseudo Messages and Real Messages

Pseudo Message	Real Message
My objective today is to brief you on the company's solid waste reduction program, its objectives, and some effective approaches to this issue in your division.	Your divisions should start a solid waste reduction program this year. Because of new regulations, not doing so would result in big financial penalties. The company has a proven approach that requires no extra personnel, and I am here to explain that program and help you implement it.
Our objective today is to review progress on the XYZ chip.	We are right on schedule and budget with development of the new XYZ chip.
My purpose today is to tell you some things you should know about purchasing policies and procedures.	You can gain a lot by cooperating with Purchasing when you order equipment, materials, or services, because we can get you a better deal and a solid contract that can be enforced — and we'll try hard to make it hassle-free.
In the next 45 minutes, I'll tell you how to give an effective presentation.	To give an outstanding presentation, you must care about the audience and do all you can to give them what they need and to connect with them as real people.

THE PLAN

The last element of your introduction is the basic plan of your talk. This is essential to reassure the audience that your presentation has a clear organization. It also makes it easier for them to process the detailed discussion, because it tells them what to expect.

It's good practice to return to this plan repeatedly in the body as you summarize each section and lead over to the next one.

Generally, your plan will be a simple list of your key points, supported by a visual. In the purchasing example mentioned above, this might look as follows:

[Main message:] *You can gain a lot by cooperating with Purchasing when you order equipment, materials, or services, because we can get you a better deal and a solid contract that can be enforced — and we'll try hard to make it hassle-free.* [Plan:] *Over the next 15 minutes, I'll discuss the main reasons for our purchasing policies and procedures; then I'll show you how to use the system properly, in a way that minimizes paperwork, delays, and other problems; and finally, I would like to hear any suggestions on how we could make it easier and faster for you to work with Purchasing. We're here to help, not to make things difficult for you.*

There is no need to get too mechanical about your plan. For instance, in the example, words such as "plan," "agenda," "key point," or "point" do not appear. Also, the numbers of the points are not mentioned, although on the supporting *visual,* the points may well be numbered — say, as in Figure 3-5.

Above all, don't dwell on the innards of construction: "I'll start with an introduction, then in the body I'll cover... And I'll conclude with a brief summary." This is offputting and uninformative, since the audience *expects* you to have an introduction, a body, and a summary or conclusion. The only exception is procedural plans that are not obvious. For example, you might say: "I'll stop after each section for questions and discussion so we can sort out any problems you might have with what I am saying." This is a useful, nonobvious addition to your content points, as it prepares the audience for essential interaction.

Tip

Always have a visual laying out your presentation plan so the audience gets a clear idea of how to process your talk.

How To Have a Beneficial Relationship With Purchasing

1. **Understand the reasons for purchasing policies and procedures.**

2. **Do it right to avoid rework, delays, and disappointments.**

3. **Share your problems and suggestions to help us improve the system.**

Figure 3-5. Supporting visual for a presentation plan.

OVERCOMING COMMON OBSTACLES TO A STRONG START

Most technical presentations don't follow the *RAMP* formula at all in their introduction. Instead, they start with a lame pseudo message, perhaps followed by an agenda — say:

> *This morning, I'd like to update you on our security improvement initiative. First, I'll review our objectives. Then, I'll discuss progress over the last six months.*

Not only does this not give the audience any substantial information, but it's also impossible to say with any kind of enthusiasm. By contrast, a good attention getter and a clear main message constitute the strongest thing you have to say about your topic, so they launch you into your talk with proper speed and force.

What makes so many people gravitate toward weak agenda-style beginnings? For the most part, *fear* — of being different, of drawing fire with a strong statement, of appearing unscientific, of losing suspense, or of dramatizing things when there is only simple information to convey. Let's take a closer look at those obstacles and see how to overcome them.

Obstacle #1: Fear of Being Different

It takes courage to be different. If everybody in the company follows the agenda style, you may be afraid to stick out. It's up to you to make a decision: do you want to be like everybody else (and give a terrible presentation), or do you want results from your presentation? You can't have it both ways!

For example, one of our students had prepared an excellent presentation, including a good attention getter and a strong main message. His attention getter was a chart clearly showing the dwindling supply of a crucial substance X and the increasing demand for it, which threatened a dangerous cost squeeze. The main message was: "We're working with a supplier on a cheaper alternative for substance X, and this alternative seems extremely promising and worthy of major financial support." The audience was the operating committee of the company (including the company's chairman), plus assorted vice presidents.

Unfortunately, at delivery time, this engineer suddenly became very nervous about being "different" in front of this top-level audience. He saw that the presenters before him all followed the agenda scheme, with the main message saved for the conclusions section. So, he skipped his attention getter and the "high-profile" initial main message and started like everybody else — with an agenda, or preview of his presentation plan. Next, he filled the audience in on some background. Finally, he inched his way toward his main message — but at that point, he was cut off by a vice president who had a political interest in sidetracking him. *He never got to give his main message at all!*

This is not at all rare; high-powered audiences often do not give you much time before they cut in with questions and objections. However, even such an audience will *not* cut you off in the very first minute of your talk! It's simply unheard of. Therefore, ironically, when you state your main points right at the beginning, you are far safer than when you try to "play it safe" and be like everybody else.

In any case, there is no reason to be like everybody else. Why shouldn't you stand out as someone exceptionally professional, considerate, and effective? Giving outstanding presentations is one of the best ways to further your reputation and career — so have the courage to excel with a strong start.

Obstacle #2: Fear of Commitment

Another common fear is that starting with a strong message puts you on the line. For instance, you might be nervous about opening with the admission that your project hasn't produced any results yet and in fact has run into unforeseen obstacles. How tempting to wear the audience down with a blow-by-blow account of all the work you did and smuggle the bad news in later, when it won't get noticed so much! Just ask yourself: how often have other people been able to fool *you* that way? And what did you think of them?

Your listeners want to hear the bottom line. So give it to them in the first 90 seconds, whether it's good or bad. At the least, you'll score points for courage! For example, consider a "bad news" main message like this:

> *After evaluating our results on the second phase of our direct marketing project, we've come to the conclusion that we should abandon this effort immediately and focus on more promising opportunities, such as expansion into the Eastern European market. Our preliminary study had suggested possible sales results from direct marketing within one year, but the Phase 2 data show that gaining a reasonable market share will take several years — and that only if we are willing to spend about twice as much on advertising as we planned.*

You may be bringing bad news — but you can still be a hero. Here, you are coming out strongly to save the company from wasting time and money on a dead-end project. That's just as positive and important as selling a winner! So, even if you don't have good news, get to the point quickly, clearly, and with confidence.

Obstacle #3: Fear of Appearing Biased or Unscientific

Many scientists and engineers feel that stating their main message first is unscientific. After all, the scientific method proceeds from hypothesis to test and only then to the conclusion. Doesn't starting with the conclusion show bias or a desire to manipulate the audience?

This fear has two components: worry about yourself — namely, your reputation as a scientist — and worry about improper treatment of the audience. Let's look at each.

Protecting Your Reputation. When you give a presentation, your listeners know very well that they are not watching you doing your research. Therefore, the fact that you present your conclusions first does *not* suggest to them that you *worked* that way. It suggests only that you know how to give a good presentation.

Different spheres of life demand different methods. In scientific research, the scientific method is universally accepted. In a presentation, the best choice is a psychological approach that considers noise, distraction, limited memory, and people's impatience. The scientific method is no more appropriate for that task than for romance, playing with a baby, or enjoying dinner.

So stop worrying about what people might think. Assume that people trust you to do your work properly — you don't have to prove it constantly. If somebody should have specific questions about the appropriateness of your method, you can answer those questions as they arise.

Treating the Audience Fairly. When you state your main message initially, you are *not* asking people to accept blindly what you are saying; you're just giving them a "fair warning" of your findings or recommendations. For instance, suppose you give them the following main message in your introduction: "Briefly, we found that topical injections with Benadryl during root canal treatment avoided some common complications, such as swelling of the gums, in more than half of the patients, so it's a worthwhile adjunct therapy to consider." Will your listeners be manipulated into accepting your conclusion? Not at all — you don't have any such power over them. Typically, they will have many questions and reservations — say, about the controls built into your study, the amounts of antihistamine administered, risks of this treatment, etc. They are intelligent people, and they will make up their own mind after listening to all your arguments.

So, you are not trying to persuade anybody with your initial message preview — you're just revealing your conclusion early so your listeners don't have to wonder what you're driving at as you talk. Instead, they can listen intelligently and evaluate all your arguments as you advance them in the body. It's really *fairer* to them — because you're giving them a better chance to formulate their own questions and be a critical audience.

Obstacle #4: Fear of Losing Suspense

People often ask us: "Won't they stop listening to me if I give them the conclusions at the beginning?" The answer is no. If you've given them a good attention getter that shows the significance, they'll be interested in understanding the *reasons* for your conclusions and to see the *details* of your proposal or results.

In reality, "suspense" in a business presentation soon turns into confusion, as everybody is trying to guess what your message might be. And the more the guessing and the confusion go on, the more people will tune you out. You simply cannot force people to listen to all of your talk by withholding the information they really want — they are the ones who control the volume button on their receiver.

That's not to say there is never room for suspense in a talk. However, in a technical or business presentation, suspense must be subordinated to clarity and simplicity — and that generally means giving away the solution to your "mystery" at the beginning.

Obstacle #5: The "I Have No Message, Only Information" Fallacy

Many speakers feel they have nothing important to say — just some routine information to convey. "I'm just bringing them up to date on my project," they say, or: "I'm just explaining the XYZ process to them — there really is no message I'm trying to get across."

Interestingly, the audience usually reacts with remarks such as: "Nice, informative talk — but we were a little confused about why we were listening to it." So, even when you feel you have no urgent message, think about giving the audience clear reasons why they should listen to you. Those reasons grow out of a good audience analysis, as we discussed in Chapter 1.

Let's look more closely at two situations where speakers often have trouble finding a strong message for their presentation: a process overview and a project update.

Process, Area, or Discipline Overview. How can you find a good, audience-related message and attention getter for something as dry and "information-oriented" as a process overview? By considering audience-focused questions such as these:

- What's interesting (to these listeners) about it?
    - Do they now (or will they in the future) interact in any way with this area? How? What do they have to know, learn, or watch out for?
    - How does this process/area affect operations upstream and downstream?
    - How does it affect product/service quality and customer satisfaction?
    - In which ways does it differ from their areas? (What makes it special?)
    - In which ways is it similar to their areas? (What are the common interests?)
- What is most challenging about it:
    - Technically
    - Managerially
    - Humanly
- How are these challenges met? Are the principles involved in the solutions significant in a general way?
- Is this a major cost area for the company? What parts are the most costly, and why? How can those costs be reduced? Are the methods of reducing costs of general interest to some or all of your listeners?
- Does this area contribute to saving the company money, time, or effort? How? Is that of general interest?
- What interesting new developments have been implemented in this area?
    - Do they relate to similar developments in other fields?
    - Are they unique, but able to inspire thinking in other fields?
- What new developments are coming along, and what will their major benefits be?

Adding a message and an attention getter based on these questions will save you from walking through the entire process from start to finish — which tends to be tedious and offputting. For example, imagine you've been asked to talk to colleagues about your group, which is responsible for developing and updating engineered standards, such as standard costs of common production processes throughout the company. You could take a straightforward "informational overview" approach — say: "I'd like to tell you all about our department, which is responsible for developing the engineered standard costs you find in various manuals." Or you could make your talk more interesting by building it around a message based on your listeners' interactions with engineered standards: "Engineered standards are not arbitrary numbers as some people think but surprisingly accurate — and they can help you justify your projects by giving you an accepted way to quantify costs and savings." A related attention getter might be: "Have you ever had a good project turned down because the accountants rejected the cost and savings numbers you put into your proposal?"

You can be sure that nobody in the audience will object: "We thought you were going to tell us all about the engineered standards group — but instead, you told us why and how to use standard costs!" And the fact is, you still *can* tell them "all about" your group; only now it will be structured around a relevant theme that gives everything focus and coherence. (Of course, once you think seriously about your listeners, you probably won't *want* to tell them everything there is to know — just what's interesting to them!)

To take another example, suppose you've been invited to talk to a general audience about biotechnology. You might choose to make it the usual rambling informational overview: "In the next 30 minutes, I'll tell you a little bit about biotechnology — what it is, how it developed, and where it is going." Or you can subordinate all your points to a single theme:

[Main message] *Biotechnology is an exciting new field that will affect us individually and as a society in fundamental ways, just as the industrial and electronic revolutions affected earlier generations.* [Plan:] *I will show you some of its major promises in medicine, agriculture, and medicine.*

An attention getter leading into this theme might be an example of a benefit, such as gene therapy to wipe out devastating genetic diseases. Or you might choose a different theme, such as: "Biotechnology poses some unique social and ethical challenges." In either case, you can still cover as much of the field as you like — but now the audience will pay more attention, because you made the information relevant to them. They can *relate* to challenges and things that affect their lives much more than to an exhaustive stream of information.

Project Update. Suppose you are updating colleagues and management on a project to recycle office and lab waste. It may be tempting to take a low-key informational approach:

1. Agenda
2. Background
3. Previous progress and obstacles
4. New achievements
5. Plans for next phase
6. Questions and discussion

What else can you do? You can consider the audience's main questions and then choose the most important ones as basis for your main message. Generally, your listeners will have questions like these about any ongoing project:

- Is it good?
- Is it on time?
- Is it on budget?
- What has been achieved so far?
- Are any of the results surprising?
- Is it going as planned, or have problems developed?
- Should we keep it going, or should we kill it?
- Should we step it up or scale it down?
- What else do you want us to do?

Let's say that in our example, you've encountered delays but also some unexpected benefits. You might then pick a main message such as:

We have run into several unexpected problems that caused substantial delays in our recycling project. It turns out that we have much to learn about this area. However, it's all worth it, because this project has already produced some good PR and other major benefits nobody had anticipated, such as improved morale, cooperation, and socialization among all the people involved in this effort.

An attention getter to go along with this might be one or two examples of benefits, such as involvement with schools and citizen groups or an interesting group visit to a deinking plant or other recycling center that improved the cohesion of the group. As in the case of process overviews, adding such a message and attention getter in no way prevents you from covering all the points you consider important, but it lends focus and interest to the presentation and makes it stand out from the dreary "informational" project updates that are inflicted on audiences every day.

EXERCISES AND DISCUSSION

Exercise 3-1. Critique and revise the following presentation openers.

(a) "Good afternoon. I'm glad to have this opportunity to talk to you, even though our topic today doesn't seem very pleasant. Because what I'm going to be talking about is *compliance* — what it means to the *company* and what it can mean to *you* personally. Briefly, I'm going to bring you up on some new developments in this whole compliance issue and give you some examples of recent experiences we had at some of our mills."

Audience: Mill or facility managers, business managers, environmental personnel, and some technology managers
Purpose: Convince them that compliance has become a much more urgent issue that should be given top priority. For instance, negligence is no longer just a company problem, but people are personally liable. To make matters worse, the government doesn't have to prove that you were negligent — *you* must prove that you were *not*. Some people at two facilities are in the middle of such legal problems.

(b) "Good morning. I'm Jim Dean, and I will be presenting on the pellet classifier evaluation. We looked at several plastic-pellet classifiers, and my objective today is to report on that evaluation. To begin with, I'll take you through the main criteria that governed our evaluation, such as accuracy, testing speed, operator time involvement, and availability of automatic data storage. Then we'll see how five major pellet classifiers stacked up against these criteria."

Assume the following: Speaker is suggesting that all production facilities switch to a more expensive plastic-pellet classifier than they're using now. This classifier costs 20% more than the cheapest of the five models evaluated, but it offers extensive automation, high testing speed, and the second-best accuracy. The plastic pellets are used as raw material for various plastic products; they must be a mixture of different sizes, with the specific mix depending on the product produced. Testing is done continuously to ensure that the pellet mix falls within the specified size ranges. The audience for the presentation consists of technical and management people from various facilities, plus some managers from Technology.

Exercise 3-2. Think about introductions you have used for your own presentations. Then answer these questions:

(a) Did you usually use an appropriate attention getter as well as a strong preview of your main message? Or did your introduction consist mostly of an agenda — a list of items you promised to cover?
(b) On a scale of 0-10, how much value did your openers have in supporting, or bringing to life, your main message?
(c) On a scale of 0-10, how much did they contribute to inspiring you to begin your talk with enthusiasm and a feeling of being in touch with the audience?
(d) Given your assessment, is preparation of an effective introduction a major improvement area for you?

Discussion 3-1. How and when should you use *demonstration objects* in your introduction? Have you ever tried it, and what was your experience? Have you watched others do it, and what successes or problems did you observe?

Discussion 3-2. Have you ever used questions to draw in the audience at the beginning of a presentation, or have you observed others who did this? What experiences and observations can you share? Are there any common problems? How could they be avoided? When questions are used properly in the introduction, how well do they work in generating interest and audience involvement?

4

The Body

If you followed our advice, then your *RAMP*-style introduction already contains (a) your message and (b) your key points (typically mentioned as part of your *Plan*). Your job in the body is to explain your key points in such a way that the audience will understand, accept, and remember them. Let's see now how to achieve that.

MAKING IT EASY TO FOLLOW

People cannot accept your points unless they first understand them. Your main tools for making your presentation easy to follow are *simplicity* of structure, intelligent *repetition*, and audience-focused *limitation of detail*.

A Simple, Linear Structure

As we discussed in Chapter 2, the structure of your presentation must be extremely simple and transparent to everyone. This is essential because your listeners are easily confused. For the body, the best scheme is a straightforward linear organization:

- Key point 1, followed by backup and examples
- Key point 2, followed by backup and examples
- Key point 3, followed by backup and examples

Here, each key-point statement should be a complete, understandable message in itself, not just a topic announcement, or the audience will again constantly wonder what you are driving at. In other words, the "main message first" principle we suggested for your presentation also applies to each section and subsection. Few speakers master this, but it's one of the most powerful ways to keep the audience with you. For instance, compare the following two examples:

[Example 4-1: Topic + Detail + Message] *Now what about "red tape"? I've heard complaints like ... [examples] Let's take a look at each of these areas. Number 1: There are endless forms to fill out. Is this true? Well, let's see what forms are actually involved.... [Leading up to subpoint 1: there are just two types, and they can be filled in quickly] OK, now let's see about Number 2: It takes too much time to get the product or service you ordered... [etc.]*

[Example 4-2: Message + Detail] *Now let's see about red tape. How much of it is there, and how can we make the whole process as easy as possible for you? As you'll see, there is very little paperwork involved and it's quite easy, and if you do it right the first time and stay in touch with us on major purchases, there are no significant delays. Let's look at the paperwork first. [Explain it.] Now, here are some of the complaints people have made about paperwork: ... [List them] Let's see if these complaints have merit and how to resolve them...*

In Example 4-1, the speaker leads up to his message about red tape through various examples and subpoints. This "stream of consciousness" development is typical — but unfortunately, it invites listeners to get lost along the way as they get either bored or intrigued with the details. By contrast, the organization in Example 4-2 lets people know right away what to expect, so they'll get your point even if they drift off later.

Helpful Repetition

No matter how well you speak, quite a few people will miss important points you mention because of distractions. This is why you must build in repetition for your main ideas. Generally, there should be no need to repeat your main message at the *beginning* of the body, since you just announced it in the introduction; in fact, restating it at this point would seem mechanical and boring. However, as you get involved in details during the body, both you and the audience may tend to lose sight of the main point. It's helpful and appropriate, therefore, to repeat your main message at least once in the *middle of the body.* The best opportunity for this is between key points, as part of transitional summaries:

So, we've seen that there are two good reasons to follow Purchasing procedures: (1) we can get you a better deal, because we have greater leverage with suppliers, and (2) we can help you avoid major troubles with guarantees, delivery delays, and fraud, because we have a lot of solid information about suppliers. Now let's see about "red tape." How much of it is there, and how can we make the whole process as easy as possible for you?

No Unnecessary or Overly Complex Details

Think carefully about what your listeners know and need. Do they have enough background knowledge to follow the technical details you are planning to introduce? If

---

Tip

Let every detailed idea or explanation pass the *purpose test:* ask if the audience must understand this detail to *accept your main idea or recommendation.* If not, omit this detail.

---

not, is it feasible and necessary to fill in the gaps in their knowledge? What would be lost if you omitted the information? Can you still get your main point across and achieve your overall purpose?

Suppose you decide that the detail is needed for persuasion, but you also realize that there is not enough time to educate your listeners to grasp the technical concepts. Then it's time for some intelligent simplification. Learn the following magical words and internalize them until they become part of your preparation instincts:

> *"To put it very simply..."*

Once you say those words to yourself, you'll be amazed how easy it is to reduce complex ideas to simple ones. Keeping your eye on your purpose, you might add an example that helps the audience understand the *significance* of your point, as opposed to the technical details.

For instance, instead of discussing hardware and software details of PC-based video capture and real-time full-motion video conferencing, you might say:

Basically, the system consists of a digital camera, a special card you plug into a laptop computer, and software that works with the camera and the computer to capture images and sound for inexpensive videoconferencing over the Internet. For instance, if you had this setup in your office in New York and a colleague had a similar system in California, you could hold a two-hour video conference for the cost of a local call. During that conference, you could share documents, write comments to each other as well as talk, and transmit digital movies of procedures, plans, drawings, production facilities, etc.

KEEPING IT VARIED

Most presentations are unbearably monotonous in content: they consist of some general statements followed by almost equally general subpoints, all presented with the aid of interminable bullet charts. The predictable result is a general sleepfest. To avoid this, you must build variation into your presentation.

Remember that during the body, the audience's natural attention is at its lowest (see Figure 4-1). Therefore, your main job during this section is to *make sleep as uncomfortable as possible.*

But don't expect continuous total attention — it's just not realistic. In most cases, you'll have to be content to bump them to attention every minute or so. Their attention curve will then look as in Figure 4-2.

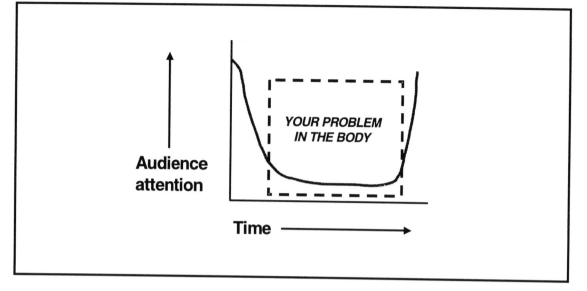

Figure 4-1. Your main challenge in the body: the audience's disastrous tendency to take turns napping while you dish up the meat of your presentation.

Now, the way to jolt people awake is through *change*. It's a simple psychological — and physiological — fact. As long as things stay the same, our subconscious mind (or, more precisely, the eternally wakeful entity known to psychologists as the "supervisor") tells us it's safe to sleep; as soon as there is any change, however, the supervisor summons us into instant consciousness. It's easy to see the evolutionary roots of this: after all, the change might be the sudden arrival of a bear in the cave.

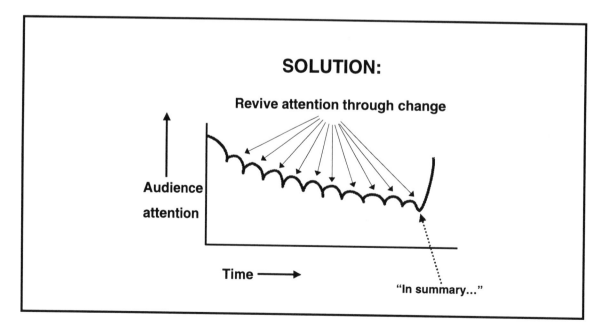

Figure 4-2. Change — your tool for reviving audience attention in the body.

Notice that it's truly *change* and not just noise that wakes us. For instance, you might sleep blissfully through the continuous hum of a hotel air conditioner, only to wake with a start as it switches *off*. This is why you can often wake up a sleeper in a large audience simply by pausing a few seconds.

So, to prevent people's attention from dropping continuously, provide enough change to keep their "supervisors" in a state of alarm. Here are three simple ways to do that:

1. ***Switch between general*** (statement of key point or a subpoint) ***and specific*** (example, anecdote, analogy). For instance, if you are proposing a computerized system for monitoring the levels in various vessels, you might switch from a general statement of improved safety to specific examples of accidents that happened when people had to climb to the top of huge vessels to check levels visually.
2. ***Switch between tell and show*** (a visual or a demonstration). For instance, to continue the example we just used, you could follow a general statement about delays and inaccuracies caused by the old method with a chart depicting the costs of these delays and inaccuracies.
3. ***Switch between lecture and question-and-answer*** (or some other interaction). For instance, in our example, you might ask some of the operators what kinds of problems *they* have experienced with the old system.

There is another important value to variety: it lets you take advantage of people's different ***learning styles.*** We don't all comprehend and learn in the same way. Instead, some of us need to *see* in order to understand; others need to interact; still others need to do some hands-on work to make a concept meaningful. By switching modes frequently, you give each person a chance to absorb some material in his or her preferred way.

Figure 4-3 depicts some of the major learning styles recognized in the literature on the subject. Most of us can use all these styles at different times — but some work better for us, and we may naturally gravitate toward them whenever possible.

Table 4-1 shows how specific tools for change tie into the different learning styles. Notice that you have met those tools before: namely, when we discussed different kinds of attention getters. Just as these devices were strong in the introduction, they can serve you well in the body.

USING THE POWER OF EXAMPLES

Examples are without question your greatest tool for engaging the audience. We sympathize with those who feel that this is somehow unfair. After all, what do a few examples really *prove?* Nothing. In fact, scientists frown upon them as "anecdotal evidence." Yet in a presentation, they seem to hold greater persuasive power than solid evidence such as statistics or other numbers. Isn't it downright manipulation, then, to make your case with examples? Yes — if you are covering up a lack of real evidence for your claims. But assuming you have proper evidence, using examples is simply smart and realistic.

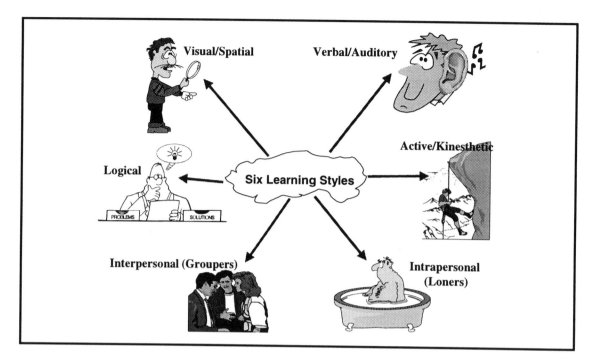

Figure 4-3. Six common learning styles your listeners may use to process your presentation. Each person tends to learn better with one or two preferred styles. Stressing variety of backup in the body increases your chances of reaching everybody.

TABLE 4-1. Your Tools for Change in the Presentation Body, and How They Relate to Your Listeners' Learning Styles

Tool	Appeals to Learning Style
Example or anecdote	Verbal
Interaction (question-and-answer)	Active Interpersonal
Demonstration	Active
Visual	Visual/spatial
Statistic	Logical
Group activity	Interpersonal

Why do examples work so well? Because they make it easy for the audience to *understand* what you are saying — and without understanding, there can be no persuasion. By contrast, numbers are hard to digest in a fast-paced presentation, and they don't *explain* anything. So, to get your ideas accepted, by all means have the numbers ready, but always present them in conjunction with good examples.

Actually, as a listener, you probably appreciate examples, too. Watch yourself as you follow somebody else's presentation. When do you get bored and lost? When do you sit up and take note? You may be surprised to find that you, too, respond strongly to that scientist's bane, "anecdotal evidence."

Why Do People Avoid Using Examples?

Most presenters overuse abstract statements out of *laziness:* it's hard work to come up with good examples for your points. But there is another, often subconscious, reason: *abstract ideas are hard to follow — and therefore difficult to falsify!* Or, conversely: when you give a concrete example of what you're talking about, people can find the weak spots in your theory immediately! So, you sometimes stay with generalities just to be safe.

However, we've never seen this trick succeed. Your listeners know exactly what you're trying to do — and they simply won't believe you until you give them a good example. For instance, in our own communication-skills workshops, we found that people just don't pay attention until we mention some real examples of managers or employees who did something right or wrong. (What they love most, of course, are examples of our own mistakes!) It's amazing how people immediately start nodding in agreement and begin to contribute their own examples.

So, don't let fear or laziness stop you from using strong examples. Remember that examples are the best way to keep the audience alert and on your side.

EXAMPLE 4-3: POORLY STRUCTURED PRESENTATION

Consider the following presentation plan, which is quite typical. Assume that there is neither an introduction nor a summary (also not unusual for this type of presentation). The only support envisioned is transparencies (word charts, lists, and tables). The approach has several severe problems: (1) it offers no variety of support, such as demonstrations or audience interactions; (2) it overuses numbers and lists and underuses concrete examples; and (3) throughout, it proceeds from one detailed point to the next, without message previews to keep the audience oriented.

Topic: *Computer Operating System and Hardware Upgrade Project*

Current situation [Several slides]
　　Number of PCs, laptops, and workstations
　　Age and capability of current systems [Table]

The current Mach 3 operating system environment
- General structure
- Limitations
- Advantages
- Life-cycle expectancy

Problems leading up to upgrade project [Several slides]

Reliability problems — frequent system crashes with data loss

Speed problems [Table of programs experiencing problems]

Memory problems, especially on laptops [Table of programs experiencing problems]

Inability to run some important advanced applications [List of programs]

Objectives of Upgrade Project [Several slides]

Ensure system compatibility with current and future releases of applications software.

Ensure reliability of systems; avoid or minimize crashes.

Ensure reasonable speed.

Take advantage of new technology, including:
- Advanced networking.
- Hassle-free Internet access from within any application.
- Smooth multimedia and Web presentations.

Status [Slides]

User survey completed [Table of questions and responses]

In-house test and evaluation of sample upgrade completed [Bar chart]

Preliminary pricing obtained [List of prices]

Projected Total Cost [Slides]

Phase 1 (selective upgrade)

Phase 2 (facility-wide roll-out)

Recommendations [Several slides]

Buy site license for Mach 5 operating system.

Upgrade one computer in each department:
- Back up all data and software.
- Expand memory if feasible; else replace unit.
- Add larger internal or external hard drive if feasible.
- Add internal or external CD-RW drive.
- Install hardware and software.
- Test and evaluate.
- Roll out facility-wide upgrade.

Next Actions [Slide]

Agree on plan and schedule.

Identify target machines in each department.

Negotiate deals on hardware and software.

Order hardware and software.

EXAMPLE 4-4: MORE EFFECTIVE PRESENTATION APPROACH AND STRUCTURE

The following describes a more effective plan for the presentation outlined in Example 4-3. In particular, the body uses fewer key points and backs them up in more varied, engaging ways. Also notice that an effective introduction following the *RAMP* formula has been added.

Topic: *Computer Operating Software and Hardware Upgrade — Mach 5 Project*

Audience: Management

Purposes:
1. Elicit and address all major questions and objections.
2. Get commitment to either go ahead now or make a decision within 2 weeks.
3. Ensure smooth implementation by
   - clearing up basic misunderstandings.
   - explaining and agreeing on overall procedure.

Major audience questions and objections considered (some of them set aside for Q&A; others covered in the body):
- What are the benefits of upgrading?
  - What will we be able to do with Mach 5 that we can't do with Mach 3?
  - What will the more powerful hardware do that we can't do now?
- Why can't we wait another year? Times are tough right now.
- All we ever get from computers is trouble. The more newfangled, the more trouble. How do we know this will *work?*
- How can we make sure the conversion is absolutely *safe* and won't corrupt important data or cripple our systems for weeks or months?
- How much will it cost?
- Exactly what will we need to do or change?
- What guarantees are there, and who will take care of problems?
- How much training will people need, and who will take care of it?
- What can we *lose* by doing this?

INTRODUCTION:
  Rapport:
  "I'm delighted to have this chance to discuss with you our project to bring our computer systems finally up to date so we all can work better with fewer glitches. I hope you'll be as excited as we are about our opportunities in this area.."

  Attention Getter [Three slides of a mock sales presentation;
  last slide = high-resolution product photo]
  "Imagine I'm a sales rep presenting to important customers. Here is my slide showing the customer's expressed needs. Then a nice 'Needs/Solutions' chart; and now a high-resolution product photo to bring the discussion to the main solution proposed. **But wait, what's this?"**

SLIDE 4: A system window pops up:

> **This program has performed an illegal action and
> will be shut down. If this happens again,
> contact the vendor.**

"So OK, we try to close down PowerPoint and restart it. But no, the Mach 3 operating system is out cold — nothing can get it to move. So I restart the computer, then restart PowerPoint, reload my presentation and get going again — *maybe* this time without crashing.

"Question: How long do you estimate it takes to get back up, with Mach 3 on our old laptops? [**About 3 minutes**] How would you feel as a sales rep in that situation? And how do you think the audience feels about the sales rep?"

Transition to main message:
"This is just one of many computer problems we cannot allow to go on any longer."

Main message preview [Slide using graphic symbolization for key ideas]:
To protect our competitiveness and technological edge, we must upgrade our desktop and laptop computers to the Mach 5 operating system *now*.

Plan [Slide]:

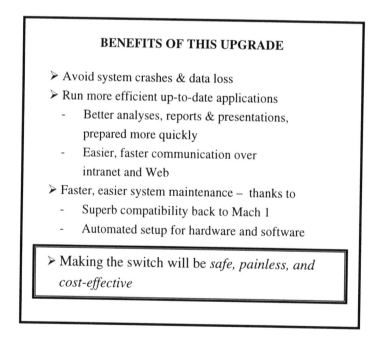

BODY:

Key Point #1 (Slide using graphic symbolization):
Upgrade will avoid system crashes & data loss.
Backup:

1. Interaction and individual exercise: "How many of you have experienced system crashes with Mach 3? OK, then I'd like you to do a simple calculation. First, apart from business loss or embarrassment as in my initial demonstration, estimate how many hours per week you lose on restarting the system and rescuing files or redoing work that wasn't saved. Then multiply that figure by 50 to get hours wasted per year. Finally multiply that by 100 to get a dollar figure." [**Record results on flip chart — to be used later.**]
2. Quotes from reviews and user surveys on **robustness** of Mach 5.
3. Our own pilot trial: no crashes; positive comments.

Key Point #2 [Slide using graphic symbolization]:
Run more efficient up-to-date applications:

- Better analyses, reports and presentations, prepared more quickly.
- Better, faster communication over intranet and Web.

Backup:

1. Interaction: "What outdated analysis programs are you using now, and how powerful and efficient do you find them to be?" [Record on flip chart, for comparison with survey shown on next visual.]
2. Visual: Top 5 outdated programs drawing user complaints, in company-wide survey:

Program	*Main Complaints*
Program A	Slow; freezes; no modules for new techniques; printing problems (missing image areas, printer errors, many attempts needed per print, low-quality print)
etc. (Prog. B – E)	

3. Visual: Same programs, up-to-date versions — showing positive user evaluations.

Key Point #3 [Slide using symbolization — e.g., car in service bay, being worked on]:
Faster, easier system maintenance — thanks to

- Superb compatibility all the way back to Mach 1.
- Automated setup for hardware and software.

Backup:

1. Show a program deletion on Mach 3, with ridiculous questions asking the user if he really wants to delete mysterious shared system files *"apparently* no longer used by any application."
2. Show the same program deletion under Mach 5 — all files removed, junk cleaned up.
3. General point [slide]: List of maintenance strengths of Mach 5:
   - Easy to install and reinstall — no need to reinstall applications, since Mach 5 arranges itself around existing programs. [Interaction: "Anybody ever had to have Mach 3 reinstalled?" Get agreement (or quote users) that it is a nightmare.]
   - Easy to add both old and up-to-date peripherals and programs. [Quote review.]

Key Point #4 [Slide — bullet chart]:
Making the switch to Mach 5 will be *safe, easy, and cost-effective.*
Backup:

1. **Safe:** Quote concern expressed in survey: "I see big risks — we can't afford upgrade snafus at sensitive time for our business." Answer:
   - Mach 5 proven compatible with programs designed even for Mach 1, so our old programs will all work, as will our peripherals. [Quote one review; note that user surveys agree.]
   - We will follow same safe, proven upgrade path as before: one key machine in each department, test and evaluate, only then roll out company-wide upgrade.
   - Many team members from last upgrade still on board. [Name some, especially those present for the talk.]
2. **Painless:**
   - One-third of desktops are upgradable; no need to reinstall applications on them.
   - Two-thirds will be new machines preloaded with Mach 5.
   - Peripherals will be set up automatically.
   - System is transparent, offers good on-line help; 1-hour training sessions adequate; Systems Group will help as needed after that.

3. **Cost-effective:**
   - Show total cost of upgrade, and rough cost per machine. [Slide]
   - Interaction/individual exercise: Have them compute time lost because of outdated, inefficient applications [return to earlier slide showing top 5 programs with problems/complaints]. **Add this yearly figure to cost of system crashes on flip chart; compare against upgrade cost per machine. [Add cost of low-quality output, presentations, etc. if needed.] Show that upgrade pays for itself within the first year.**

SUMMARY
Main message and key points: [Slide]
   Upgrade to Mach 5 will
   1. Avoid system crashes, slow, unreliable computing.
   2. Allow users to run up-to-date applications that will lead to better and faster analyses, reports, presentations, etc.
   3. Make system maintenance much faster and easier thanks to superb compatibility and automated setup for hardware and software.
   4. Be safe, painless, and cost-effective.

Next Actions: Agree on plan and schedule.
"I hope we can reach that agreement right now!"
[Refer to **handout** for details on schedule and costs.]

Handout [to be distributed at end, just before Question and Answer]:
Details of schedule, implementation, and costs.

EXERCISES AND DISCUSSION

Exercise 4-1. Develop a presentation outline for the following theme and background. Start with an Audience & Purpose Analysis, then develop an effective main message and key points. Outline the introduction, body, and summary. For the body, think of effective *examples, ideas for visuals, and ways to interact with the audience.* Use these ideas to support your points in varied ways.

Topic: Recommendation to install a security system using miniature closed-circuit TV cameras

Audience: Management and employees

Background: The company wants to cut down on security violations by employees and outsiders and also prevent crime in the parking area. Restaurants have used this kind of system, which made customers feel safer. The equipment is easy to install, light, easy to use, and not expensive. Costs have come down sharply: $200 per camera/microphone, each of which is hooked up to a VCR/TV. (Restaurant paid $2,600 for 2 cameras and monitors.) Everybody will get involved in security as they notice things on the monitors; in the case of restaurants, customers got involved in watching the parking area (it competed with TV for entertainment value). Liability is also lessened: the system avoids lawsuits by people who get hurt in an attack. Finally, it can save on security guards. An alternative considered is VideoEye: $6,000 for equipment, then $300/month to have premises monitored by VideoEye staff 24 hours a day, in their central location. They contact police, describe what's going on, even fax still of video to police.

Alternative topic: Any real presentation which you need to prepare soon, or which you may find useful in the future.

Discussion 4-1. What are *your* preferred learning styles? What does this mean for a presenter who wants to hold your attention, make it easy for you to follow the discussion, and persuade you?

5

The Summary

One of the most common problems in a presentation is running out of time, either because you underestimated the length of your speech or because your time allowance suddenly was shortened. At this point, many speakers fly into a frenzy. They rush through their remaining overheads — and almost always skip the summary (if they did, in fact, prepare one).

This is a big mistake. Don't ever omit the summary. Instead, be prepared to shorten your presentation by condensing parts of the body.

There are three very good reasons for always summarizing:

1. As mentioned earlier, there is a well-established rule of thumb: the audience takes in only about one-third of what you say. So, if you want to make sure everybody has heard your main points at least once, you need to state them three times. The summary is a natural place for the final repetition.
2. The best chance to get your main message across is when the audience is naturally most attentive, which is at the beginning and the end of your presentation.
3. Audiences tend to remember best whatever they heard last. Therefore, a strong summary of your main points makes it more likely that people will remember your main ideas and act on them.

HOW TO SUMMARIZE

Your summary is simply a restatement of your main message and your key points. If you can manage to add an interesting final thought or a call to action, your closing will be even stronger. The whole thing should take no more than a minute.

It's essential that you use the words "In summary," "In conclusion," "To summarize," or something similar. Why? Because without some such expression, not all the listeners will come back from their daydreams and join you for your closing thoughts. That is, their attention curve will look as in Figure 5-1, and your summary will get at best subliminal attention.

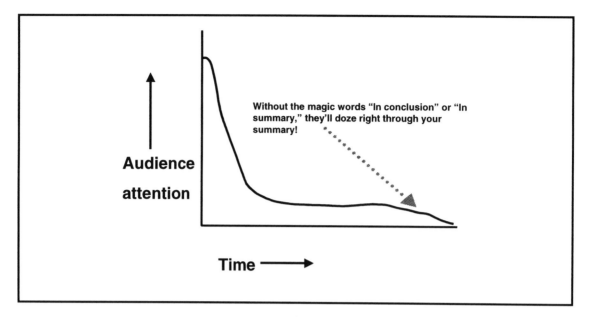

Figure 5-1. Always summarize — and don't forget the "wake-up call"!

Finally, plan to close with an enthusiastic invitation for questions, such as "And now I'd be glad to answer your questions." "Questions?" or "Any questions?" does *not* qualify as enthusiastic invitation. "That's all, I guess" is even worse — yet it's one of the most common "closing remarks" in technical presentations. If this is one of your favorites, then include in your notes a more upbeat request!

Here are two examples of summaries. In the first, the final extra idea is an assertion of personal commitment to a project; in the second, it is a request for suggestions beyond the question-and-answer period.

Example 5-1: *In summary, we should add an extended-nip press to paper machine #2. This will reduce drying costs 25%, decrease our rejects by 70%, and create exciting new product opportunities, such as.... I urge you to move on this immediately so we can avoid the escalating customer complaints related to our current press section. Brenda and I are committed to implementing this upgrade as quickly and smoothly as possible. And now I'd be happy to answer any questions you might have.*

Example 5-2: *In conclusion, I've tried to show you that our purchasing procedures are there to help **you** as well as the company. They'll usually get you a better deal and an enforceable contract from a proven, reputable vendor. Yes, there's some paperwork — but no more than you'd have to complete to order products or supplies on your own. And there needn't be any delays, either, provided you fill out the requisition order correctly. It's not difficult, and we're happy to answer any questions you have. Of course, there's always room for improvement, and you've already pointed out a number of changes you'd like to see, such as more input into vendor choices. We'll consider all these carefully. Now, there's one more thought I'd like to leave with you. The story is not finished with this presentation. We want to do* *whatever we can to make the system as good as possible. So, if you think of any suggestions or problems after today, I urge you to call me or come by my office and share your thoughts. I'd really appreciate it. And now I'll be glad to answer any additional questions.*

A CARDINAL ERROR: OUTSTAYING YOUR WELCOME

We said earlier that the summary should take no more than a minute. Many speakers violate this rule — and they pay for their mistake with a loss of goodwill, even if their *total* time is right on target. Above all, don't introduce a number of new points at this late hour, no matter how important they may be (you can always try to raise them during the question-and-answer session).

Figure 5-2 illustrates the reason for the one-minute limit: mental exhaustion. When you say the magical words "In conclusion" or "In summary," the audience shifts into high-attention gear. Unfortunately, they can maintain this high level only for a minute or so; after that, they crash.

Think of them as long-distance runners going for the final 50-yard dash. You can't suddenly move the finish line by 400 yards just as they get to it! They'll either collapse or just stop and walk off the track, crying "Foul play!" Your audience is just like that.

So, do summarize — but don't spoil your last impression by outstaying your welcome!

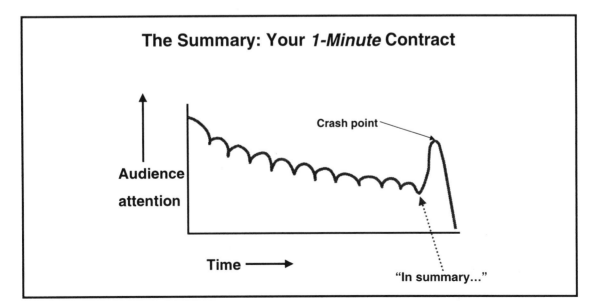

Figure 5-2. You have only about one minute to summarize, or the audience will crash.

EXERCISES AND DISCUSSION

Exercise 5-1. Critique and revise the following summary and closing:

"So, I hope you can see the benefits of this project — the impact on the product line for the next two years and the lower production costs by 3 percent — which more than pay for the costs of $420,000. Questions?"

Exercise 5-2. Imagine you've been asked to give an *overview of your job or area of work*. The audience consists of managers and fellow employees who know little or nothing about your specialty; however, their work may impinge on yours, and your work affects them in some ways.

1. Find an interesting main message for your presentation — something useful or challenging.
2. Decide on 3-5 key points based on your analysis of the audience.
3. Outline the introduction, including an attention getter.
4. Outline the body; choose varied support for your points (visuals as well as audience interaction and other devices drawing on different learning styles).
5. Outline the summary.

Discussion 5-1. You are a presenter at a conference. Speakers before you in your group have used up too much time, so the moderator asks you to cut 5 minutes of your talk, from 15 to 10 minutes. What do you do? Talk faster? Omit introduction and summary? Other options? Has this ever happened to you? What did you try that *worked*, and what did you do that did *not* work?

6

Preparing Effective Visuals

Good visuals can strengthen your presentation tremendously — but unfortunately, they're rare. Here are three key attributes to remember:

1. *Few* and to the point.
2. *Big,* so they're easy to see.
3. *Simple,* so they're easy to understand.

To these, add one more principle:

4. Make the *important* visuals *memorable* so your key ideas stay with the audience long after the talk.

We'll look at these properties in more detail in this chapter and show you how to achieve them.

BEING SELECTIVE: KNOW YOUR PURPOSE

People often ask us how many visuals they should use per minute of speech. They are usually disappointed with our answer: No more than you *really need.* There is no magical number; the true criterion is that each visual must have a clear *purpose.*

There are only a few legitimate purposes:

- To get a difficult technical point across — say, with a flow diagram or line chart
- To make a process or concept more concrete with an example
- To make a key point easier to remember through a strong symbolic image
- To make the structure of your talk more transparent by listing the major points to be covered
- To provide a prompt for yourself so you don't forget the next point

The last purpose is the least legitimate — yet in many presentations, it seems the only reason for most of the visuals. Imagine writing every word of your presentation on transparencies and just reading the whole speech off the screen. Well, the more overheads you use as prompts, the closer you get to this absurd extreme!

How Many Visuals?

Common advice has it that you should use about one slide for each 2-3 minutes of talk. That would mean 7-10 visuals for a 20-minute presentation. In many cases, that proportion is quite reasonable. However, *varied support* works much better than a constant stream of visuals (see Chapter 4 for guidance and examples). So don't apply rules mechanically, but always check your purpose and choose the strongest support (example, anecdote, quote, interaction, visual, etc.) for your point.

Just decide *exactly how you will use each visual.* If it doesn't serve a legitimate purpose, throw it out. Sometimes, that leaves just three or four visuals. That's fine. Many presentations can be improved dramatically just by omitting half the visuals. For one thing, it encourages you to talk to the people rather than hide behind your visuals.

Of course, some of your visuals may be objects, such as samples or tools. Such demonstration objects can be very effective. If possible, avoid passing them out while you speak, though, as this always creates some distraction. The same holds for handouts: unless people need them to follow the discussion of a detailed technical point, try to hand them out after rather than before or during your talk. (We'll have more to say about handouts in Chapter 7.)

Tip

Use each visual for a *clear purpose*. The most legitimate of these are

- Persuasion
- Enlightenment
- Explanation of difficult concepts
- Orientation (show where you are in a process or in your presentation plan)

Then choose the *type* of chart or graphic that serves your purpose most strongly.

CHOOSING THE RIGHT CHART TYPE

Your material (say, numbers or ideas) usually suggests a certain *range* of chart types (e.g., tables, pie charts, line charts, or bar charts for numerical material), but within that range, there can be many choices. Table 6-1 lists some of your major options and their most appropriate uses.

The most overused chart type undoubtedly is the word chart; the most inappropriate, the numerical table. Just correcting your habits in these two areas may give you a major presentation improvement without much effort.

TABLE 6-1. Some Major Chart Types and Their Proper Uses in a Presentation

Chart Type	Purpose
Word charts	To highlight ideas, problems, etc. *(Pure word or bullet charts, without graphic support, are weak but OK for routine points. For major points, consider replacing them with symbolic graphics.)*
Numerical tables	To bring together a *few* important numbers. *(Number tables are very weak—always consider replacing them with stronger graphics.)*
Pie charts	To show parts of a total, with ratios or percentages.
Cut pie charts	To emphasize one element of the total. (May be combined with a *column chart* to show components of the slice.)
Line charts	To show fluctuations or trends over time.
Horizontal bar charts	To rank many similar items.
Vertical bar charts	To show changes over time.
PERT or Gantt charts	To show project schedules.
Drawings or symbolic graphics; "concept charts"	To illustrate processes, concepts, equipment, etc.
Photographs	To show buildings, equipment, people, etc.
Video clips	To show actions or processes, or complex layouts not well illustrated by one or two photographs

MAKING TEXT AND IMAGES BIG AND BOLD
(THE 18-POINT RULE)

Unreadable charts are one of the most common complaints. For instance, how readable is the chart in Figure 6-1 going to be for the audience?

As *recipients* of such visual assaults, we have not a second's doubt that such a chart is unreadable and therefore pointless. Yet as *presenters,* we are all too often tempted to inflict similar visuals on our audience!

Is there a simple guideline for avoiding this problem? Yes: make typed text bold and at least 18 points. Anything smaller is hard to read from the back of the room. Here are some samples of text in proper size:

This is 18 points (the minimum)
This is 24 points

Too small: 12 points   Also too small: 14 points

Using type of at least 18 points means you can't fit more than about 16 lines (including title) on a slide (assuming you are using "landscape, " or sideways, format, which is the default in today's presentation software). That works out fine — anything more would be too much information for the audience to absorb at a time.

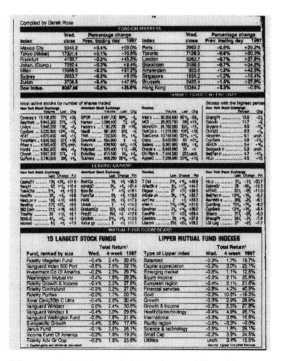

Figure 6-1. Unreadable charts like this one are still a common problem.

In a bullet chart, keeping items to a reasonable length usually forces you to use short phrases rather than full sentences. That's again all for the better: You don't want to turn your presentation into a speed-reading exercise or insult your audience by reading verbatim what's on the screen!

If you are an accountant or controller, *please suppress the urge to photocopy that 12-column computer printout!* Are you really going to read all the invisible numbers in all 12 columns to your audience? Perhaps you need just a list of the 12 column headings and then the numbers for one or two interesting or representative examples.

Tip

You may be aware of the *Arm's Length Rule:* If you cannot read all parts of your visual (including text) while holding it at arm's length, you've made it too small. This may work for 35 mm slides, but it is much too forgiving for computer slides or transparencies. For instance, you can probably read 10-point or 12-point type at that distance — but people in the back of the room never could.

Some Common Mistakes To Avoid in Preparing Visuals

- *Don't overuse word charts.* If you need several word charts, you can disguise some of them as "concept charts" by enriching them graphically.
- *Avoid tables.* People don't have time in a presentation to read many numbers. Also, after reading the numbers, they usually still need to translate them into *relationships*. In most cases, a bar, pie, or line chart will show the relevant relationships more clearly and quickly.
- *Avoid unreadable transparencies made by copying computer printouts or other busy material.* Instead, decide exactly which portions of the original chart you want to discuss in detail, then use only those items. (If time is short, you can cut and paste, then enlarge the result on a copier until the size is right for projecting.)
- *Throw out unnecessary visuals for minor points.* Using too many visuals becomes monotonous. Often, an example will support your point more strongly than yet another dull word chart.

KEEPING IT SIMPLE AND EASY TO PROCESS (THE THREE-SECOND RULE)

As much as possible, avoid competing with your visuals for the audience's attention. Anything that takes them away for more than three seconds constitutes destructive competition. Therefore, it's crucial that you make all charts simple and immediately understandable. Here is the rule for you to remember:

The Three-Second Rule for Visuals

**If viewers can't get the big idea of the visual
in three seconds,
you must revise the visual.**

This means cutting out all clutter (unnecessary grids, numbers, and details). Include only what you need to make your point. In most cases, it also means you should replace numerical tables with other types of charts, such as bar or line charts. These charts are more quickly absorbed, because they show *relationships* visually. Use numerical tables only when you're talking about simple numbers rather than trends or relationships — say, when giving a short cost breakdown.

For instance, in the following examples, notice how much longer it takes to extract the key relationships from the table in Figure 6-2 than from the bar chart in Figure 6-3.

Some Simple Ways To Make Visuals Easier To Process

One of the hardest things for the audience is *cross-referencing,* or having to go back and forth over certain sections of your visual. A *legend* asks them to do just that. The smarter approach is to label things directly, if possible. Even though it may be a little extra work for you, you'll be rewarded by better audience attention.

For instance, consider the line chart in Figure 6-4, which is characteristic of traditional scientific illustrations. It will take the audience quite a few moments to get the facts, because the three line styles and markers have to be correlated with the legend.

All that work has been done for the audience in the next version (Figure 6-5), which also has thicker, more visible lines and does away with distracting grid lines. The labels are placed directly next to the curves (no leading lines are needed if you choose the right spot, where there can't be any ambiguity). Unless you are operating in a very low-tech environment, without access to color, you would of course use a different color for each line to make distinction easier; the labels (*Fresh, Frozen, Canned*) would then be in the same color as their corresponding line.

The same principles can be applied to pie charts. For instance, Figure 6-6 relies on a legend for the pie slices (usually, this is the software default). Using direct labeling as in Figure 6-7 greatly speeds up processing of the chart for the audience and helps you keep their attention.

U.S. Population
1986 and 1990

Region	1986	1990
Northeast	50,000,000	50,600,000
Midwest	59,300,000	59,800,000
South	83,000,000	87,300,000
West	48,800,000	52,300,000

Figure 6-2. Tables are ineffective at any size in a presentation. How long does it take viewers to grasp which item is the biggest and how the others compare? Even for just a few numbers, as in this case, several seconds — enough to take attention away from your talk.

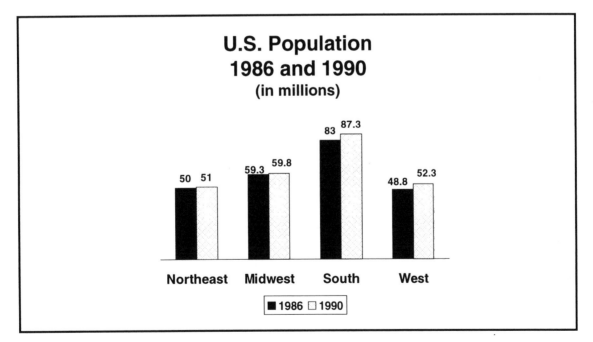

Figure 6-3. A bar chart conveys the same information more effectively. Notice that size relationships are immediately obvious.

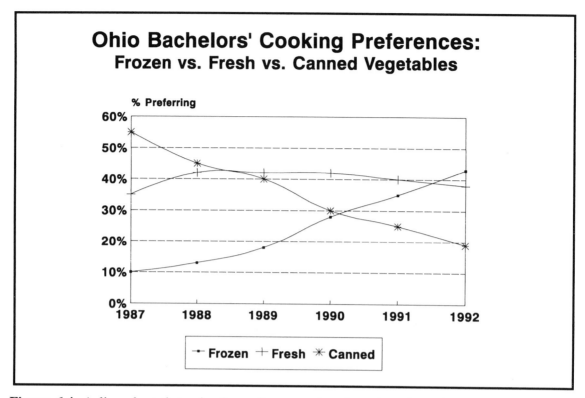

Figure 6.4. A line chart that asks the audience to do a lot of work: make out thin lines, cut through the clutter, recognize and distinguish poky line markers, and correlate the legend with those line markers.

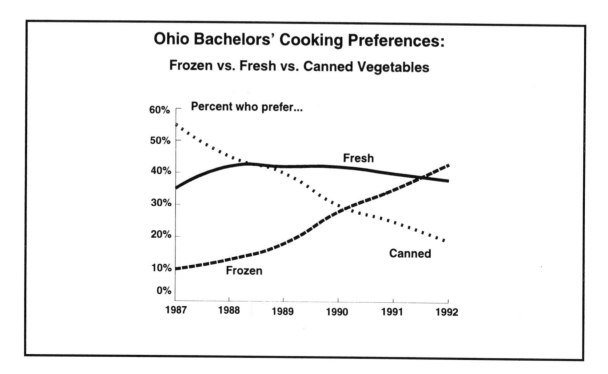

Figure 6-5. Line chart cleaned up so it passes the Three-Second Rule: grid and legend omitted, thick, clearly distinct lines used without markers, and curves labeled directly.

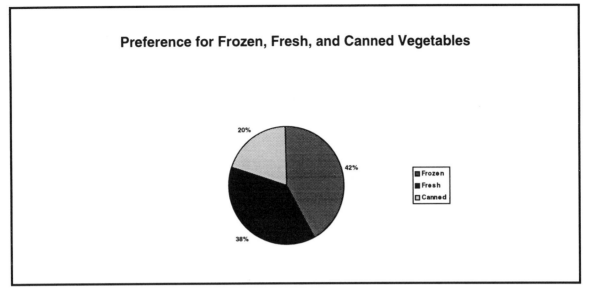

Figure 6-6. A standard pie chart with legend (usually much too small, as provided by the software default) and small percentage numbers keeps the audience occupied for quite a few seconds as they try to figure out what goes with what and how big it is. Also, the title does nothing to focus viewers on the main point.

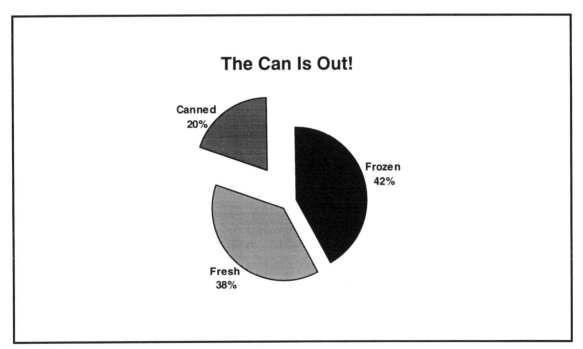

Figure 6-7. Direct labeling combined with using cut slices to emphasize the main idea (here, the "canned" portion) helps the audience get the picture instantly. The snappy, to-the-point title also helps.

The Limits of Direct Labeling

Consider again the cluster bar chart shown earlier as Figure 6-3, reproduced here as Figure 6-8. Notice that despite direct labeling of some aspects, there is a *legend* for the two data series: 1986 vs. 1990. Each of the four regions has a pair of bars, and viewers must study the legend to understand which bar refers to which year.

Conceivably, we could get rid of the legend by labeling each bar directly for the year, as in Figure 6-9. However, at this point a trade-off between clutter and direct labeling begins to kick in: there may be too much to read for the audience. Certainly, if *four* years were compared, putting four year-numbers on each bar cluster would be overwhelming — and three or four bars per cluster is quite common.

This should make it clear that there is a natural limit to direct labeling. Use common sense: if the overall effect looks too busy, you need to use standard referencing methods, such as a legend.

However, the basic problem has not disappeared: the audience spends quite a bit of time cross-referencing things on your chart, and that takes attention away from you. What can you do about it?

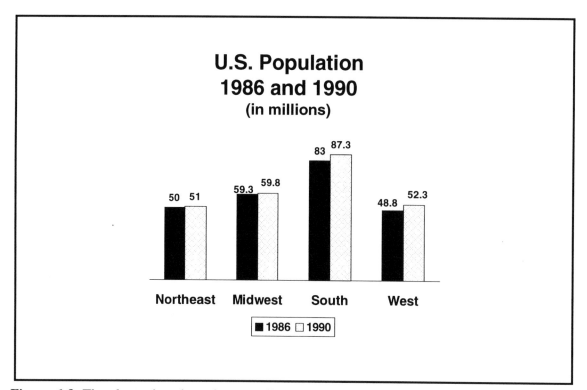

Figure 6-8. The cluster bar chart shown earlier, using direct labeling as far as appropriate (i.e., for U.S. regions and the population data above each sales bar). Notice that there is nonetheless a *legend* for one item — 1986 vs. 1990 data.

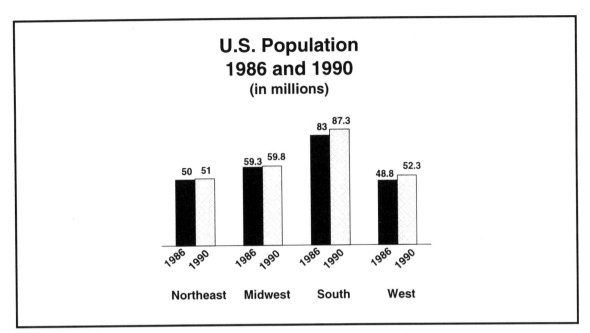

Figure 6-9. The same chart as in Figure 6-8, with direct labeling taking to an extreme. Note that there are now too many numbers to read, even though each cluster has only two bars. With three or four bars per cluster, the number clutter would be overwhelming. The better approach is to live with a legend and "walk" the audience through the meaning of the first bar cluster.

The best solution lies in smart delivery: Recognize that the audience needs help, and *give* it. This simply means taking 10 seconds to *clearly explain what each bar in a cluster stands for.* Obviously, you only need to do this for the first cluster; all the others follow the same pattern. By explaining matters in this fashion, you keep the audience with you and pace their analysis of your chart. Otherwise, they'll be trying to figure out the clusters while you're talking, and then you've lost them.

Word Charts and the Three-Second Rule

Remember our Three-Second Rule for visuals:

The Three-Second Rule for Visuals

**If viewers can't get the big idea of the visual
in three seconds,
you must revise the visual.**

This applies not only to tables and complex line or bar charts but also to word charts. For instance, test the word chart in Figure 6-10 against the Three-Second Rule. Notice that this chart takes much too long to process — surely more than three seconds. Also, if

---

CORPORATE MISSION STATEMENT
"Our corporate mission is to provide superior products and services that provide complete customer satisfaction, with zero defects passed on to end users, at a price that meets or beats competitors' prices, while providing maximum return to shareholders through proactive exploitation of technologies that reduce production costs."

Figure 6-10. Word charts containing whole sentences make for slow, cumbersome processing.

Tip

In word charts, use only key words, not complete sentences. Sentences take too long to read and interfere with processing what you are saying.

---

you are reading the chart out loud, your voice will be conflicting with audience members' inner voice as they read the chart silently — at a speed that clashes with yours!

The way to avoid the problem is simple: ***don't use complete long sentences — just key words.*** (And certainly avoid reading a whole chart out loud verbatim — it's intrinsically slow and boring. Instead, paraphrase the points on the screen.) Figure 6-11 shows a key-word version of the verbose chart in Figure 6-10. Beautiful as the Corporate Mission Statement might sound to some ears, in our experience the audience will thank you for not plastering it full-length on the screen.

OUR MISSION

- **100% customer satisfaction**
- **Zero defects**
- **Competitive prices**
- **Maximum shareholder returns**
- **Aggressive application of technology to reduce production costs**

Figure 6-11. Improved word chart that passes the Three-Second Rule.

MAKING KEY IDEAS MEMORABLE THROUGH GRAPHICS

So far, we discussed how to create clean visuals that support your points. In essence, this involves

- Keeping text big (at least 18 points) so it can be read easily from the back of the room
- Minimizing clutter (grids, numbers, legends, and unnecessary details)

If you do these two things, your visuals will work *for* you rather than compete *against* you. Now let's see how to make some of your visuals not just effective but *memorable*.

Why Create Memorable Visuals?

A strong visual can help your listeners *remember a key point.* This is especially important when you want to persuade them to do something. By the time they are in a position to act, they may well have forgotten everything you said! However, if you give them one interesting image, they often can reconstruct your message from it. (Of course, it need not always be a visual — often, a demonstration or vivid example is more effective.)

Tip

Don't overuse "memorable" symbolic treatment, or *none* of your visuals will be remembered!

For instance, what are the chances of anybody in the audience remembering a table such as the one shown in Figure 6-12? This is just a bunch of words arranged in columns and rows — nothing memorable about that at all. On the other hand, the same idea expressed with the help of the symbolic image of "scale," as in Figure 6-13, may well stay with the audience. (In fact, it did with us — we could easily reconstruct the essence of the entire talk from that one core visual.) Therefore, even if it takes an extra 20 minutes to prepare, it's well worth the effort.

**Environmental Impact Factors:
Nonrecycled vs. Recycled Paper**

	Nonrecycled paper	*Recycled paper*
Energy	Yes	Yes +
Emissions	Yes	Yes +
Chemicals	Yes	Yes +

Figure 6-12. Unmemorable table.

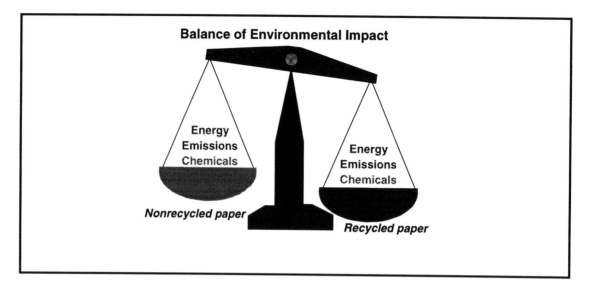

Figure 6-13. Symbolic treatment that has a better chance than a table or bullet chart to be remembered by the audience at the time when they have to make decisions.

Using Symbolic Images As a Layout Element

On the simplest level, symbolic images can serve as a basis for a layout that avoids the standard bullet format. The chart is still a basic list, but its character is disguised to give the audience a break from the tedium of bullets.

For instance, Figure 6-14 shows a standard bullet chart that will probably wash right over the audience. The same content arranged around a star symbol that expresses the speaker's "star presence" will get much more attention (Figure 6-15).

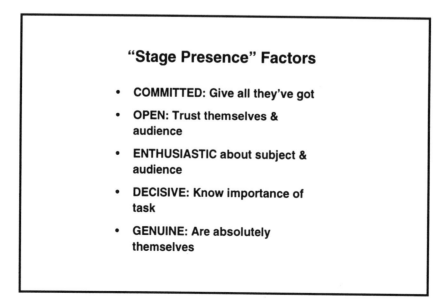

Figure 6-14. If this is bullet chart #20, will the audience even notice it?

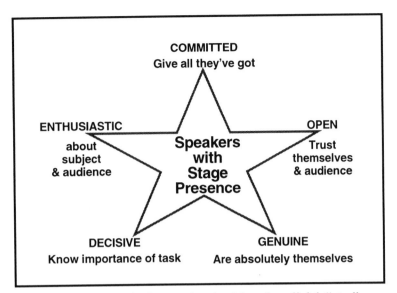

Figure 6-15. Graphic layout inspired by the cliché "star" can relieve "bullet overload" and draw more attention.

Symbolization: A Key Skill

Symbolization involves finding a concrete image for an abstract concept. For instance, an iceberg can serve as an image for the abstract concept *problem* and suggest "dangerous stuff lurking under the surface." Good images often illuminate the abstract concept in interesting ways, so they're not just "add-ons."

Unfortunately, symbolization is difficult for many of us, because we're not used to thinking in images. However, since it can add so much power to your presentations, it is a skill worth developing.

Word charts can profit most from symbolization. This doesn't mean you have to go to the trouble of creating graphics for each word chart. Just pick your *key visuals* and think of strong images for them. It's worth the effort, because with strong visuals for your key points, you can

- Get your listeners to wake up and pay attention.
- Make them *remember* your key points later, when they are in a position to take the kind of action you may be recommending.
- Lighten the atmosphere while giving serious information.

Here are some possible sources of inspiration:

- Thesaurus (look up synonyms that are *picture words*)
- Clichés ("road to success," "barking up the wrong tree," etc.)
- Catalogs (e.g., household products), magazines
- Cartoons (*The New Yorker* and other magazines)
- Ads (many elaborate on a cliché; e.g., a "jail bird" trying to break the window bars, which are actually cigarettes; the caption asking "Can you break the habit?")
- Different spheres of life (sports, hobbies, nature, weather, animals, etc.)

Using Graphics for (Tasteful and Gentle) Humorous Effect

Sometimes, you can also use a symbolic visual to *introduce humor* without diluting your credibility — a great benefit especially when you're presenting to a nontechnical audience. Most audiences are secretly hoping for relief from boredom or tension. Even the gentlest touch of humor in a visual will immediately improve their receptiveness to you.

The simplest approach to devising a humorous visual is to search your clip art collection under the category "cartoons" for appropriate images that you can use or customize. For instance, Figure 6-16 is a customized combination of a cartoon depicting a sleeper and images for a wasp and a "dream cloud." The humor is of the gentlest variety — it derives mostly from the cartoonist's skill in drawing a blissful business sleeper. Yet the resulting slide can do much to lighten the atmosphere and at the same time leave the audience with a lasting image reminding them what to do in a difficult situation.

Tip

Don't overuse humor in visuals, or it will detract from the seriousness of your message.

How To Produce Memorable Visuals

Creating the kinds of visuals we are talking about requires two skills:

1. Symbolization
2. Graphic execution

Figure 6-16. Graphics can help you lighten the atmosphere without the need for verbal jokes or anecdotes. If well done, they can also leave the audience with a lasting image that reminds them of your message.

Executing graphic ideas has become possible even for nonartists, thanks to improved graphics software that includes plenty of electronic clip art and powerful, easy-to-use drawing tools. We'll offer some detailed suggestions on how to make the best use of modern software in Part 3 of this book.

Symbolization is the skill of finding symbolic images for the concepts you want to express. For instance, we wanted to illustrate the idea that the key to powerful delivery is *connection* with the audience. A natural image for *connection* was that of a plug connected to an extension cord so that power could flow. It was simply a matter of asking: *Where do power connections occur?* In the realm of everyday household objects, plugs and extension cords immediately offered themselves. Furthermore, the cliché "plugged in" seemed ready-made for the purpose, leading to the symbolic chart in Figure 6-17.

You will find similar clichés useful in many cases. Table 6-2 lists some examples to get your thinking going.

Other useful sources for symbols are simply all the different areas of life. Here are some examples:

Sports	Hobbies	Nature, landscapes
Boating	Food	Weather
Everyday objects	Construction work	Office
Hospital	Buildings	Shops
Transportation	Tools	Traditions and their symbols
Animals	Gardening	Plants
War	Violence	Weapons, archery, etc.
Food preparation	Restaurants	Street, city
Playground	School	Church life

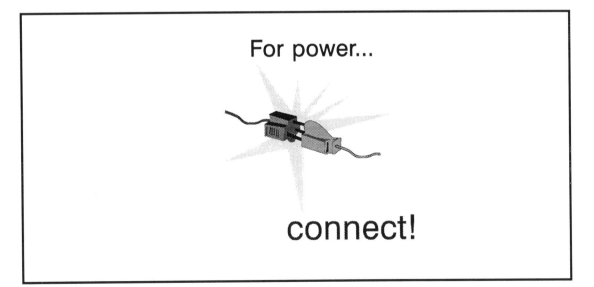

Figure 6-17. Clichés can help you find an effective image quickly, as in this example expressing "connection to power," which was developed from the cliché "plugged in."

TABLE 6-2. Some Examples of Clichés That Evoke Useful Images for Symbolization

Cliché	Possible Application
Taking a swing at … (bureaucracy, corruption, etc.)	Business person swinging baseball bat; background or stadium elements can be labeled to denote the target.
Obstacle course	Show one, with obstacles labeled to express the issues to be addressed.
Bull in a china shop	Show things being broken — label them as appropriate.
Tip of the iceberg	Cruise boat hitting an iceberg; boat and iceberg may be labeled to denote the concepts you are talking about.
Dog fight	Dogs fighting over bone; label dogs as needed — e.g., *Accounting* and *Production*
Take off like a rocket	Show it; label the rocket with the concept you're interested in.
Out of synch	Rower stroking out of synch; shirts of rowers may be labeled with different department or group names.
Climb the ladder of success	Each rung of a ladder being climbed can be labeled to show the path to success.
Blind to danger	Blindfolded person and some peril (truck, manhole, etc.); danger may be labeled as appropriate.
Blinkers	Show things being ignored left and right; label them as appropriate.
Building blocks	Show some; label them as needed.
Burst the bubble	Show it; label the bubble as needed.

Finally, just browsing through the clip art in your software may give you ideas. Take a little time to do this as a fun project — not just when you are under pressure to design visuals for tomorrow's presentation. You may come across some images that are inherently useful for your sphere of work. If so, copy them all into a presentation file and keep them there for future use; it may save you hours of drawing or searching six months

---

Tip

If you have trouble thinking of symbols, study billboards and ads in technical and business journals; you can learn a lot about effective symbolization from them. You may even want to save some ads in a file to spark ideas later.

---

from now. Figure 6-18 shows a few typical examples of such clip art, with annotations added to suggest ways to use it.

A Caveat

By definition, a memorable visual draws attention to itself — and therefore away from you. Isn't that just the sort of competition we urged you to avoid? Yes — and that's why you should be careful not to overdo this. Besides losing your audience to your graphics, you risk getting a reputation as someone who likes to play on his computer instead of working on the real problems. Consider a special visual only for your main message or the most important key point — and even then only if the ideas naturally lend themselves to strong symbolic representation. So build the skill, but use it sparingly!

USING COLOR TO ADVANTAGE

Color can be very helpful to the audience by heightening distinctions and drawing attention to different portions of a chart. It also sets a mood and projects a certain image of you and your presentation. The keys to using color effectively are *restraint* and a basic understanding of the *color wheel*.

Figure 6-18. Some common images available in presentation software, and sample uses for a presentation. Making yourself a file of annotated images such as this for future use can be a smart timesaver.

A Balanced Palette: How Your Software Can Help

Color becomes distracting rather than helpful under three circumstances:

1. There are too many colors.
2. The colors chosen clash.
3. Colors are used inappropriately, producing insufficient distinctions (e.g., between different lines in a line chart, or between background and text) or misdirecting attention (e.g., by using a natural foreground color as your background).

Tip

Don't base a distinction solely on red vs. green — remember that color-blind audience members see these two colors as the same. If you do use red vs. green, you can add a difference in pattern to avoid confusion.

The best way to avoid these problems is to *restrict the number of colors* and to *exploit the expertise embedded in your software.*

As a starting point, use one of the major color schemes your presentation software offers. These schemes are usually safe and well balanced. If you don't have a lot of categories of data that you must distinguish visually, you usually don't need to add or change colors in that scheme.

If you find that you must indeed add colors, follow these simple guidelines:

- Add as few colors as possible, using the color wheel as your guidance (see below).
- Consider working with *shades* (light vs. dark) of the same color rather than adding new colors. However, make sure there is strong color contrast between distinct chart elements, such as lines or bars.

The Color Wheel

Working with color becomes easier when you understand the color wheel (see Figure 6-19), which expresses basic relationships among colors.

The solid triangle inside the color wheel connects the three *primary colors: red, yellow, and blue.* These are pure colors that can't be produced by mixing other colors. The broken triangle connects the *secondary colors orange, green, and violet,* which are mixed from adjacent colors. Lighter and darker shades of any color result from adding white or black.

Complementary colors are two colors that occupy opposite positions on the color wheel. Examples are red and green, orange and blue, or yellow and violet. Complementary colors contrast sharply with each other.

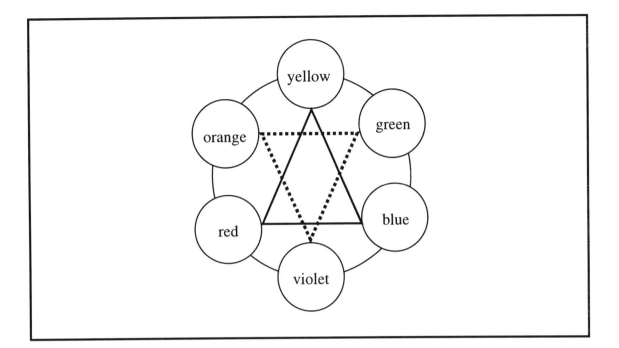

Figure 5-19. The color wheel is the basis for understanding how colors work together to produce contrast and aesthetic balance.

Common Color Schemes Based on the Color Wheel

Study the color schemes of your presentation software. Many of them will be based on five schemes commonly used by artists: (1) monochromatic, (2) analogous harmony, (3) complementary, (4) perfected harmony, and (5) triad harmony. To any of these schemes, you can add white, gray, and black.

A *monochromatic scheme* uses lighter and darker shades of one color. To produce the shades with your software, add white or black as needed. This color scheme produces a unified effect, but it does not allow for much contrast. Therefore, if you need to make a lot of distinctions between different sets of data, a monochromatic scheme is not a good choice.

The other four schemes are shown in Figure 6-20 and discussed in more detail below. The arrows in each scheme illustrate only one example; by rotating the constellation of arrows, you can work out other possibilities. For example, analogous harmony uses any three adjacent colors on the color wheel.

Tip

Avoid bright, "hot" backgrounds such as pink or yellow; they tend to overwhelm any elements in the foreground.

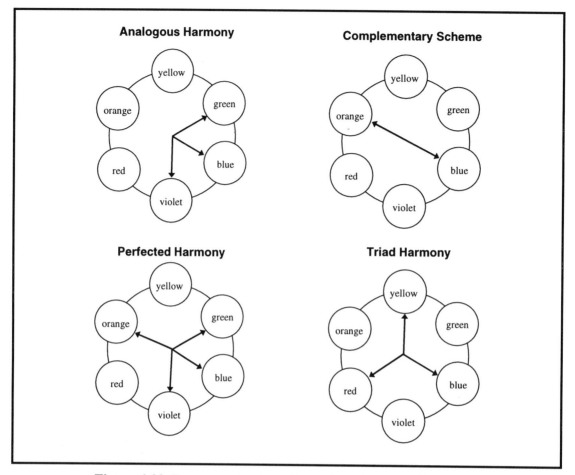

Figure 6-20. Four general color schemes based on the color wheel.

Tip

Safe color combinations for slides include dark blue background with yellow or white lettering and black or dark purple background with yellow lettering. The background may be graduated from a lighter to a darker shade or from one dark color to an adjacent one, such as from dark blue to dark violet..

Analogous Harmony. Choose one color as your dominant color and supplement it with other colors adjacent to it on the color wheel. For example, if violet is your dominant color, you can use it with blues and reds. To achieve greater contrast, you can make some colors lighter (more intense). An analogous scheme produces a sense of harmony.

Complementary Scheme. This scheme uses colors that are opposite each other on the color wheel, such as blue and orange. Mute your predominant color and reserve the lighter shade for emphasis. For instance, use a dark blue background with light blue and orange, plus the neutral tones white, gray, and black. Because of its sharp contrasts, a complementary scheme tends to stimulate interest.

Perfected Harmony. This is a combination of analogous harmony and the complementary scheme. Because it offers more choices, it is useful when you need to make a greater number of distinctions. In the example, blue might be your dominant color, used with its analogous colors green and violet; for contrast, the complementary color orange is added. To take another example: if blue is your dominant color, you might contrast it with its complement orange and the colors adjacent to orange, namely, red and yellow.

Triad Harmony. This scheme uses any three colors (such as the primary colors red, yellow, and blue) on the wheel that form an even triangle. Choose a dominant color for your chart and reserve the other two for contrast and highlight. For instance, a dark blue background goes well with yellow and red chart elements, plus white, gray, and black for separating chart elements as needed.

Psychology of Colors

Colors can evoke moods, feelings, or ideas. Table 6-3 shows some examples. Before settling on a color scheme, you may want to consider the occasion (serious vs. light, informative vs. persuasive, young audience vs. older audience, etc.) and the image or mood you are trying to project. For instance, if you want a calm, conservative effect, magenta is not a good key color for your scheme.

TABLE 6-3. Some Colors and the Moods, Feelings, Or Ideas They May Suggest in Western Cultures

Color	Mood, Feeling, Idea
White	Cold or cool, pure
Gray	Conservative, solid
Black	Serious, sad
Cyan	Cold or cool
Blue	Calm, loyal, honest, pure
Violet	Royal, grand
Magenta	Intense, lively, nervous
Crimson	Angry
Red	Warm, passionate; angry; danger; money loss
Orange	Stimulating, warm
Gold	Wealthy, glamorous
Yellow	Warm, gay, festive; sunny
Green	Cool, relaxing; spring; money
Dark green	Peaceful, in harmony with nature

EXERCISES

Exercise 6-1. Review Table 6-1, which shows chart types and their uses. Evaluate your own presentation habits. Do you overuse certain chart types? Do you always use the best chart for your purpose? Note two major improvements you can generally make:

1. _____

2. _____

Exercise 6-2. Choose three of the following concepts to *symbolize graphically,* using the principles discussed in this chapter. You may put a few words on the visual you develop — but overall, let the image, not the words, convey the main concept.

1. Finding a solution that fits the problem
2. Celebrating success
3. Problem
4. Taking risks
5. Courage
6. Promoting our service
7. Understanding the elements of a system
8. Brute force approach
9. Pollution
10. Out of our element
11. We keep repeating the same message, but ...
12. We must stop this
13. Natural enemies
14. Persistence
15. The sky is the limit
16. We must use the momentum
17. Competition
18. Speed
19. We must give our very best
20. Team work
21. Insensitivity
22. Precision
23. Time is running out
24. Are we just full of hot air?
25. Losing perspective
26. We must take the plunge!

Exercise 6-3. Experiment with modifying preset color schemes in your presentation software, using the guidelines discussed in this chapter (see especially the sections on the color wheel and general color schemes based on it). To do this, choose one of the following approaches:

a. Copy an existing presentation file that you produced using one of the predefined color schemes. Save it under a new name so you don't damage the original file. Now find the menu option (often under *Format*) that allows you to change the slide background or color scheme. Then change various elements, one at a time: slide background color (including gradient and other effects), title, text, fills. Next, go into general chart options and change the color of a data series (e.g., one line in a line chart, or one series of bars in a bar chart).

b. Create a simple presentation containing a bar chart, word chart, and line chart, then choose different preset color schemes and modify them one step at a time.

Exercise 6-4. Critique the following visual and revise it roughly by hand (or, if you wish, on your computer).

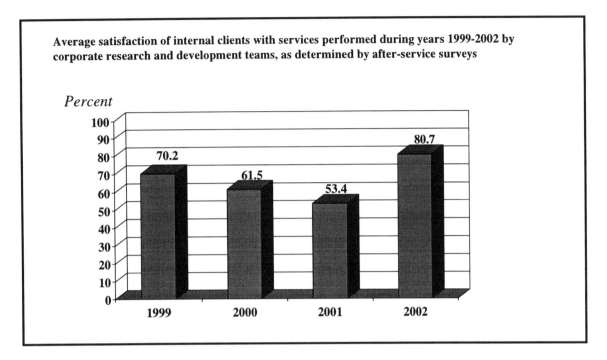

Exercise 6-5. Critique the following visual and revise it roughly by hand (or, if you wish, on your computer).

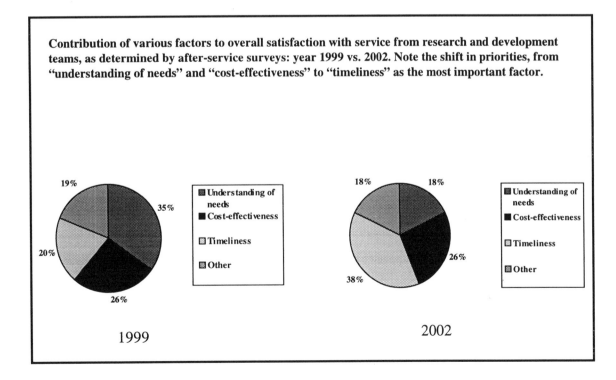

Exercise 6-6. Critique the following visual and revise it roughly by hand (or, if you wish, on your computer).

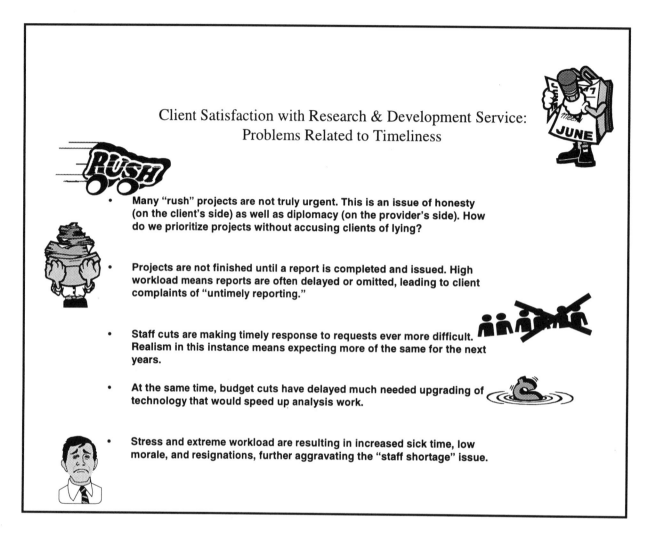

Client Satisfaction with Research & Development Service:
Problems Related to Timeliness

- Many "rush" projects are not truly urgent. This is an issue of honesty (on the client's side) as well as diplomacy (on the provider's side). How do we prioritize projects without accusing clients of lying?

- Projects are not finished until a report is completed and issued. High workload means reports are often delayed or omitted, leading to client complaints of "untimely reporting."

- Staff cuts are making timely response to requests ever more difficult. Realism in this instance means expecting more of the same for the next years.

- At the same time, budget cuts have delayed much needed upgrading of technology that would speed up analysis work.

- Stress and extreme workload are resulting in increased sick time, low morale, and resignations, further aggravating the "staff shortage" issue.

Exercise 6-7. Critique the following visual and revise it roughly by hand (or, if you wish, on your computer).

Frequency of reportable safety incidents at company locations A, B, and C over the last four years

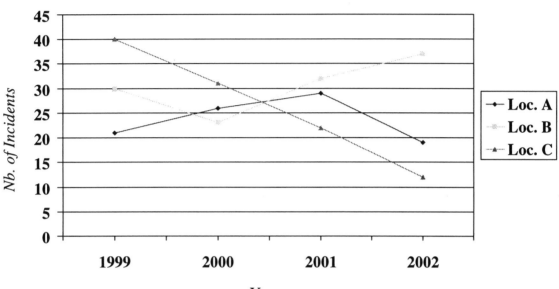

7

Notes, Rehearsing, and Handouts

The ultimate outcome of all your preparation is mental and physical material: namely, ideas and plans in your head, slides and props or demo objects, handouts, and notes. We have dealt with the ideas and visuals; now it's time to attend to the final touches — notes and handouts, and the proper way to put everything together in sensible rehearsal.

PREPARING NOTES AND REHEARSING

Poor notes produce two common disasters. One, you may get muddled and omit important parts of your message. Two, you may lose your connection with the audience — especially eye contact. You can minimize both problems by following three simple principles:

1. *Have the right type of notes* — short key words or phrases, in big type, on just a few pages or index cards, or on transparency frames or the visuals themselves.
2. *Practice from those notes* to
   (a) test their usability
   (b) discover weak spots in organization
   (c) check your timing
3. Use any additional practice time you may have to *wean yourself from your notes*.

Let's look in more detail at these principles now.

Right and Wrong Notes

Notes are nothing to be ashamed of, especially if you had only short preparation time for a complex presentation. Your job is to get your message across to the audience, and if this requires notes, that's fine. However, people tend to have the *wrong kinds* of notes:

many pages covered with full paragraphs, written in small lettering. Such notes are impossible to use without getting confused or losing the connection with the audience.

No matter how short your preparation time, you must keep your notes down to a *few points in phrase form.* Don't even start writing sentences or whole paragraphs. Write only words and phrases, and practice from those. Besides being the only thing that works, it will save you lots of preparation time.

Tip

To save time and ensure meaningful practice sessions, have notes **only in key word form**, never in sentences. It takes less time to produce such notes, and it forces you to *trust yourself* when it comes to practicing. We tend to think we'll forget points unless they're fully written out—but that's usually not true.

Proper type size and layout will help you find your place quickly if you should get lost. If you type your notes, choose 14-point type and use plenty of white space and bolding to help you navigate. For some people, handwritten notes work better; some even prefer to lay out their points as a "pictorial roadmap."

Your notes should contain

- Your main message
- Your three or four key points expanding on that message
- Examples or other backup for each key point

Tip

Don't forget notes (and/or visuals, if appropriate) for the *question-and-answer period.* In particular, you may expect some questions that involve complex numerical facts; these would be difficult to answer authoritatively without a visual or proper notes.

In most cases, this should fit on two or at most three pages. Furthermore, most of this information should also be on your visuals; in that case, there is no need to duplicate it in your notes.

Whether you put your notes on regular paper, index cards, or the frames of your transparencies is strictly a matter of personal preference. To some extent, your visuals will usually serve as your notes, too; however, don't let that lead you to use too many otherwise unnecessary visuals.

Practicing From Your Notes

Practicing does much more than implant portions of your talk in your memory for smoother delivery:

1. It gives you a chance to check how helpful your notes are.
2. It makes you aware of awkward, rough, or illogical spots in your organization that need revision.
3. It allows you to check if the length of your presentation is right.

However, you'll reap these benefits only if you practice correctly, using proper notes. If you do it wrong, you're probably just wasting your time — you might as well give your talk without rehearsing at all.

The most common mistake made by nervous speakers is to write out large parts of their talk and practice from that script. They hope that by delivery time, they'll be able to remember their text by looking just at the visuals or perhaps a condensed version of the notes. However, that hope is rarely fulfilled, because the practice situation was simply too different from the real event. (Also, the time to condense the notes somehow never materializes, leaving only the full script as a cumbersome crutch.) Not surprisingly, then, these speakers end up with their head buried in their notes, trying to read their speech.

The intelligent approach is to practice strictly from your "key word" notes, speaking freely from them *so that your brain is fully engaged.* You want to *practice thinking* while you present, because in the real situation, that is what you're aiming at: interacting intelligently with the audience, not parroting some words.

Visualize your actions as you walk through your presentation, and hold each transparency (or activate each computer slide) as you introduce it. Your goal is to *see exactly what you will be seeing during the actual presentation* — no more and no less.

If you get stuck at certain points, your notes or visuals for that passage may be unclear or incomplete. If so, fix them and practice again. If the trouble persists, it may be because that part of your talk is intrinsically convoluted and therefore impossible to remember. Make sure your arguments are as simple as feasible and your organization is linear — key point after key point, each backed up by examples and evidence.

Practicing in this way will focus you on likely trouble spots and avoid nasty surprises at delivery time. It will also encourage you to talk naturally, using simple conversational language. Finally, it should give you a realistic time estimate for your talk.

Weaning Yourself From Your Notes

If you have extra time for practice, you can use it to wean yourself gradually from your notes until you need only the points shown on the visuals. Try covering the easier portions with Post-It™ stickers; if you get lost, you can simply "lift and peek." There is nothing more impressive and authoritative than a speaker who talks freely and fluently, without dependence on notes other than perhaps one brief "completeness check." If you have enough preparation time, your goal should be to work toward that ideal.

Answers to Some Common Questions About Notes

Should I use my visuals as my notes? Yes, but don't let that lead to a monotonous proliferation of slides. Remember that props and demo objects are just as good a memory jogger as slides. On the other hand, if you plan to use audience interaction as support for a key point, you may need some note of the question to ask or the instructions to give to the audience. Putting it on a visual may be awkward.

Notes or No Notes?

There is no question that a truly connected, smooth delivery is impossible if you must consult your notes continuously. Therefore, your personal strategy should be to *learn to give presentations without notes.* It may not happen overnight, and it may not be feasible when somebody assigns you a presentation to give that very afternoon — but you can work toward it. In fact, many of our clients had to learn this because their group or organization simply did not allow notes. It's surprising how people facing such pressure can make progress *very quickly* on living without notes.

Here is a general strategy for becoming a "noteless" speaker:

- Have *short* notes (1-2 pages) as "insurance policy" only. Consult these notes directly before speaking, but then set them aside as backup.
- Have a visual for your attention getter if appropriate.
- Have visuals for your main message and your plan (preview of key points), as part of your introduction.
- Have a visual for each key point and for your summary.
- To remember examples, key numbers, and the main point about each graph, put them directly on the graph if possible without producing clutter.
- Use your visuals as notes during rehearsal and final delivery.

Should I use regular 8 1/2 × 11 paper or index cards for my notes? It doesn't really matter. However, don't take a whole pad — even if you plan to leave your notes on the table, purely as backup. You may end up needing the notes more than you expected, and having a bulky pad with you is distracting. Quite often, we've watched speakers balancing a big pad on the five fingers of their open hand. Nobody in the audience looked at anything but that pad, making private bets on whether it was going to fall down or stay up!

Is it a good idea to put my notes on the transparency frames? That's a good solution if you are using overhead transparencies and have the time for framing. Flip-Frames from 3M are a quick solution to the framing problem — however, they are cumbersome to handle at delivery time, so you need to practice a bit how to do it smoothly.

Should I ever write out a whole speech? Yes, if every word is politically or legally sensitive and may be held against you by opponents or the press. Usually, that's not your situation. Generally, reading a speech is deadly and thoroughly out of fashion.

I have a foreign accent (or a speech impediment) and am not always easy to understand. This can cause trouble, especially with technical terms. What can I do to overcome this? Give your audience a break: put any important term that you might mispronounce on a visual. That way, people can see what you're talking about. In addition, they can learn what your spoken version of this term sounds like, so when they hear it again, they recognize it more easily. For instance, we listened to an engineer from the South who kept mentioning a "bohler" in his talk. It left us without a clue, until he put on a visual that contained the word *boiler!*

Should I ever memorize my talk? No. Memorization is immediately obvious to the audience and puts them off even more than if you read the speech. It creates an atmosphere of a circus performance rather than honest communication.

However, if you are very nervous and likely to get off to a poor start, there is one section you may want to memorize a little — namely, the introduction. The idea here is to familiarize yourself thoroughly with that most difficult first minute. To avoid the trap of an unnatural "written speech," try this approach:

1. Write out key word notes (no whole sentences) for the introduction.
2. Rehearse this section several times from your notes. Listen carefully to check if the wording sounds strong, positive, and natural; if not, do it over, choosing better words.
3. Once you are happy with the wording, memorize it roughly; if necessary, add the most important phrases to your notes.

Note that even if you write out some portions in detail using these three steps, your starting point was not a script but your free speech based on key word notes. Therefore, the result, even if memorized, will sound quite natural. Anyhow, if you are using a strong attention getter, chances are you'll throw away the semi-script at delivery time and just talk freely and enthusiastically.

BEING PREPARED FOR TROUBLE

Presentations are inherently prone to nasty surprises of all kinds. Part of your preparation is to be ready for those surprises.

Problems with Equipment or Facilities

To begin with, equipment may be different from, or more complex than, what you imagined, or may turn out not to work. Basically, you should *expect* that things will go wrong in that department and be prepared for it. Notice we don't say "fully prepared"; if it happens to be Murphy's day, even the most ingenious, foolproof arrangements and backup will be laughably inadequate! Still, here are two things that will help in many situations, and will at least buy you some peace of mind:

1. If you plan on using complex equipment, test it and be familiar with it.
2. If you plan on a computer slide show, make backup transparencies at least for your key visuals (e.g., complex process diagrams) and arrange for an overhead projector.

Some Useful Accessories To Own
—And To Bring to the Presentation

If you present frequently, you can avoid many problems by keeping a few useful items in a small bag, ready to travel with you to the presentation. Here are some things you may find particularly helpful:

- Three-prong extension cord (handy if you must quickly move equipment forward or backward)
- Adapter plugs and converters for electrical equipment and telephone if you plan to present abroad
- Masking tape
- Pushpins
- Extensible pointer
- Cellophane tape
- Transparency markers in different colors, *tested to work*
- Monitor cable to connect your laptop computer to an LCD projector
- Flipchart markers, *tested to work*
- Remote control for computer slide shows — preferably one that controls *your laptop* rather than the projector

---

You may also need to make proper arrangements for the presentation room. If you don't reserve well in advance, you may find yourself squashed in some small meeting room instead of the comfortable, well-equipped facility you had envisaged! Here are some common items that may need your attention:

- Room of proper size for expected audience
- Appropriate setup of the room (e.g., U-shaped for a smaller audience, classroom or herringbone for larger audiences)
- Enough chairs — but not too many extra ones cluttering up the room
- Refreshments
- Water in jugs; water glasses for attendants
- Paper and pencils for attendants
- Place cards with names
- Flip chart(s) and markers
- Whiteboard with correct whiteboard markers and eraser
- Pointer (an extensible pointer is a useful accessory to own — and bring)
- Overhead projector and projector table
- Blank transparencies and transparency markers
- Projection screen
- LCD projector
- Microphone, amplifier, and loudspeaker(s)

Problems with Time or Audience Resistance

If they told you to give a 20-minute talk, what are the chances that you will actually *get* those 20 minutes on the Great Day? In our experience, dim indeed. Certainly during a conference of any kind, or during a morning of presentations to upper management, there are always several presenters before you who go well over their allotted time. When it's finally your turn, the operative phrase is: "Could you please cut that to ten minutes? We'll need to get going on that lab tour."

Now what? The answer is simple: Use Plan B! That's right — you need not one plan but three:

- Plan A — the full talk, taking the allotted time
- Plan B — a shortened version if your time gets cut or the audience appears bored with your details or examples
- Plan C — a version that adds explanations or arguments (while dropping minor points to make room for the additions!) if the audience appears confused or unconvinced

We don't mean to say you need to prepare three different presentations. Rather, you should spend some time reviewing your notes and visuals and making a list of candidate points to *drop* (Plan B) and possible backup to *add* for clarity or persuasion (Plan C).

PREPARING HANDOUTS

Don't underestimate the power of handouts to do a long-term job of persuasion for you. Your words and your flashy visuals come and go, but the handout is there as a permanent reminder and may help you get the action you want.

Unless you are going to use the handout to work through examples, give it out *after* the talk, or people will leaf through the handout instead of following you. Another good solution for a smaller audience might be to distribute it just before the question-and-answer period in order to get more useful, informed questions.

Once you've decided exactly how you're going to use the handout and when you'll distribute it, prepare it so the content goes along with your planned use — for example, as a discussion aid, a question focuser, or just a reminder of your main points.

It doesn't really matter how you prepare your handout (say, with your word processor or with your presentation software); what counts is that it contains the appropriate reminders and details for your audience. Be warned about today's audiences, though: they seem to have become addicted to having an exact copy of all your visuals, whether or not that reflects your talk in a sensible way. (Most visuals that we have seen are more mystifying than illuminating without the accompanying verbiage.) Giving them right away what they want will save you the trouble of making a second handout of your visuals and sending or e-mailing it to half the audience.

One last point: If the audience includes people who don't know you, be sure to include complete contact information, including your e-mail address.

EXERCISE AND DISCUSSION

Exercise 7-1. In Chapter 1, Exercise 1-2, you did a self-assessment, which included items relating to notes and rehearsing. Since losing one's point in a presentation is a major worry to many presenters, you may profit from doing the following more detailed assessment and developing a specific plan for yourself.

Improvement Areas (*Degree:* 0 = OK, 1= minor,…, 10 = big problem)	**Possible Approaches** (Note details of problem & ideas for improving, based on the discussion in this chapter)
Dependent on notes throughout the presentation__	
Notes too long (>3 pages)__	
Tend to lose point even with notes__	
Tend to lose point especially in the introduction__	
Notes duplicate the visuals; confusing to handle both__	
Notes consist of sentences and paragraphs — hard to find place if lost__	
Even repeated practice doesn't make material familiar — just reading script or sentences doesn't engage the brain__	
Not enough information on the visuals to serve as proper notes — too much need for extra notes__	
Tend to overdo visuals (word charts) just to avoid notes of any kind; monotonous for audience__	

Discussion 7-1. Discuss the following questions relating to notes and handouts:

- What do you consider advantages and disadvantages of notes?
- When would you use them?
- What's the best way to use them during rehearsing?
- What kinds of notes work best?
- What problems have you experienced yourself with notes?
- What problems with notes have you observed in others?
- What do you consider the three most important principles of effective notes?
- What problems have you experienced or observed with handouts?
- What are some effective uses of handouts?

Discussion 7-2. Consider the situation of a nonnative speaker of English. Assume this speaker has a strong accent that makes him or her difficult to understand at times. What special advice would you give this person on the use of supportive visuals?

PART 2

PERSUASIVE DELIVERY

8 The Magic of Connection 109

9 The Winning Attitude 113

10 Connecting Through Body Talk 121

11 Connecting Through Voice and Language 139

12 Staying in Touch Through Eye Contact 151

13 Handling Notes 157

14 Handling Visuals 161

15 Handling Questions 175

16 Dealing with Unpleasant Surprises 195

17 Moderating a Conference Session 203

8

The Magic of Connection

Do you wish you were a powerful, persuasive presenter? Do you envy people who can address a large audience with casual ease and charm, as though conversing with a few good friends? In the next chapters, we will show you how to turn wish into reality and become one of that select group of exceptional presenters. It's surprisingly simple, as you'll see — and you don't need any special natural talent.

THE TRIANGLE OF POWER: REAL YOU, REAL AUDIENCE, REAL PURPOSE

The real secret to powerful delivery is a strong, positive, uninterrupted *connection* with the audience. Figure 8-1 shows the three sides of this connection.

There is a great temptation to treat a presentation as something artificial: a "production," show, or lecture. When you fall into that trap, two unfortunate things happen. One, you feel strangely divorced from the presentation, because it isn't really *you* giving the audience something — it's an abstract event playing itself out with your participation. In particular, you tend to lose sight almost immediately of your purpose and of your audience. Two, your listeners relate to your presentation in the same abstract, noncommittal way. They sense your lack of honest involvement and respond in kind. As a result, you will have a hard time reaching them and getting results.

To sell your ideas and recommendations, you need to step out of that abstract space and establish honesty, trust, and goodwill. That's what the magic triangle is all about: remind yourself of what you're there to achieve, dare to be yourself (at your best, of course), and *enjoy making continuous contact* with the real people in your audience. You don't need any special skills to do this — you just need the right *focus*. And once you learn how to stay within that magic triangle, you'll surpass many polished presenters who don't understand the prime importance of connection.

So, remember: for truly powerful delivery, **connect the real you with the real audience, for a real purpose** — and don't let anything break that connection.

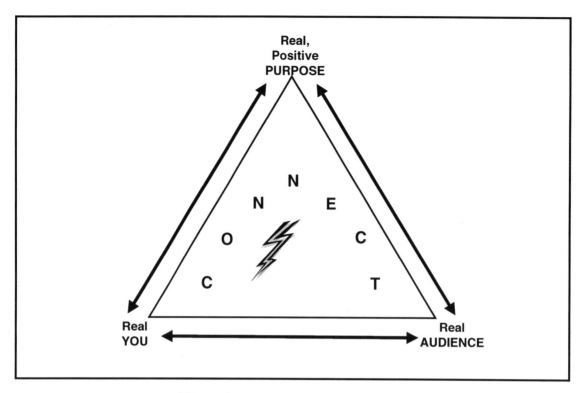

Figure 8-1. The magic triangle of power.

FOUR ASPECTS OF AUDIENCE CONNECTION

To build your connection with the audience, you first of all need the right *attitude*. Then you need to *express* that attitude with your body, voice, and eyes. Figure 8-2 sums up these four elements of connection.

> **Tip**
>
> More than anything else, work on your *attitude* toward the audience. It will make the rest of delivery infinitely easier, because you'll do the right things naturally. With the wrong attitude, everything positive you're trying to do will be forced, and the audience may in fact not trust your "mixed signals."

Attitude is by far the most important factor. If you can manage to keep your mind focused on giving your listeners something that is valuable to them and on liking and respecting each member of the audience, you will naturally do the right things with your body, face, voice, and eyes. So again, no special skills are necessary; all you need is a willingness to like people and to do something for them. If you think you can develop that willingness, then you can become an outstanding presenter.

In the following chapters, we will look in more detail at each of these four elements of connection, as well as special issues, such as handling notes, visuals, and questions.

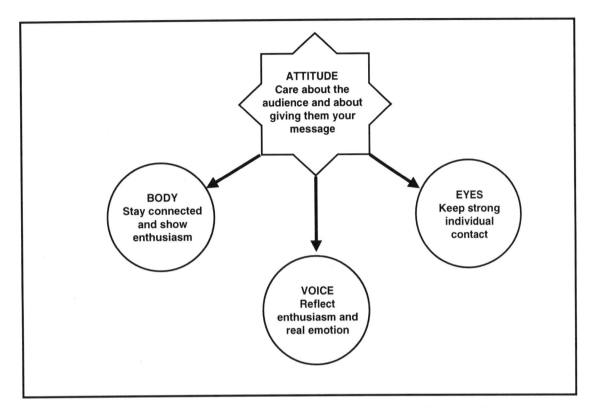

Figure 8-2. The four elements of persuasive connection with the audience.

9

The Winning Attitude

As we saw, the master key that opens the door to powerful delivery is *honest connection* with your audience. Outstanding speakers know that they must at every moment be connected with the real people in the audience, for a real purpose that matters to those people, and without hiding behind any slick stage personality. This is what generates the trust essential for persuasion.

You may object that in most of your presentations, you're only selling *technical information,* with persuasion rooted entirely in objective criteria. But our experience with many organizations strongly suggests that this is the wrong view. You're always selling a *package:* people want the facts, but they also want to know that you are *trustworthy* and *committed* to helping them or to seeing a project through. And they get this essential information about trustworthiness and commitment not from the numbers and charts you present but from the way you connect with your listeners.

THE STARTING POINT: A CARING ATTITUDE

Getting properly connected begins with the right attitude. Do you really *care* about your listeners and about giving them something they need? Once you have that attitude, you'll find it easy to *express* it with your body, face, eyes, and voice. If you *don't* have it, even the best "performance" will seem fake and leave your listeners uncomfortable and suspicious.

Check Your Preparation

From the outset—while *preparing* your presentation—you should have developed a real appreciation of your audience (see Chapter 1). Just who are they, and what do they want? How does that fit in with what *you* want them to do or believe? As you get ready to deliver your presentation, once more review your material. Have you found the best angle, the one that connects you most strongly to this audience? If not, are there any quick adjustments you can make in your message or some of your key points? For instance, are *discussion* and *problem solving* most important to many people in this audience? Then how about dropping some minor point or detailed backup and using some *interaction* instead? It's a change easily made at the last minute.

In particular, *keep your message positive,* even (or especially) when you bear unwelcome news. Your listeners are never yearning for negative news or criticism. So, if you want them to change, give them positive, not negative reasons for doing so.

Check the Setup

Exceptional presenters do everything they can to make the audience feel *comfortable.* Be early and check that the room is clean and inviting. Remove extra chairs, and get rid of flipchart pages left over from a previous presentation. And, of course, check all equipment and lighting. The cumulative effect on the audience is a sense that you respect them and are totally in charge of the occasion.

Removing extra chairs and clutter will also make it infinitely easier for you to connect physically with the audience. (How connected can you be when you address a lot of empty chairs?)

Room and Equipment Checklist

Here are some common items to check before you start, to make the audience comfortable and the presentation successful:

- Room clean?
- Extra chairs removed?
- Optimal room setup for your purpose? (e.g., U-shaped to allow visibility and interaction)
- Equipment set up correctly and working?
- Projector focused properly?
- Flip charts set up?
- Markers ready and tested to work?
- Lighting adjusted to show screen image clearly yet leave enough light in the room to allow interaction and discourage napping?
- Water, paper, and pencils provided for attendants, if appropriate?
- Contact available in case there is trouble with equipment?

In a *conference setting,* some of these adjustments may not be possible — especially if you just show up for your session, hoping that all is well! The smart thing to do is to check on the setup in a *previous* session, so you can decide:

- What quick adjustments you need to make at the beginning of your talk. (For example, do you need to dim the front lights somewhat to make the screen more visible? Or must you shift the overhead projector to the other side of the projection table, in order to place the transparencies in the proper spot for working at the screen?)
- What changes in setup or equipment you should try to arrange through your moderator or some conference official. (For instance, do you need an extra flip chart or a more up-to-date LCD projector?)
- What you have to live with — for example, limited lighting control, an elevated presentation stage that will place curbs on your movements, or general room setup, such as classroom style with projection screen in the right corner.

Learn To Love *Any* Audience

Really appreciating your listeners and their needs presupposes that you *like* them. This is where some people have a big problem. Their thoughts are dominated by *fear* of the audience (or some powerful audience members), and that leaves no room for liking. Or they may *resent* a particular audience, or *look down* on them. This is sure to transmit itself, no matter how polished your style, and the audience will turn against you. Many will not even hear what you have to say, let alone accept it.

We witnessed one corporate staffer (a smooth, experienced presenter) ruining a carefully prepared presentation because of this basic mistake. He was talking to a group of engineers about the importance of Total Quality Control. It soon became apparent, from subtle signals, that he neither liked nor respected his listeners but saw them as *obstacles* to his quality goals. They promptly became resentful and resistant to his suggestions.

Tip

To win the audience over to your view of things, work on your attitude:
- *Care* about your audience.
- Even with difficult listeners, find something *likable* in everybody.
- Be *enthusiastic* about your message and about getting it across to this audience.
- *Smile* to express your enthusiasm for the audience and for your message.
- Put your message in *positive terms* that will make it easy to accept for the audience.

So, as you get ready to give your presentation, take a look around and *find something likable about everybody*. One thing we've found helpful is simply to notice how *different* everybody is. For some reason, this seems to make it easy to start with a smile. Something similar may work for you.

THE POWER OF A SMILE

A smile is perhaps the greatest connector. Unfortunately, some people find it hard to smile, especially in a technical presentation. When we discuss this with them, they object that there's nothing funny about their subject. That may be true—but the secret is to derive the smile not so much from the subject matter as from the company! We have witnessed plenty of presentations about dry, "unfunny" subjects in which the presenter beamed brightly throughout, with the result that the audience was totally won over. There was nothing at all unnatural or inappropriate about the smile. It simply expressed enthusiasm about the work or product, the audience, and the chance to make this presentation to them.

The Winning Attitude: Friendly Respect

There is only one attitude toward the audience that is uniformly successful: friendly respect. This attitude implies that you are **on the same level with the audience** — neither talking up to them (even if they are upper-level managers) nor talking down (even if they are first-line employees or children).

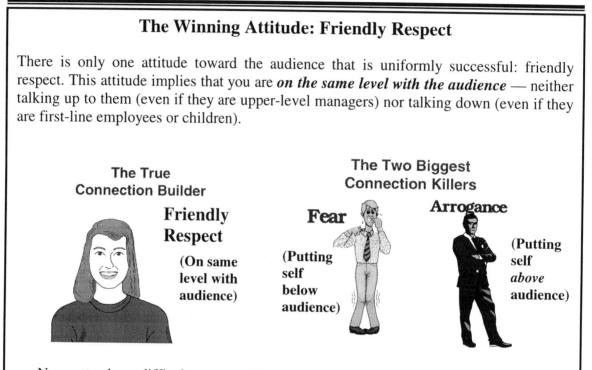

No matter how difficult or powerful the audience seems, find something likable or interesting in them. You might not be able to maintain this idea for a week — but you can certainly do it for a 20-minute presentation. In particular, "interesting" is an attribute you can easily apply to any extreme character, including irascible table-pounders or cynical snipers. Practice a little *detachment:* whatever these people do, they do it to *everybody,* not to you personally.

Here is a common piece of advice that does *not* work well: imagining the audience, or feared members of the audience, in their underwear. Whatever it is, it's neither friendly nor respectful, and if you are blessed with good visual imagination, you may find it quite distracting, too!

On the other hand, we have talked to many people in our seminars who found their careers threatened by their inability to smile. They were dismayed that peers and superiors interpreted their unwavering "seriousness" as unfriendliness, arrogance, aloofness, or some other form of negativity. Their subordinates didn't want to obey their instructions, and their internal clients ignored their recommendations. The same thing

Tip

Just as using the right kind of smile will lift your mood, you can improve other aspects of your attitude by working on your body language. In particular, you'll feel stronger and more assertive if you employ a straight *posture,* steady *eye contact,* comfortably *close distance* to the audience, and *strong volume.*

happens in a presentation: the audience will tune you out or fight you if you're sad, somber, or even just bland.

So smile as broadly as you can. It will not only charm your listeners but also lift your own attitude!

The Right Kind of Smile Is the One That Also Lifts Your Own Mood!

Not all smiles are the same — and in fact, only one will really do the job for you in a presentation. That smile is a full "eye-smile," which has been shown to lift your own mood (quite apart from the benefit of making the audience comfortable with you).

According to research reported in *The New York Times* ("When Is a Smile Really a Smile?" Oct. 26, 1993, C1), the truly happy smile involves mainly two muscles: "the Zygomaticus major, which runs from the cheekbones to the corners of the lips, and the Orbicularis oculi, which circles each eye." A smile that does not involve both (like the one on the left below) does not "activate the centers in the brain that regulate pleasant feelings."

Most important, the research has found that even if you produce the right kind of smile *artificially* (as actors did during experiments), it will still produce the brain changes that go along with delight. Therefore, ***you can gain from practicing this smile*** — for instance, in front of a mirror — until you can use it routinely in a presentation.

The following two cartoon faces may help you develop the right kind of smile:

On the left, you see a smile involving only the mouth, with lips pulled to the side. The eyes remain fully open, with a serious or worried expression. On the right, the smile involves the face from mouth to eyes, with lips pulled upward so that smile-creases reach the eyes. It is this kind of "eye smile" that has been shown to lift your own mood — and it's also the only one that sends an unambiguous signal of pleasure to the audience.

BEATING STAGE FRIGHT

Stage fright is simply the result of caring too much about yourself and not enough about the audience. That implies the best cure: redirect your focus where it belongs.

Most people don't realize how radical you have to be about this. "Caring a bit" will do nothing for you; you need to go all the way and love the audience without reservation.

We often observe this failure of "under-caring" in technical presentations when a speaker feels it unnecessary or inappropriate to relate strongly to the audience. At first, things may go well; but soon the audience returns the lukewarm feelings. The speaker picks this up and becomes increasingly unsettled, until stage fright has him firmly in its grip.

Don't let this happen to you. Make sure you're well prepared, with a message of value to your audience. Then keep firmly focused on getting that message across to a bunch of people whom you like and respect a lot. There won't be any room left in your mind for that presenter's dread, stage fright!

Beating Stage Fright

To beat stage fright, concentrate on your message, not yourself.

- Pick a message you *care about.*
- Keep focused on that message, no matter what. *(Think of yourself as a "window to your message.")*
- Be *enthusiastic* about your message and about the chance to give it to this audience.
- Remember that the audience is there to *learn* something from you, not to "get you."
- Make contact not with the audience as a whole (which tends to be impersonal and overwhelming) but with *individuals* in the audience; get your point across to *each* of them.
- Don't try to be somebody else; don't try to "be" *anything* other than yourself.

**"Obstacles are those frightful things you see
when you take your eyes off your goals."**
– Anonymous

EXERCISES

Exercise 9-1. Evaluate your relationship with different kinds of audiences and the influence of this factor on your relative success in presenting to these audiences. Here are the questions to consider.

What **type of audience** gives you the greatest difficulties?

    High-level audience, such as management_____

    Operators, blue-collar audiences_____

    Subordinates_____

    Mixed: management and other employees_____

    Customers (sales presentations etc.) _____

    Children or young adults_____

    Other: _____

What is the **nature** of the difficulties?

    Nervous_____

    Rarely successful/persuasive with that audience_____

    Cannot control them; no authority_____

    Audience tends to be hostile to me_____

    Other: _____

What do you see as the **cause** of the difficulties?

    Faulty relationship to the audience:

        Talking up; afraid_____

        Talking down; arrogant; teacher-like; etc. _____

        Trying too hard to please them_____

        Can't relate to them; different universe_____

        Don't really care about giving them value_____

        Other: _____

In view of your answers, and the information contained in Chapters 8 and 9, **what are the biggest changes you could make** to solve these problems?

_____

_____

_____

_____

Exercise 9-2. Assess your habits relating to setup and arrangements. (Answer *yes* or *no* to the following questions.)

Generally, audience comfort ensured? _____

Clean room? _____

Extra chairs removed? _____

Optimal table setup for your purpose: e.g., U-shaped to allow visibility and interaction? _____

Equipment set up correctly beforehand and checked? _____

    Projector focused properly? _____

    Flip charts set up; markers ready and tested? _____

Lighting checked or adjusted as appropriate for your purposes? _____

Contact available in case there is trouble with equipment? _____

Overall, **in what areas relating to setup do you need to improve most?**

_____

_____

10

Connecting Through Body Talk

You've seen that the real secret to powerful delivery is a strong, positive, uninterrupted *connection* with the audience. To build that connection, you first of all need the right *attitude:* appreciation and respect for your listeners and enthusiasm about getting your message across to them. Now let's look at ways to *express* that attitude with your body and face.

GETTING PAST THE "TERROR LINE" INTO COMFORTABLE CONTACT ZONE

There is an invisible "line of terror" in front of the projector table. Many speakers never make it past that line for their entire talk — they just shuttle between the projector and the screen (see Figure 10-1).

For a number of reasons, it's essential that you cross this line of terror at the outset and move into the audience:

- Staying behind that line when you don't have to signals to the audience that you are not comfortable with them. But for you to connect with the audience, they *must* feel you're comfortable with them, or they'll be suspicious of you.
- When you keep far away from the audience, you need to speak that much louder to be heard and understood. For many speakers, it means half of what they say is actually lost.
- From that far away, it's harder for you to get good eye contact with individuals in the audience or to read their expressions.
- Especially near the screen, with the front lights partially dimmed, you will be poorly visible. Whatever eye contact you make, or whatever smiles you manage, won't make any impression on the audience.

So, after you've deposited your slides and/or notes where they belong and perhaps refreshed your memory on your main message and key points, *step past the projector into the audience* and get ready for your opening. Taking that step may create a momentary "white-out." This is perfectly harmless. Simply smile and wait until your senses return to you.

Once you're over the shock, you'll find that the audience is much less frightening when you're close to them. Just *remember not to talk while you're in a white-out!* One client confessed to us that he started giving the *wrong speech* — not once but on several occasions — precisely because he did not have the nerve to wait until he had collected himself.

Of course, once you've made it past the line of terror, the question arises: how far should you go? How close to the audience should you get? The answer is, *reasonably close.*

We say "reasonably" because like everything else, this can be overdone. For instance, in some fancy restaurants there seems to be a new theory that you should get *really* close to the customer — a theory that is put into practice by waiters *squatting* at your table to take your order. That way, they're right at your level, showing you the

---

Tip

Don't wait to move into the audience but do it at the very start of your presentation. Remember, the longer you wait, the more awkward you may feel about crossing the "line of terror." Also, if the audience has sized you up as a "distance presenter," they will be shocked if you suddenly change style in the middle of your presentation and charge past the projector!

---

closest smile you ever saw. Now, we witnessed presenters doing the same thing with audience members — kneeling down in front of them, and in the meantime showing their back side to the rest of the room for several minutes.

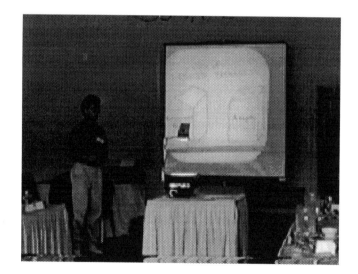

Figure 10-1. The position preferred by speakers who don't want to be with the audience: safely behind the "line of terror" that runs in front of the projector table. Note how the speaker blends into the wall to become a non-presence. Can you even see his eyes? If he tried to make eye contact with you, could you tell?

Clearly, this is not productive. It puts an uncomfortable focus on one person, and it excludes others. It won't happen to you, though, if you follow a simple rule: *Never turn your back on any audience member for more than a few moments.*

KEEPING IN TOUCH THROUGH MOTIVATED MOVEMENT

Some presenters move naturally; others seem to grow roots wherever they plant themselves. There are two problems with not moving: (1) it again conveys a sense of discomfort, and (2) it makes it impossible for some people to see your visuals, if you are using any (unless you are spending all your time next to the screen, of course).

So, you have to move—but with some *reason.* Senseless movement is distracting. Fortunately, you have several good reasons to move:

- To get closer to the person you're making eye contact with at the moment
- To put on a new visual
- To guide the audience through a visual you're discussing
- To get out of people's way so they can see a visual you may have blocked

Even people who feel awkward about moving around during a presentation (because they're afraid it might come across as a song-and-dance routine) can easily get used to this approach.

ENERGY — THE LANGUAGE OF SUCCESS

We advised you repeatedly in this book *not to try to be anything but yourself.* Now it's time to qualify this somewhat: don't try to be anything but yourself, *at your most energetic.* Audiences will not get excited about your cause if you seem hardly able to keep awake talking about it! So, learn to put some energy into your body, and half your persuasion job will be taken care of. Anybody can do this — and we'll give you some step-by-step guidance to make it painless and surefire.

Finding Your Base: The Athletic Stance

To use your body effectively in a presentation, you first of all need a solid base. That base is the *athletic stance.* Table 10-1 shows its various elements, as well as typical deviations and the impressions they may convey.

The athletic stance is a good base from which to start, or to which to retreat, when you are not moving or handling visuals. To audiences, it suggests energy, flexibility, comfort, and balance — and those are also the benefits it offers you directly. In particular, by standing firm and straight, you can generate feelings of security and assertiveness for yourself — just as smiling can make you feel happier (see the discussion of smiling in Chapter 9).

Motivated Movement vs. "Movement Disorders"

Motivated movement makes it easier for the audience to pay attention to you and harder to tune out. It's another case of the principle of *reviving attention through change* we discussed in Chapters 2 and 4.

By contrast, *senseless* movement is merely distracting, and *lack* of movement (unless compensated for by otherwise animated delivery) is sleepifying. Here are three "movement disorders" to avoid:

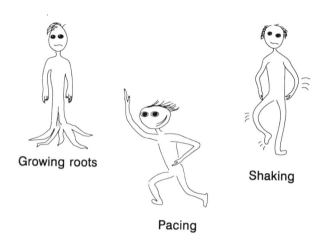

Growing roots

Pacing

Shaking

Growing Roots. Remember that a moving target is more interesting than a stationary one. There is no need to breeze around the room if that is not your style; just move naturally, to stay in touch with audience members and help everybody see the visuals you're showing.

Pacing. Charging back and forth in the room projects a frenetic state of mind, not energy or a desire to connect with the audience. Your energy should come mostly from the *upper body,* not your legs.

Shaking. Some speakers have a way of "loosening up" by shaking out their legs. It's a curious mixture of being cool and shaking off nervousness. Like other senseless movements, it does nothing to connect you to your audience or project enthusiasm and energy.

Contrast the athletic stance with typical faulty postures. At one end of the range, you have *excess nervous energy,* expressed by shuffling, rocking on your feet, and other fidgeting. At the other, you have *lack of energy,* as evidenced by slouching. In between, you have various degrees of awkwardness, tension, and aloofness. The athletic stance is the happy medium: it keeps you ready, alert, and comfortable and gives off no negative vibrations.

TABLE 10-1. Elements of the Athletic Stance, and Common Deviations From That Stance

Athletic Stance	Ineffective Stance & Possible Interpretations
Feet planted firmly, unless you are moving purposefully to a new position	Shuffling your feet; shifting uneasily from foot to foot (projecting *nervousness*)
Feet a little less than shoulder width apart for good balance	• Heels slammed together like soldier at roll call (*formal* or *subservient*) • Feet crossed (*nervous* or *timid*)
Standing straight	• Slouching (*nervous* or *trying hard to be cool or laid back*) • Standing ramrod straight, inflexible (*rigid with fear*)
Weight on balls of feet; ready to move	• Rocking from heels to toes; other movements an effort from that rhythmic action (*nervous; in your own world* — not related to audience) • Weight on one foot and hip; other foot forward (*arrogant/aggressive, "cute," or awkward*)
Toes turned *slightly* outward	• Toes turned inward (*awkward*, perhaps *trying to be cool*)
Arms hanging down loosely, or gesturing as needed	• Arms crossed (may seem *arrogant* or *defensive*) • Hand(s) resting on hip(s) (*arrogant, cool, laid back, aggressive*) • Hand(s) in pocket(s) (*insecure, nervous,* or *trying to be cool*)

Of course, this is only a general ideal, and we are in no way suggesting that everybody needs to be in that position every time he or she is not moving. However, here is a simple suggestion for you to try out right now. Stand up and follow the directions for the athletic stance completely. Stand like that for a while. Now compare this to how you think you stand habitually (a) in everyday life and (b) in a presentation. *Does it feel very different?* Then you will profit from practicing this stance repeatedly, especially a few days before a presentation. Pay particular attention to those elements (e.g., weight on balls of both feet) in which you know you tend to deviate most from the ideal.

How To Forget About Your Hands

Do your hands grow into huge, heavy appendages as soon as you start giving a talk? It doesn't have to be that way. The key is, once again, "motivated movement." Your arms and hands are tools of expression; to move them naturally, you need something worthwhile to express. That's all you need to concentrate on—and it's more a matter of *preparation* than of delivery.

Since the problem usually is worst at the beginning of the talk, you need to *plan strong, lively material for the first minute.* (That was one reason we recommended having an attention getter and your main message in the introduction of your presentation.) When you have something exciting to say right at the start, you'll never even think about those beastly hands! And once you've started waving them around, they'll keep right on going until you make your final point.

If you think stance is a minor matter, you are severely mistaken. Take the case of a woman presenter we know. She had an important talk to give to an audience of middle and upper management. Throughout most of it, she was standing with her weight on her left foot; the right foot was nicely crossed in front of the left, in the manner preferred by some women. At the end of the talk, she asked a friendly colleague how he thought the talk had gone. "Mary," this man said, "I couldn't tell you. I didn't hear a thing you were saying. All I could think was, is she going to fall over, and am I going to have to rush up to catch her?"

In our experience, this is not at all an unusual case. *Any* extreme or affected posture will have a terribly distracting effect on the audience, because unlike a poor visual or a bungled sentence, it's there all the time, asking to be noticed. So, make sure you don't handicap yourself with some easily corrected fault of your basic stance.

Focusing Energy in Your Upper Body

The athletic stance is a good starting point. However, you can go a bit further than that to inject your physical delivery with infectious energy — namely, by working specifically on *upper-body energy.*

Think of it this way. When you watch a presenter, what gives you the impression of high energy? The fact that he is jogging around the room? Or the fact that he is using his upper body for lively, supportive gesturing?

If you can't answer this question, think about it in yet another way. Imagine one presenter keeping his upper body stiff, but continuously running around the room. Then think of another presenter not moving around at all, but just reaching out with his arms toward the audience, sometimes reaching up or reaching down to illustrate something, and otherwise gesturing with deliberate, forceful movements. *Which of these speakers will seem to transmit more energy from himself or herself to the audience?* Obviously, our answer is: the second speaker — and when we ask audiences about it, they agree.

Movement for the Not-So-Agile

If movement is physically difficult for you, your presentation need not suffer from that fact. First of all, remember that your limitation is not unique — after all, anybody addressing a large audience from a podium, using a microphone, is in the same situation of not being able to move about freely. Yet many excellent talks are delivered that way.

Here are some ways to take advantage of easy, small movements or to compensate by other means:

- Lean and gesture toward the audience. This indicates quite effectively where your focus is, even if you are perfectly stationary. By contrast, clutching a lectern or burying your head in your notes shows that you want to be alone with your material and/or terror.
- Shift out of the way of visuals occasionally—even if you take just a single step.
- Pivot on your heels toward different audience members.
- Make up for lack of movement with upper-body energy, eye contact, and a generous smile.
- Use your voice to convey enthusiasm.

The challenge, then, is to *get the energy from your feet up to your tummy, chest, arms, and head.* This is done easily by

- Taking a full breath that expands your chest fully
- Keeping the chest expanded like that by doing diaphragm breathing
- Raising your hands above the belt line and mostly keeping them there
- Slightly tightening the muscles in your arms so you are aware of them

You can try a mental trick to achieve the same thing: Imagine you're bending down to pick up all your energy from your feet. (Note that we said "Imagine..." Please don't try to actually do this at the start of your presentation, or they'll cart you off to the nearest emergency room!) Now take that energy and push it up above the waist line. The result should be just as described above.

Now once you are in that energized body position, you'll look pretty puffed up *unless you immediately put your energy to use for supportive gesturing.* That's the whole point of upper-body energy: it's there to be *used,* not to be *displayed.* In the next section, we'll see how to do that.

Unfortunately, at the very start of your presentation, when you feel most vulnerable, you may not have a need for any gesture. Therefore, you must find some way to bridge the first few seconds. Here are a few suggestions that may work for you:

- Start with your hands lightly clasped or steepled (but not folded as in prayer — unfolding is too unlikely to occur). However, don't continue this endlessly but move on to more helpful gesturing as soon as possible.
- Start by *moving into the audience* as you greet them. The momentum may carry you through the uneventful first ten seconds. Make sure, however, not to keep your back turned to one side for all that time. Rather, pivot so you greet everybody.
- Start with both hands comfortably hanging down, as in the athletic stance, and move to full upper-body energy only when you reach worthwhile material — namely, your attention getter. (In that case, you may find it helpful to rest the thumb of one hand on the tip of the index or third finger. It's an unobtrusive mini-version of wringing your hands or folding your arms.)
- Start with one hand holding your notes and the other hanging down loosely as in the athletic stance.

DEVELOPING NATURAL, USEFUL GESTURES

Effective gestures are not things you do with your hands. They are energetic, deliberate movements involving your arms and often the entire upper body. (In fact, a vigorous presenter demonstrating, say, "high" may stretch his *whole body*, rising on his toes.)

Just try this. Stand in front of a mirror, with your hands folded in front of your tummy. Now flap one hand to the left (using only wrist action, not the whole arm) and then the other to the right as you say "On the one hand ...; on the other hand ..." Does that look like an effective gesture, or does it look more like a penguin impersonating a presenter?

Now try the same thing by using your entire upper body. First, put one arm way out as you say "On the one hand...," then the other hand to the other side as you say "On the other hand..." Then go further and put *both* arms to one side as you say "On the one hand...," then *both* arms to the other side as you say "On the other hand..."

Can you feel and see the difference? In the first case, you look as if you are *embarrassed to use your body at all.* So you just flap your hands quickly and return them to their safe position. In the other two cases, you put a lot of energy into *taking the audience with you* — first to the one side, then to the other.

Why is that second approach so good? Precisely because of this business of *taking the audience with you!* A whole-body gesture is not something an audience can ignore — people are simply *programmed* to take note. "What's this?" their subconscious says, and so they look — and *thereby pay attention to what you are saying.* By contrast, if you just stand there, or flap in minuscule ways, they are free to look out the window or otherwise tune out and miss everything you say. It's such a simple thing, but it can make all the difference between being heard and being tuned out!

Besides just keeping the audience with you, good gestures also *help people understand your ideas better.* For instance, gestures for physical actions or relations allow people to use their *visual* and *kinesthetic learning styles* (see the discussion of learning styles in Chapter 4). Some people understand and learn much better when they can use these learning styles instead of having to follow only your words.

Your task as you develop useful gestures, then, is to *get in touch with the expressive possibilities of your upper body.* Look at it as "almost pantomime": you don't want to act out everything to the extreme, but you do want to give *supportive hints,* and do it with *energy and enthusiasm.*

Certainly, you won't have great success with this if you keep your hands in your pockets for security, like the speaker in Figure 10-2. (A variant of this is to have one hand in a pocket and the other holding the speaker's notes. In that case, we usually just find the speaker waving the notes around and creating a little breeze in the room.) If this is your habit, kick it in a hurry and get those hands out and ready to move!

Another habit that can interfere is continuous wringing of the hands (see Figure 10-3). You can see it on TV all the time, even from professional media people — but that doesn't make it any better. It's repetitive, and it expresses nothing useful. Similarly, periodically beating the air with a "down-up flap" is useless and soon becomes annoying in its monotony.

You need to go beyond all these crutches and develop gestures that are specific, energetic, and helpful to the audience. For instance, compare the fruitless hand wringing in Figure 10-3 with the specific gesture expressing the concept of "layer" in Figure 10-4. Notice how not just the hands but both arms and shoulders, and in fact the entire upper body, are involved in Figure 10-4. This kind of deliberate, forceful gesturing is something the audience simply cannot ignore, and it keeps their thinking on track.

Figure 10-2. How much supportive gesturing can you do with one or both hands in a pocket?

Figure 10-3. Wringing your hands throughout your talk does not illustrate anything except that you're nervous! It's all right as an initial or occasional crutch, but remember to move on to more helpful gestures as soon as possible.

To get some practice with this skill of specific, energetic, and helpful gesturing, try expressing the words listed below. In the right column in each block, there are some suggestions for possible gestures; however, you'll profit most if you try your own gestures first and consult the suggestions only if you are stuck. You will see that you already have all the skills needed to express ideas with gestures — you just need to get into the *habit* of using those skills in a presentation context.

Figure 10-4. Aim for this: use your body to help the audience understand your points and stay focused on you. (Here, the speaker is illustrating the concept "layer.")

1. Common Action Verbs

Surround	Two hands forming circle, with fingers spread open
Oppose	Two fists moving toward each other
Intermesh	Open fingers of two hands moving to intermesh
Compare	Open hands alternating in moving out; two open hands alternating in "weighing" motion (palms up)
Weigh	One hand, palm up, going up in weighing motion
Suppress	Open hand (palm down), or thumb, moving down
Elevate	Open hand, palm up, moving up
Alternate	One or two hands showing right and left side (the two alternatives)
Hear	Thumb or several fingers bending one ear forward
Combine	Open hands moving together; fingers may be curved
Build	Same as "combine"
Destroy	Curved fingers of two hands touching, then moving apart quickly
Demolish	Moving two hands forcefully apart; palms may face outward
Pick up	One or two hands moving up, palm(s) up
Drive down	Fist or open hand moving down
Throw out	Throwing motion (quick sideways movement) with one hand
Pull up	Pulling-up motion with one hand (imagine holding a rope)
Bend	Two fists showing bending motion (imagine holding a flexible stick)
Stick together	Touching fingertips or clasping hands
Rotate	Circling motion with hand or index finger

Say the following sentences out loud, supporting the underlined words with appropriate gestures:

(a) We <u>pour</u> this emulsion into a large vessel, <u>stir</u> it with highly efficient titanium blades, and <u>pipe</u> it off to the forming section.

(b) Basically, we had to <u>demolish</u> the existing structure, <u>pick up</u> all the pieces, and <u>rebuild</u> the whole thing.

Pour:	Pouring motion with one hand (imagine you are pouring milk from a jug)
Stir:	Slow stirring motion with one hand
Pipe it:	Show diameter of pipe with thumb and index finger, then pull hand away to show motion
Demolish:	See description above
Pick up:	See description above
Rebuild:	See description of "build" above

2. Other Common Words and Phrases

Pronouns referring to people in the room:

I, my	Hand toward or on chest
We	Circle with one or two hands
You	Open palm toward audience (be careful not to *point* at the audience, especially with international audiences — in many cultures, this is considered very rude)

Quantity and Count Words:

All	Circle with one or two hands
Nothing	Draw two open hands apart; wave one open hand from left to right and back
Three	Three fingers
First ... second	Count off on your fingers (note that *thumb*, not pinky, is #1)

"Good/Bad" Adjectives:

Successful	Thumb(s) up; move open palm up
Failure	Thumb(s) down; open palm down; making "throwing out" motion with one hand

Direction and Limit Words:

High	Raise open hand high up (be energetic about it)
Low	Lower open hand
Up	Move open hand up
Down	Move open hand down
From the ground up	Move hand, palm up, from a low position upward
Outward	Move open hand out
Inward	Move two hands inward

Contrast Words:

On one hand ... on the other hand	One or two hands all the way to left, then all the way to right
Either ... or	Same as "on one hand ... on the other hand"
This ... that	Same as "either ... or"; or point down at two different spots

Behavior of Things Over Time:

Suddenly	Sharp down movement with one hand, as if cutting
Repetitive	Continuous circles or other repetitive hand motion
Even, constant	Draw hand evenly from left to right
Variable, fluctuating	Wavy motion

3. Abstract Ideas Made Concrete

Many abstract concepts can be made easier to understand through *physical analogies* that you can demonstrate with gestures. This is important to realize especially in a technical talk, where you mostly discuss just such abstract ideas. Without the skill of working through physical analogies, you would be left with long stretches of dry material unsupported by any gestures. As a result, your presentation style would become stiff, and the audience would soon tune out.

We will show you three general classes of abstract ideas that you can easily treat in physical ways: (1) processes, (2) cycles, and (3) systems. In each case, however, the *general skill* is the same:

> **Turn abstract concepts into a concrete space**
> **or object that you can manipulate physically**
> **with energetic gestures.**

3a. Processes

What we have is a continuous process in which we chip the logs in the chipper, clean them in high-speed cyclone cleaners, cook them with chemicals in a digester, then manipulate the fibers physically in refiners ...

This describes a complex process in a rather long sentence — an open invitation to listeners to lose track of things and tune out. Unfortunately, the elements of the process are too specific and numerous for useful gesturing — the result would be a frantic kind of overdone pantomime acting out *chip, clean, cyclone, cook,* and *manipulate* in rapid succession.

The solution is to **work with the process as one concrete object** and simply **demarcate its segments**. Here is one way to do that:

1. Optionally indicate the *continuous* nature of the process by showing it as a *stretch* (move hand straight across from left to right).
2. Treat the process as an *imaginary long sausage.* Now *cut that sausage into segments,* using the right open hand like a knife and the left hand like your cutting board.
   Cut 1 = chip the logs in the chipper
   Cut 2 = clean them in high-speed cyclone cleaners
   Cut 3 = cook them with chemicals in a digester
   Cut 4 = manipulate the fibers physically in refiners

This has three benefits: (1) it keeps you busy and energetic, (2) it involves the audience visually and therefore prevents tuning out, and (3) it keeps the audience *visually informed* about when the "next step" in the process begins.

This third benefit is perhaps the least appreciated by presenters, yet it may be the most important. As a speaker, you can easily forget just how difficult it is for the audience to follow any complex thought. External and internal distractions abound, and there is no chance to go back over what you said. By cutting a thought visually into manageable chunks, you make processing that much easier.

So, watch out for process discussions in your own talks and apply the simple technique we've given you here. You'll find audience attention greatly improved.

3b. Cycles

Cycles are, of course, just special cases of processes. The visual treatment is similar, with these two exceptions:

1. The overall process motion is a cycle, not a straight line.
2. The first element should start at "12 o'clock," and the last should end up in the *same spot* so that the audience understands visually just *when the cycle has been completed.*

Here is an example. Try for yourself to indicate the elements of the cycle with appropriate gestures, such as pointing into the imaginary circle with several fingers. Make sure you begin and end at "12 o'clock."

The way it works is like this: We want more customers, so we offer higher credit limits and less background check; customers <u>use</u> those higher limits; they don't pay their bills, because they're not responsible customers; so we drop them; now we have fewer customers; and once again we try to get more customers by offering higher credit limits and less background checks.

3c. Systems

Technical presentations are full of talk about systems, so you should often be able to take advantage of the following suggestions. Think of a system as a *pizza pie* hanging in front of you. Then poke your way through that pie, picking out elements anywhere you like or, if appropriate, in some structured way that reflects real relationships (such as "opposition") among the elements.

Here is a simple example:

Over here we have Finance; here, Production; and here, Sales — and they just don't communicate quickly and completely.

In this case, imagine the different groups as occupying different spots in the overall system — the pizza pie. Then point at those spots (e.g., with a rotating action of several fingers).

UNDERSTANDING AND CONTROLLING BODY LANGUAGE

As a presenter, you must learn to control body signals that may transmit negative attitudes or feelings to your audience. For instance, listening to an audience member's question with a lopsided grin or furrowed eyebrows suggests skepticism or disapproval, respectively. No matter what words you use, those signals may overwhelm your message. Similarly, any repetitive automatic gestures, such as adjusting your glasses or necktie, or jingling coins in your pocket (an all-time favorite!) project discomfort with the audience.

At the same time, you need to be sensitive to your listeners' signals, because they can tell you a lot about how your presentation is being perceived. Are some people shifting restlessly, looking at their wristwatches, or fiddling with objects? Then you may have to switch to Plan B and tighten the pace by skipping inessential details.

Exercise 10-1 gives you a chance to evaluate body signals of speakers and/or listeners (some signals don't apply to speakers but only to listeners). Most people are quite good at reading such signals. In fact, being *unable* to interpret body language is part of a severe communication disorder that makes it almost impossible for people to form relationships. Of course, each signal usually has a fairly broad range of meanings; however, the context may narrow this down a lot in any given situation.

Using Your Body To Connect with the Audience

- *Move into the audience* immediately, to break the isolation. (If the setup does not allow that, move or lean *toward* the audience.)
- Don't spend a long time with your back toward any member of the audience.
- Translate your excitement for your material into *upper-body energy,* and use that energy to demonstrate your concepts with helpful gestures.
- Translate your enthusiasm for the audience into *motivated movement;* in particular, move to get in touch with different individuals.

EXERCISES

Exercise 10-1. Understanding and controlling body language: a body language test

Fill in the meaning and importance for the following body language signals. Note that the meaning and importance of most body language signals depend on **context** — in particular, facial expression and tone of voice. *Not all signals in the list are negative.*

SIGNAL	LIKELY MEANING	IMPORTANCE* (0-2)
Constantly clearing throat, without sign of a cold or cough		
Crossing arms over chest		
Tightly crossing legs		
Stroking chin while looking intently at the other		
Avoiding eye contact		
Very long eye contact (steady stare)		
Looking at other person's forehead rather than eyes		
Slowly removing eyeglasses, then cleaning them (although they don t seem dirty)		
Abruptly taking glasses off and putting them on the table		
Peering over top of eyeglasses		
Partially covering mouth with one hand while speaking		
Rubbing eyes, ears, or side of nose		
Leaning forward while sitting on the edge of the chair		
Folding hands on top of table, rubbing thumbs together		
Leaning back, putting hands behind head, stretching		
Sucking on a pen		
Tapping, jiggling, fiddling with objects		
Yawning		
Wringing hands		
Raising eyebrows		
Rubbing back of head		
Biting lower lip		
Narrowing eyes		

* Relative importance of signal: 0=unimportant; 1=moderately important; 2=very important (avoid it yourself; watch carefully if others do it)

Exercise 10-2. Review the body signals in Exercise 10-1. Then answer the following questions.

Which of these signals do *you* often use in a presentation?

_____
_____
_____
_____
_____
_____

What does this indicate about your attitude?

_____
_____
_____
_____
_____

What changes in attitude or behavior might therefore be beneficial to you?

_____
_____
_____
_____

Which of these signals do you often notice in *listeners* when you give a talk?

_____
_____
_____
_____
_____
_____

What does this indicate about your presentation content or delivery?

_____
_____
_____
_____

What changes would be most helpful?

_____
_____
_____
_____
_____

Exercise 10-3. Have a colleague videotape you as you rehearse a presentation. In reviewing the tape, evaluate your gestures. If there are weaknesses in this area, then practice *all* the gestures described in this chapter in front of a mirror *in an exaggerated manner* — as many times as it takes to get comfortable with them. **Repeat this exercise the *day before* any presentation.**

Exercise 10-4. Stand in front of a mirror (or, in a group setting, get up and observe one another as you do the exercise). Now use energetic upper-body gestures that support the following words or phrases:

Compress
Tease apart, disentangle
Down
Bottom
Up
Wide
Narrow
Circular
Evolving
Interwoven
Erratic
Smooth
Two
Backward
Comes back
It makes you think
Spread out
Concentrated in one spot/area
Stay
Move
The center
At the periphery
Isolated instances
Over here ... over there
Segment
Stack

Exercise 10-5. Review the *athletic stance* and practice it. Compare it to how you think you stand habitually. ***Does it feel very different?*** Then practice the athletic stance repeatedly, especially a few days before a presentation. Pay particular attention to those elements (e.g., weight on balls of both feet) in which you know you tend to deviate most from the ideal.

11

Connecting Through Voice and Language

You've seen that an attitude of appreciation, respect, and enthusiasm is the key to achieving the all-important connection with your listeners. One way to *express* that attitude is with your body and face, through appropriate position, movement, gestures, and smile. Now let's consider the contribution your voice and language can make.

Briefly, you must be *heard* and *understood;* you must talk at the *right speed* that invites the audience to stay with you; and you must maintain an *emotional bond* by expressing appropriate emotions and using appealing, natural language. Finally, you need to avoid *distracting verbal habits.*

THE BASICS: BE HEARD AND UNDERSTOOD

You can't connect with your listeners at all if you talk so softly that they can't hear you, or so indistinctly that they miss half your words. Unfortunately, these are common problems.

The cure for the volume problem is simple: talk to the people in the *back of the room.* If projecting that far is hard for you or drives up your pitch too much, try the exercise described in the box. You'll be amazed how quickly you can develop more volume and depth.

Be aware of a delicate "sound barrier," though: if you talk much louder than necessary to reach everybody, people will feel that you're addressing *nobody* but giving a "ceremonial speech." It's a most disconcerting experience for the audience.

IMPROVING YOUR ARTICULATION

The other basic prerequisite beside volume is *clarity.* Do you move your mouth enough for consonants like *t, p, s,* or *f* — especially at the ends of words? If necessary, slow down until your speech becomes clear.

A Simple Exercise To Strengthen Your Voice

Here is an exercise that will help you develop volume without raising your pitch. It's particularly appropriate for women with soft, high voices.

1. Stand in front of a wall, about 6' away from it.
2. Say a resonant word such as "Wonderful!" at a comfortable volume. Feel it bounce back at you.
3. Move back one step and say the word again, but this time *louder and at a slightly lower pitch*. Listen as it bounces back at you.
4. Repeat Step 3 until you have reached your limit. However, *don't slip into shouting*, which involves a dramatic increase in chest and throat pressure. (You can probably avoid shouting automatically by *maintaining a smile* — which is a nice thing to practice in any case!)

By actively *lowering* your pitch in this exercise, you'll be countering the natural tendency to speak higher as you talk louder.

Here is an exercise to improve clarity: take some poems and *whisper* them forcefully. Because in a whisper the sound comes only from the consonants and not from vibrating vocal cords, you'll be forced to put a lot of articulatory energy into your consonants. If you do this frequently, you will improve your pronunciation dramatically.

To start you off on this program, here are a few short verses for practice. Notice the underlined letters; these are consonant clusters or word-final consonants to which you should pay particular attention.

From Psalm 23

The Lord is my shepherd; I shall not want.
He maketh me to lie down in green Pastures;
He leadeth me beside still waters.
He restoreth my soul.

Stanza 1 of "Auguries of Innocence"
(William Blake)

To see a World in a Grain of Sand
And a Heaven in a Wild Flower,
Hold Infinity in the palm of your hand
And Eternity in an hour.

"On the Beach at Fontana"
(James Joyce)

Wind whines and whines the shingle
The crazy pierstakes groan;
A senile sea numbers each single
Slimesilvered stone.

(Anonymous)

Amidst the mists and coldest frosts,
With barests wrists and stoutest boasts
He thrusts his fists against the posts
And still insists he sees the ghosts.

Two Simple Ways To Improve Your Clarity

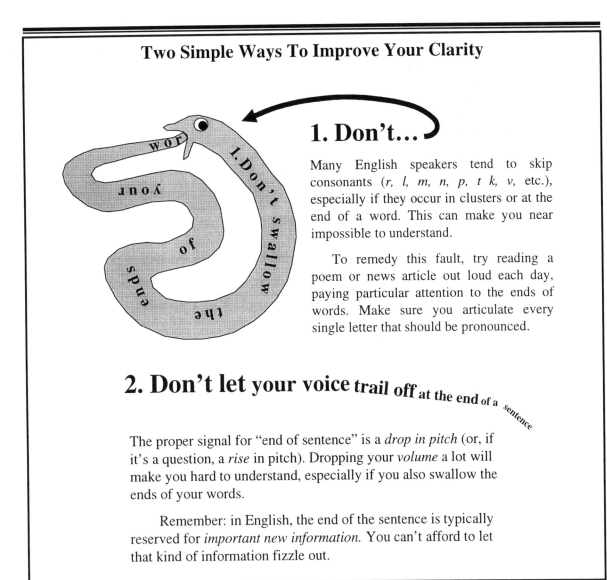

1. Don't...

Many English speakers tend to skip consonants (*r, l, m, n, p, t k, v,* etc.), especially if they occur in clusters or at the end of a word. This can make you near impossible to understand.

To remedy this fault, try reading a poem or news article out loud each day, paying particular attention to the ends of words. Make sure you articulate every single letter that should be pronounced.

2. Don't let your voice trail off at the end of a sentence

The proper signal for "end of sentence" is a *drop in pitch* (or, if it's a question, a *rise* in pitch). Dropping your *volume* a lot will make you hard to understand, especially if you also swallow the ends of your words.

Remember: in English, the end of the sentence is typically reserved for *important new information.* You can't afford to let that kind of information fizzle out.

One of the greatest things you can do for your general clarity is to develop the habit of reading something aloud each day, articulating as clearly and vividly as you can. Perhaps you have a young child who would enjoy having a story not just read but *read well*. Even reading part of an interesting news article out loud will do the job — and since you probably read the newspaper anyhow, you don't have to spend any extra time on this exercise.

THE RIGHT SPEED

There is no one best speed for a presentation. If you talk slowly the whole time, the audience will soon escape into daydreams, because they think much faster than you can speak. On the other hand, if you talk fast from start to finish, you'll lose them, too, because (a) the monotony is killing and (b) your clarity usually suffers greatly at high speed.

What works is *variety:* slow down (and speak louder) for important points, and hurry through routine material (e.g., paraphrases of ten items on a simple bullet chart that they're reading as you talk). This skill is easily learned, and it makes your presentations infinitely easier to follow, because it gives the audience strong clues about what's new and important and what is old and fairly obvious.

A related skill is the intelligent use of *pauses.* A pause is a good way to signal that you're starting a new section or thought. Without the pause marker, the audience may get confused and interpret the next material as if it belonged to the point before it.

Tip

If you have a problem with rushing through presentations at out-of-control speed, don't just try to slow down but **super-articulate**. This slows you automatically *without making you self-conscious about speed.*

Pauses also convey *power:* they show that you feel entitled to "occupy time." So, if you lose your point or need to think for a few seconds, don't fill the air with nervous noises like "uhm" or filler words like "and"; just pause calmly until you're back on track.

EMOTIONS AND VOICE

Even technical projects involve dramatic feelings, such as frustration, determination, fear of failure, and the joy of success. Listeners connect to those emotions much more powerfully than to numbers. So, to reach people, you need to express proper emotions with your voice.

Many technical presenters feel uncomfortable putting emotions into their voice and therefore end up with a monotone. They often pay for this with a stalled career, because their superiors misread their attitude as lack of enthusiasm or commitment. So, it's essential to overcome any reluctance to share emotions.

Great presenters make you feel as if you are a friendly partner in an *animated conversation*. Think about how *you* would talk to a friend. Would you use a robot-like monotone? Would you be afraid to show some emotions? Of course not! Then if you want your listeners to be your friends, why not treat them the same way?

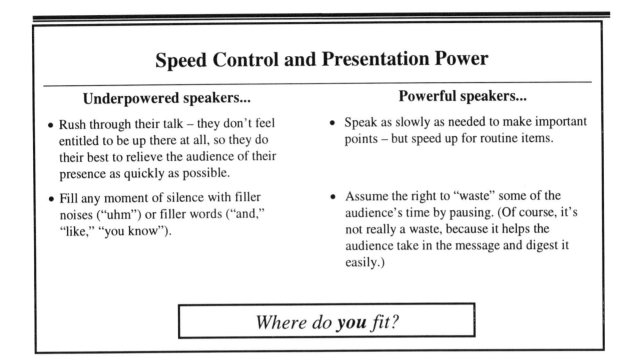

Speed Control and Presentation Power

Underpowered speakers...	Powerful speakers...
• Rush through their talk – they don't feel entitled to be up there at all, so they do their best to relieve the audience of their presence as quickly as possible.	• Speak as slowly as needed to make important points – but speed up for routine items.
• Fill any moment of silence with filler noises ("uhm") or filler words ("and," "like," "you know").	• Assume the right to "waste" some of the audience's time by pausing. (Of course, it's not really a waste, because it helps the audience take in the message and digest it easily.)

*Where do **you** fit?*

A Simple Exercise To Improve Your Expressiveness

In a workshop setting, we often make participants ham up a dramatic poem. In the private review of their presentation tape, they're surprised when we point out the many places where one of the emotions they practiced on the poem would have been appropriate in their own technical presentation.

You may want to do a similar exercise on your own if you feel that your delivery tends to be "flat." For instance, copy the following poem and mark it up with words describing the emotions governing different lines. Then read it aloud, acting out those emotions as well as you can with your voice and body.

Lord Hippo
By Hilaire Belloc

Lord Hippo suffered fearful loss
By putting money on a horse
Which he believed, if it were pressed,
Would run faster than the rest:
For someone who was in the know
Had confidently told him so.
But on the morning of the race
It only took the *seventh* place!

Picture the Viscount's great surprise!
He scarcely could believe his eyes!
He sought the Individual who
Had laid him odds at 9 to 2,
Suggesting as a useful tip
That they should enter Partnership
And put to joint account the debt
Arising from his foolish bet.
But when the Bookie — oh! my word,
I only wish you could have heard
The way he roared he did not think,
And hoped that they might strike him pink!
Lord Hippo simply turned and ran
From this infuriated man.
Despairing, maddened and distraught
He utterly collapsed and sought
His sire, the Earl of Potamus,
And brokenly addressed him thus:
"Dread Sire — to-day — at Ascot — I…"
His genial parent made reply:
"Come! Come! Come! Come! Don't look so glum!
Trust your Papa and name the sum….
WHAT?… *Fifteen hundred thousand?*… Hum!
However… stiffen up, you wreck;
Boys will be boys — so here's the cheque!"
Lord Hippo, feeling deeply — well,
More grateful than he cared to tell —
Punted the lot on Little Nell: —
And got a telegram at dinner
To say that he had backed the Winner!

The Heavy Price of Shunning Emotions

Being afraid to show emotions in a presentation can have severe consequences. For instance, a lab director in an electronics firm was being considered for a major promotion. As part of putting this into the works, his boss arranged for him to present to the board on an important project. The lab director was a low-key, highly professional person. He delivered his talk in a smooth but flat, "objective" tone. At the end, he declared in the same tone that the project was "very exciting." At this point, one of the directors slammed the table and said, "Then for God's sake, man, *show* it!" It sealed the fate of the promotion: with that kind of negative attention, the boss did not dare even bring it up to the president again.

Note what happened in this case: the presenter was sending *conflicting signals*. His words said that the project was exciting — but his voice denied it. Audiences can get extremely unsettled by that kind of inconsistency. So, as you can see, emotion is not an extra nicety to add to your presentation; it's an essential element.

Controlling Your Pitch

Pitch is used in English to distinguish questions from statements: "Good?" (rising pitch) vs. "Good." (falling pitch) But pitch also has some other functions speakers do not always appreciate:

1. Keeping your pitch up in the middle of a sentence signals that you are not yet finished.
2. Using large pitch intervals expresses strong emotions such as surprise, pleasure, or annoyance.

If you don't understand aspect #1, you will keep getting interrupted, because listeners think you've finished talking. So, *lower* your pitch at the end of a simple (non-question) sentence, but *keep the pitch up* if you hesitate in the middle of a sentence.

Tip

Never drop your pitch in the middle of a sentence — it invites interruptions because it suggests that you've finished your sentence or thought.

The second use of pitch — as an expression of feelings — relates directly to issues of *trust* and *authority*. On the one hand, we don't trust people who *don't* express feelings. So, if you talk in a monotone, we may just not believe you. (We'll also be bored.) On the other hand, in business talks or conversations, *too much* feeling as expressed by pitch variation may make us doubt your credibility or authority. Apparently, Americans expect you to keep some reasonable control of your emotions.

The safest approach is to *develop a habit of using three reasonably distinct levels of pitch.* This will help you sound professional and credible yet also persuasive and emotionally committed.

Now, there is an interesting difference between the sexes: women tend to use more pitch levels (four vs. two or three) and greater pitch intervals than men. Do our guidelines mean that women should talk like men? Yes — if they want to make it easier for themselves to succeed in business! In fact, if they enter the world of radio or TV as announcers, they may be specifically trained to reduce their pitch levels to

---

Tip

Work with three levels of pitch.

---

two so they sound more like men. It may not be fair or rational, but for now, that seems to be the social reality.

USING LANGUAGE THAT REACHES PEOPLE

To speak naturally, as to a friend, you have to use the kind of *language* you would use with a friend: straightforward words and simple sentences. Obviously, this means no *scripts* or *memorized talks*. Think about it: would you memorize your half of a conversation with a friend and then try to impress him with your polished contribution? You wouldn't keep many friends if you did — and you won't keep audiences with you that way, either.

Here are some things to do and to avoid in your language.

Do:

- Use short, snappy sentences.
- Get to the point quickly. *("There's going to be a severe shortage of engineers. Study after study has come to this conclusion over the last few years...")*
- Use direct questions. *("Who do you think will have to pay?")*
- Use contractions (*wouldn't, haven't, don't, isn't,* etc.).
- Use personal pronouns (*you, I, we, they*).
- Use concrete, colorful words.
- Quote people.
- Use active voice, few prepositional phrases, few adjectives.

Don't:

- Use long, complex sentences.
- Start sentences with long phrases. *("Although, as we all know—or at least should know, since we have been told many times over the last few years—there will soon be a shortage of engineers...")*
- Use only dull declarative statements. *("The costs will inevitably be borne by the general public.")*
- Use tongue twisters.
- Use long strings of adjectives.
- Use lots of numbers.
- Use formal, technical, or bureaucratic language.
- Use flowery or affected language.
- Use an impersonal style (passive voice, no personal pronouns or names).

Yes:	No:
I think we should boost our advertising budget.	*It is my opinion that our advertising budget ought to be increased.*
Last year, our shipping department planned to expand the Night & Day Service.	*It was last year that plans were formulated by our shipping department for an expansion of the Night & Day Service.*
The problem of employee injuries demands our immediate attention.	*The subject of injuries to employees is a most important matter and therefore ought to be considered immediately.*

Word Choice and Your Listeners' Learning Styles

Your word choice can also help listeners grasp material better because it targets different *learning styles* such as the kinesthetic or logical styles (see the discussion of learning styles in Chapter 4). Table 11-1 describes some of the relationships between word choice and learning styles. It's not something you will be able to control spontaneously during delivery, of course. However, your choice of key words in your notes, as well as your word choice on your visuals, can take this consciously into account, and the language you'll use during delivery will naturally be colored by the choices you made during preparation.

OVERCOMING DISTRACTING VERBAL HABITS

Anything that repeats itself over and over is distracting to the audience. A verbal habit such as sprinkling your speech with *uhm, and, like, basically,* or even just clearing your throat noisily, can ruin your entire talk. Of these *uhm* is perhaps the least damaging (for instance, you'll hear it on radio and TV from people who are constantly in the public eye). Unfortunately, however, many bosses have the nasty habit of *counting* those *uhm*s in your presentation and then saying: "You know how many times you said *uhm??!*" So, in your business life, you don't even have the luxury of this relatively inoffensive sin.

Getting Rid of "Uhm," "You Know," and Other Verbal Crutches

First of all, identify your favorite verbal or semiverbal crutches. Then pay attention to them *the day before* a presentation. For instance, you might ask a friend or your spouse to help you catch it. In the meantime, while that friend is trying to catch you at it, what *you* are trying to do is simply to *pause* briefly instead of saying "uhm, like …"

TABLE 11-1. Words You Can Use To Appeal to Different Learning Styles

Active Learning Style	**Visual/Spatial Learning Style**	**Verbal Learning Style**	**Logical Learning Style**
Action words/ metaphors: • *Fix, shape, stretch* • *Drop, shatter* • *Clash, push,* etc.	Spatial metaphors: • *Layout, pyramid* • *Branch out, grounded,* etc. *Any* good visual metaphor: • *Grain, cloud, mountain,* etc.	Attractive, memorable words Good rhythm Alliteration (starting words with the same letter): • *Law of Logic,* etc.	"Reason" words: • *Average, trend, variation* • *Proof, method,* etc. • *Problem, solution,* etc.

Don't put all your focus on this problem at delivery time — you need your mental energy to think about the audience and your message. The truth is that these habits get better only over time, so you need to be content if you can make a little progress each time.

Here is special help with one common problem: the annoying overuse of *and* as a verbal crutch and all-purpose connector. In some cases, of course, your solution is simply to omit the *and*. Often, however, a *more specific transition word* will make your talk more meaningful and easy to follow.

Here is a list of such specific, informative transitions:

accordingly	however	so
also	moreover	still
besides	nevertheless	therefore
hence	otherwise	thus

If overuse of *and* is a severe problem for you and you find it difficult to overcome it spontaneously during a talk, then you might consider ***putting some appropriate transition words right into your slide titles***. That way you won't forget them. For instance, if slide #6 is entitled

General Market Outlook for Next Year Is Down

then the next slide might have as its title

However, Our Chosen Niche Is Growing

and the one after that may be headed

Therefore, We Are Expanding the Specialty Product Line

Four Aspects of Vocal Connection

1. Loud
- Speak loud enough to be heard without effort in the back of the room.

2. Clear
- Move your mouth; articulate clearly.
- Don't let your voice trail off.

3. Expressive
- Speak naturally, as you would to a friend.
- Reflect enthusiasm.
- Express other appropriate emotions (urgency, concern, empathy, frustration, doubt, determination, satisfaction, confidence, etc.).

4. Varied
- Speak fast for routine items; slow down for important points.
- Pause between sections and thoughts.
- Vary volume and pitch.

EXERCISES

Exercise 11-1. On the basis of your own impressions and/or feedback from other people, answer the following questions about your use of voice in presentations. Use a simple verbal scale of *no, rarely, often, always.*

Volume generally **adequate** and **varied**? _____
Ends of sentences loud enough to ensure comfortable understanding? _____
Speed varied (slow for important points, faster for routine information)? _____
Comfortable using pauses? _____
Articulation generally clear? _____
Ends of words sharp? _____
Enthusiasm projected through variety of pitch, volume, and speed? _____
"Uhm" and other filler noises or words avoided (replaced with pause, if necessary)?
_____

For any items rated negatively (answers of "no" or rarely"), review the advice and exercises contained in this chapter.

Exercise 11-2. Have a colleague videotape a dry run of one of your presentations. Then evaluate the videotape as to your **use of voice and language.** For guidance on evaluating your use of voice, see Exercise 11-1 above. For language use, answer the following questions, using *yes/no, often, rarely.*

Word choice:
Conversational yet precise? _____ If not, indicate problems you see:
    Too formal? _____
    Too informal (sloppy or slang)? _____
    Spontaneous speech leading to many wrong or imprecise words? _____
    Complicated word choices (double negatives, difficult or long words, etc.)?
    _____
    Uncomfortable using personal pronouns (*I, we, you*)? _____
Enough specific **transition words** (*however, nonetheless, therefore,* etc.) _____ If not:
    Overuse of *and* or *but*?
    Often no transitions at all?
Concrete, colorful words preferred over abstract ones? _____

Sentence structure:
Sentence length appropriate? _____ If not, indicate problem:
    Mostly too long? _____
    Mostly too short or choppy? _____
Sentence structures simple? _____ If not, indicate problem:
    Long introductory clauses or phrases? _____
    Sentences broken up with too much qualifying or explanatory material? _____
Questions used as well as declarative statements? _____
Active voice (e.g., *We did this,* vs. passive *This was done*) preferred? _____

*For word choice problems, **review your notes for the presentation.** Did they contain overly formal words and phrases that led to poor language during delivery? If so, change your style of preparing notes: use the kind of words you want to **say** in your talk.*

12

Staying in Touch Through Eye Contact

The most powerful way to reach people is to talk to them on a *personal* level, in a one-to-one conversation. This creates a great challenge for you in a presentation, because the obvious reality is that you are talking in front of a *group*, not just one person. The challenge is to beat that reality and *create many special moments of privacy,* so that at the end, each listener feels he or she had some important personal interactions with you. Eye contact is your tool for achieving this.

THE ART OF CONVERSING WITH YOUR EYES

For eye contact to do this tremendous job, it can't be a half-hearted affair. Yet that's how most speakers approach it. They engage in it as little as possible; they drop it before it can make any impression; and they seem to get nothing out of it — no information, no confidence, no pleasure.

Think of eye contact as a *silent, private conversation that goes on in parallel with your talk.* The thoughts you are transmitting are things such as

> *Was this clear?*
> *Do you accept this idea?*
> *Does this interest you?*
> *I'm enjoying this — are **you**?*
> *I like you.*
> *I'm comfortable with you.*
> *I am interested in what you think.*

The thoughts you are getting back are answers and reactions:

> *I'm confused.*
> *I'm skeptical — give me more evidence.*
> *I'm convinced.*

I'm interested.
I'm getting bored — move on.
I'm enjoying this, too.
I appreciate your interest in my thoughts.

The ideas exchanged may be rather simple — but they are crucial to the success of your talk, because they tell you how your presentation is being received. And eye contact is your only elegant access to this information.

Here are some specific guidelines on the art of "eye conversations":

- *Always be in touch with some individual.* The only time you're excused is when you have to get your next point from your notes or a visual. Specifically, remember that the floor, the walls, or the scenery visible through the windows *never* need your attention — your *listeners* do.
- *Focus sharply on the eyes of one individual — and **enjoy** the contact.* You may be able to *see* more than one person at a time, but you can't have *eye contact* with more than one. So, give just one person your full attention and get pleasure out of learning more about him or her.
- *Hold the eye contact until you have had a complete interaction with the individual.* This will take several seconds. Does the person agree with your point? Is she bored or confused? Have you belabored your point? Spend the time to find out!
- *Shift eye contact randomly, making sure to get to everybody.* Any pattern, such as left-to-right or "ping-pong" across the room, is unsettling to the audience. Also, people will react negatively if you look only at the highest-ranking listener or a few well-meaning friends.
- *Don't hold eye contact too long, as this tends to make people uncomfortable.* Similarly, singling out certain people for repeated eye contact can make both them and others apprehensive.

EYE CONTACT AND FEAR

The main reason speakers avoid eye contact is fear. They are afraid to see signs of disagreement, disapproval, or pity; and they worry that their own discomfort and nervousness are apparent in their eyes. So, they look at anything but the audience.

Unfortunately, people in our culture react powerfully against lack of eye contact, both in speakers and listeners. They automatically suspect criticism, aloofness, arrogance, or guilt — and none of these is appreciated.

To avoid trouble, therefore, some speakers try to *fake* eye contact: they stare just above the head of some person in the back of the room. From that distance, it's hard to tell the difference between real and fake contact.

There are two problems with this:

1. You are giving up vital feedback from your listeners, because you are in fact trying hard **not** to see their eyes.

2. You are not breaking out of the circle of fear — and that's what you most need to do.

Eye contact allows you to break down the fear-inspiring "crowd" into a number of individuals with whom you can have a casual conversation. If you're not already in the habit of keeping full eye contact, you simply have to force yourself to do it next time so you *experience* the benefits. After the initial shock, you'll feel connected, in control, and confident instead of terrified. In short, good eye contact can turn a nightmare into a pleasant affair!

Using Eye Contact To Maintain a Strong Audience Connection

In our culture, eye contact is probably the most important way to connect with your audience. Here are some pointers on how to make it work for you.

- Throughout, keep eye contact with different members of the audience.
- Lock in on a person before you start a thought block.
- Maintain eye contact for several seconds, until you feel you had a *complete interaction* with the person.
- Shift the focus of your eye contact in a *random pattern;* avoid scanning the audience or "ping-ponging" in a regular manner from side to side.
- When showing visuals, do not lose touch with the audience.
- If some listeners seem very uncomfortable with eye contact, don't force it. Just move on and check again later to see if it signals resistance, disagreement, or perhaps just general discomfort with eye contact in any public situation.

HOW TO ACHIEVE STRONG EYE CONTACT

You might think that it's obvious how to make eye contact: you just look in the other person's eye. But in a presentation situation, it's not as simple as that, because your conversation partners are constantly changing, and are in different parts of the room. The common temptation is to face more or less down the middle of the audience and look at people either fully if they are straight ahead of you, or *out of the corner of your eyes* if they are on your right or left. By contrast, in a regular one-on-one conversation, the other person is usually facing you, so that eye contact is always full and straight.

Tip

If you are shy, you can overcome your fear of people simply by working "from the outside in": practice strong eye contact, get reasonably close, and speak in a firm, loud voice. These are all signals of assertiveness and being comfortable with people, and they will activate patterns in your brain that go along with these signals.

Now, most presenters simply don't appreciate the difference between straight and crooked eye contact. (If they did, they would avoid the latter like the plague.) However, we want *you* to understand it clearly, so that you may have an incentive to work on the skill of *facing people squarely.*

Take a look at Figure 12-1. The two drawings (a) and (b) illustrate how you look to some of the people (those straight ahead of you) when you make eye contact with people on the right or left. To the people you are favoring with that eye contact, the view is even more extreme, since they see you almost in profile. How do you think they view you and your thoughts? Specifically, what do they think is going through your mind? How about

I don't trust you. (You might sneak up on me from the side!)
Who are you anyway, over there?

Tip

Turn to *face the person squarely* as you make eye contact. This is much more effective than looking at people out of the corner of your eyes. It will make you feel that you are having a casual, personal discussion with individuals rather than addressing a frightening mass of people!

In return, they probably don't relate to you or trust you much either. Certainly, they won't feel that every individual in the audience is really important to you.

Compare this with the very different effect of full, straight eye contact, illustrated in Figure 12-2. Here, you can see that the speaker pivots toward an individual and, for some seconds, addresses this person as in a private conversation.

By focusing eye contact rigidly on one person in this whole-body fashion, the speaker overcomes the uncomfortable "mass" reality and replaces it with a "private chat" reality.

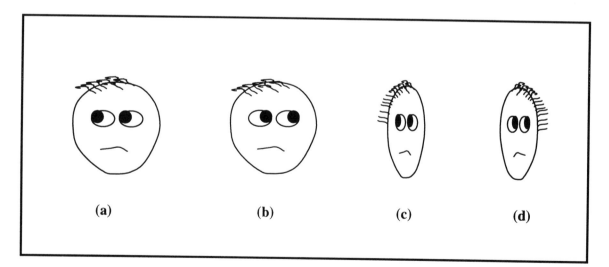

    (a)   (b)   (c)   (d)

Figure 12-1. The effect your eye contact gives if you do *not* face an individual squarely: (a) and (b) as seen by the people *straight ahead* of you; (c) as seen by the person on your *right* with whom you are making eye contact; (d) as seen by the person on your left with whom you are making eye contact. How do *you* react when a speaker looks at you like that, or when you see her looking at others in that fashion?

Figure 12-2. Combine strong eye contact with turning toward the person with whom you are "conversing" at that moment. This speaker is doing it. Notice how connected to the audience he appears as a result.

EXERCISE AND DISCUSSION

Exercise 12-1. Evaluate your habits relating to eye contact. Answer *yes* or *no* to the following questions.

In *regular conversation* with another person, what are your eye-contact habits?

- Never any contact_____
- Rarely_____
- Often but brief; not comfortable with it_____
- Regular, natural: 3-4 seconds at a time, then breaking briefly_____
- Often looking over the other person's shoulder (*Note:* This is very unsettling; usually, the person will turn around to see who is standing behind him or her!) _____

Now consider what you usually do in a *presentation*.

- Always make sure to include everybody_____
- Try to make "general" eye contact with the whole group (*Note:* This is not really possible; eye contact is necessarily focused on **one person's eyes**!) _____
- Tend to look at just a few people with whom I am comfortable _____
- Tend to look mostly at the decision makers in the audience (*Note:* This is going to cost you the goodwill of everybody else!) _____

- Tend to look at the floor, especially when trying to think of the next point or an answer to a question (*Question:* What is written on the floor that is so helpful? Learn to look at people while you are thinking; or, if you need to consult your notes, do that briefly.) _____

Considering your answers, what are the greatest improvements you can make in this area?

_____
_____
_____
_____

Discussion 12-1. As an *audience member,* what experience have you had with eye contact? In particular:

- How much do you think your reaction to a talk has been influenced by strong, weak, or absent eye contact?
- How much influence does eye contact have on holding your attention?
- Have you ever been made *uncomfortable* by eye contact from a speaker?
- What kinds of inferences have you drawn about a speaker's character from the way he or she handled eye contact?

13

Handling Notes

Everybody admires the speaker who talks freely and animatedly, without referring to any notes. Unfortunately, when you have little time to prepare a talk on a complex technical subject, you often can't do without notes. This chapter, therefore, will offer some advice on handling notes smoothly and effectively. (For *preparation* of notes, as well as ways to develop independence from notes, see Chapter 7, which also discusses effective rehearsing.)

PARK OR CARRY?

If you think you'll need to refer to your notes just once or twice, you can park them on the projector table or wherever they are easily accessible. Presumably, your notes

- Are short
- Are easy to read because they're written or printed in large letters with helpful underlining and highlighting
- Consist of key words and phrases rather than long sentences or paragraphs
- Don't duplicate points you can read off your visuals

With such notes, you'll be able to find your point quickly if you should get lost, even if you have to walk over to them and turn one or two pages. By contrast, with the wrong notes you'll be shuffling through many pages or sifting through long paragraphs to get back on track.

Unfortunately, many people are deluded about their grasp of the material. They think they can give the presentation with just occasional reference to their parked notes—say, before each major section. However, when they start speaking, they soon find that they need to consult their notes much more often. But do they then change their strategy and pick up their notes? No way. In our experience, once they've parked their notes on the overhead table, they'll leave them right there, no matter how confused they get. The effect of this is that they face the audience sideways for most of the presentation while reading points off the notes or the visuals (see Figure 13-1).

Others experience only occasional blanks but are too embarrassed to return to their parked notes. Therefore, they try to improvise — and promptly forget whole chunks of their talk.

The remedy is simple. Once you find you need your notes a lot, just *take them with you* so you can move around. Hold them in one hand and consult them openly when you need them. (Don't take a whole pad of paper with you, though; it's too obtrusive and too awkward to handle.) If your notes are good, the break in audience connection should be very brief. Or, if you need your notes only very occasionally to overcome a blank, walk calmly over to them and get your point.

Tip

Make sure your notes or visuals contain at least

1. The strong *attention getter* you want to use in the introduction
2. Your *main message,* which you will repeat several times
3. Your *key points,* which you should also repeat as part of your transitions between sections

Your notes may also need reminders on examples, anecdotes, quotes, statistics, and other elements you plan to use, unless these reminders are built into your visuals.

RECOVERING FROM AN OMISSION

If you do park your notes and consult them, say, only at the end of each major section, you may sometimes find that you've skipped some material from the section you just concluded. If it's important, don't be embarrassed to add it. Just use a nice, *nonapologetic* transition such as "There's one more point on this subject I want to add: ..." Remember, looking smooth won't help you one bit if it means omitting your most persuasive argument or example!

Figure 13-1. Reading extensively from notes or transparencies parked on the projector table often leads to this situation: showing the audience your profile for the entire presentation.

Living with Notes

If you think you will need your notes at delivery time (say, because you had almost no time to rehearse), don't be ashamed to use them. Consult them calmly and openly at the start of each new section. Here are some additional pointers:

- Above all, *keep your cool* when you first get to the front. Don't rush into the presentation while you still suffer from a "stage-fright blank." Calmly arrange your notes and visuals, look at people in the audience, consult the notes again to remind yourself of the first two points to make, then start *with a smile.*
- Medium-size index cards are a good choice if you plan to carry your notes with you. However, if you end up with more than, say, 20 cards, or you find during rehearsal that you never turn the cards until you are lost and then have trouble finding your place, then condensing the material onto three or four letter-size sheets is better.
- If you use transparencies and have the time to *frame* them, you can put a few notes (keywords, in *large letters*) on each frame. Then you can read the notes just before you put on the visual, so you can give a smooth transition.
- If you would prefer to keep your notes on the table rather than carry them around, you *must* condense them on two or three sheets—otherwise, you will not find your place in your pile of sheets when you do get lost.
- Your visuals can, of course, serve as memory joggers. However, practice smooth transitions so you don't seem to "hobble behind" your visuals.
- If you plan to quote from newspapers, books, or magazines, bring the original (if you have it) and read directly from it. Seeing the book or magazine will remind you of the point to make—and for some reason, handling the original adds interest to the presentation (whereas reading from notes never does).

EXERCISE

Exercise 13-1. Assess your handling of notes during delivery; also, review the kinds of notes you usually prepare in order to evaluate their usefulness for delivery.

What kinds of notes do you usually keep?
- Short words & phrases? _____
- Large letters? _____
- Few pages or index cards? _____
- Mostly on visuals; additional notes don't duplicate visuals? _____
- Do these notes work well at delivery time? _____
- If not, what problems do you tend to have?

_____

_____

_____

_____

How do you handle your notes?

- Park them and usually don't need them_____
- Park them but usually need them a few times_____
- Park them and often need them — but leave them parked_____
- Park them, but usually pick them up soon and keep them with me, as I need to consult them often or continuously _____
- All or most of my notes usually are on the visuals — no need to take notes along_____
- Use a mix of visuals and other props to keep myself on track; check notes perhaps for completeness at the end of a section or before the summary_____

Review all your answers in this exercise. In light of the discussion in this chapter, what are the biggest changes you should make in this area of preparing and using notes?

_____
_____
_____
_____
_____
_____

14

Handling Visuals

Visuals have a way of overwhelming you. Instead of paying attention to the audience, you spend all your time putting on transparencies or changing computer slides and then running to the screen and talking into it.

The main challenge you face is to *stay connected to the audience while getting the full benefit of your visuals*. Three simple steps will help you succeed in this:

1. Check your preparation and setup.
2. Keep in touch with the audience while working with visuals.
3. Avoid distractions that disrupt the connection.

REVIEWING YOUR PREPARATION AND SETUP

Visuals can reinforce your major points and make complex ideas more accessible. However, when you have too many visuals, you spoil their impact. So, as you get ready, take a last look at your visuals. Are there any that would only slow you down and take you away from the audience? Then throw them out.

Also, check that the equipment is set up in the right way. Are you going to spend time at the screen, helping the audience understand sections of your visuals? If so, make sure there is space next to the projector for your transparencies, *on the proper side*. This will save you from constantly walking through the projector beam or having to work on the wrong side of the screen.

Figure 14-1 shows a workable setup for a U-shaped room if you're planning to work at the *left* side of the screen — in which case you also need to put on the transparencies (or operate your laptop computer) from the *left* side of the projector. If you prefer to work on the *right* side of the screen, then set up the projector to leave room for transparencies on its *right* side. (All the figures and the discussion in this chapter will take the *overhead projector* as the normal case. Electronic slide shows will be discussed in detail in Part 3, Chapter 20.)

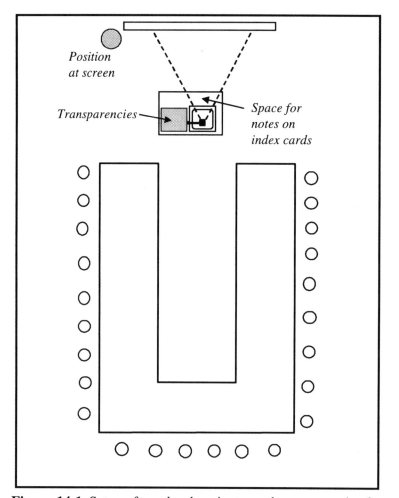

Figure 14-1. Setup of overhead projector and transparencies for a U-shaped table arrangement if you prefer to work on the *left* side of the screen. This setup avoids your walking through the beam of light when changing slides. If you want to work on the screen's *right* side, place transparencies to the *right* of the projector.

While *not* working with visuals, you are free to move some way into the audience — but avoid showing your back to the people in the front chairs for more than a few moments. This can be a difficult restraint for natural movers who like to breeze confidently into the middle of the U, or perhaps even farther in order to get close to a key decision maker at the end of the table. However, we have observed over and over that in these situations, the people in the front of the room are severely turned off from the whole presentation: they simply feel left out!

Figure 14-2 shows similar left- and right-side setups for a boardroom-style arrangement. The main challenge in this setting usually is the dearth of space for your essentials: projector, transparencies or laptop computer, notes, and props or demo objects. Often there is no space for the transparencies you've just shown, making it necessary to shuffle transparencies like a deck of cards. All this makes it extra important that you check the setup beforehand and adjust it while you can. Move front chairs back a little to create a little sphere of privacy (after all, you may not be comfortable having the people in the front reading your notes ahead of you!), move the projector into the best spot and refocus it, and certainly remove extra chairs.

In this setup, you are severely restricted in your movements, even when not working with visuals. It's impossible to start walking around *behind* audience members without making them very uncomfortable. (For one thing, it's too reminiscent of school teachers sneaking up behind you to check on your work!) Therefore, you can basically only stray to the edge of the table and back to the projector, or, of course, to the screen when necessary. However, even in this setup, you must manage *some* movement, so you don't block one person's view of the screen continuously. As explained in Chapter 10, your most effective movements serve to bring you into full eye contact with one person at a time — with you *facing that person squarely*. This means that even in this restricted setup, you will need to move and *pivot* so that you face different audience members.

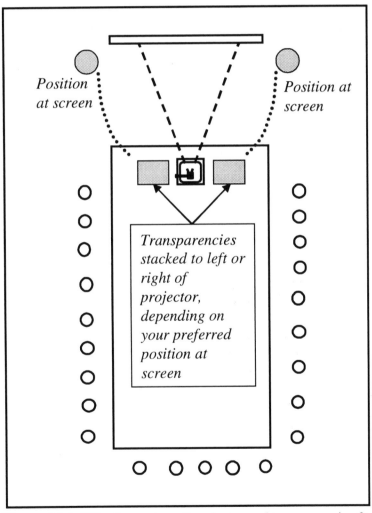

Figure 14-2. Effective setup of projector and transparencies for a boardroom-style arrangement. As in the U-shaped arrangement, set up your transparencies (or laptop) on the side (left or right) where you want to work at the screen so you avoid having to walk through the beam of light to change slides.

Figures 14-3 and 14-4 show two common classroom-style arrangements — one with the screen at center, the other with the screen in the right corner. The setup for the arrangement with screen centered (Figure 14-3) is the same as in a U-shaped room: pick your favorite screen side to work with visuals, and set up transparencies on that side of the projector. By contrast, you don't have that choice when the screen is set up in the corner (Figure 14-4). Here, you want to be positioned toward the *middle* of the room rather than be squashed all the way in the corner where you can't see anybody and many in the audience can't see you.

In either case, you are free to move some way into the audience, as in the U-shaped arrangement. Again, however, avoid turning your back to the people in the front for more than a few moments.

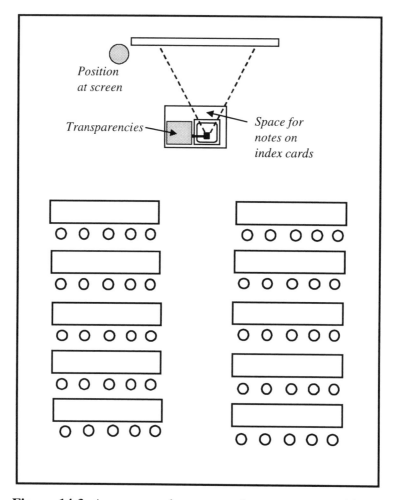

Figure 14-3. A common classroom-style arrangement with the screen at center. As in the U-shaped arrangement, you can choose the side of the screen to work on (shown here is the position at left of screen). If you prefer to work on the right side of the screen, then you set up the projector on its table so that there is space for transparencies on its right side.

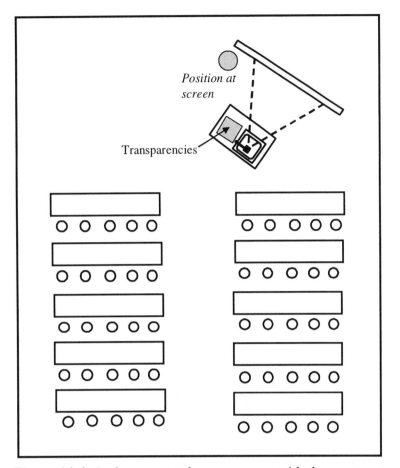

Figure 14-4. A classroom-style arrangement with the screen set up in a corner. In such an arrangement, you must avoid boxing yourself into a tiny corner where you have no mobility and hardly any visibility. That means you need to work at the left of the screen when the screen is set up in the right corner.

You might think that all this is obvious — so that, for instance, at a conference, things will be set up properly by the organizers anyhow. Nothing could be farther from the truth: this is an area continuously bungled both by organizers and by presenters. ***Your job is not to take the setup you find as fixed but adjust it quickly to your needs.*** Otherwise, you'll stumble through a presentation that could have been smooth sailing.

We'll give you just two real examples to illustrate this point. At a conference, the hotel staff had set up the projector as shown in Figure 14-5, leaving space on the projector's right side. This would be appropriate for working on the screen's right side — a bad choice with the screen set up in the right corner. Neither the organizers nor the moderator for the session had changed this setup.

Speaker 1 appeared, placed his transparencies on the right side, and headed straight for the screen's left so he could be in touch with his audience. To change slides, he had to walk through the beam of light. He had quite a few slides, and after a few of these light-beam-crossing trips, he grew embarrassed about the huge shadows he was creating. So, he repositioned himself to deliver the rest of his talk squashed into the *right* corner, becoming more of a voice than a bodily presence. The talk itself was quite interesting, but without speaker contact, many in the left half of the room tuned out completely and read their conference proceedings instead.

Speaker 2, having witnessed this fiasco, seemed determined not to fall into the same trap. But did he adjust the projector to make room for transparencies on the *left* side? Not a chance! He placed his slides on the right side but parked himself on the *left* to have a bit of audience contact. Now, to change slides, he was not going to repeat the previous speaker's initial mistake, walking through the light beam. Instead, he reached over with a v-e-r-y long arm and gingerly picked up the old transparency, then maneuvered the next one onto the projector stage (see Figure 14-6).

This in itself was already quite fascinating, generating much audience interest. However, the clincher was that he wore a *nice long tie* that dangled in tantalizing ways in front of the projector as he manipulated his slides. It's a good bet that 90 percent of the audience took in nothing of that talk other than the speaker's intriguing balancing act and his Animated Dangling Tie Screen Show!

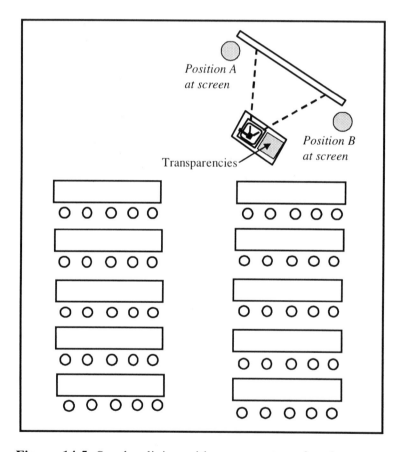

Figure 14-5. Speaker living with a poor setup of a classroom-style room with screen in the right corner. First attempt was to change slides from the right side but deliver the talk on the left side (Position A, and moving past projector into audience). Because of the distraction of walking through the light beam, the speaker abandoned this for a boxed-in position (B) in the right corner.

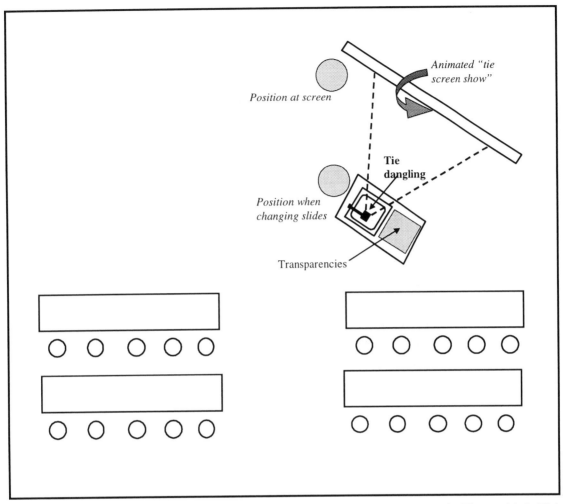

Figure 14-6. Another speaker's attempt at defeating the impossible setup in Figure 14-5. This speaker stayed on the left side, but *leaned over the projector* to change slides. This proved most distracting, especially because of intriguing shadows produced by his dangling long necktie.

What's the lesson from all this? One, *be early and change what you can.* Two, make a note of what you'll have to adjust quickly before you begin your talk.

KEEPING IN TOUCH WITH YOUR AUDIENCE

The well-known formula for working with visuals is *Touch-Turn-Talk* (see Figure 14-7). This means you look at the screen to find your place and point at it ("touch"), then face the audience and make eye contact with somebody ("turn"), and *only then* continue to speak ("talk"). The main point to remember is this: *whenever you talk into the screen, you show lack of concern for your audience.* You may still come across as enthused about your *subject,* but the connection to the *audience* has been broken.

Figure 14-7. Aim for this: when needed, *touch* your point on the visual, then *turn* to the audience and make eye contact, and only then *talk!* This is what is meant by the well-known formula Touch-Turn-Talk.

Of course, many times you don't have to point at a visual at all. If a chart has three simple bullet points, you can stay close to the audience while talking about those three points. On the other hand, if you're illustrating a process with a complex flow diagram, pointing precisely at each item as you explain it is essential.

Achieving Cohesiveness Through Your Visuals

To make your talk cohesive and reinforce your main points, always *give clear transitions to and from your visuals:*

- Explain the *reason* for the visual — what it is supposed to illustrate.
- Tie that reason back to your main message or the key point you are discussing, if there is any chance that it might have been lost in the details of the discussion.
- Discuss the visual.
- When you've finished with the visual, make a clear transition to your next point.

The most common error is the one illustrated in Figure 14-8: being glued to the screen, which serves as the speaker's notes. There is nothing much wrong with using visuals as your security blanket; just remember to return to the audience once you've refreshed your memory so you don't lose connection.

Figure 14-8. Avoid facing the screen while talking to the audience — even if you're using your visuals as your notes, as this speaker does.

Many speakers treat the screen almost as if it held magical powers of focusing their thinking and restoring their sense of balance. In fact, we've seen quite a few presenters gazing fondly at the *blank* screen, for a minute at a time. They seemed to *remember* the last, or some earlier, visual they'd put there, and it gave them the sense of security they craved. Invariably, the audience also stared at the blank screen, and a few people actually laughed. Surely, that's not the kind of response you want to generate!

The point is: gazing at the screen at great length has *no* value for your thinking. On the contrary, it puts you into a *reading* mode, which is the opposite of what you need: flexible thinking and interacting.

Tip

Treat visuals as you would regular notes: consult them briefly, *then look at the audience and talk.* Once you've seen your next point, there is nothing gained by staring at it further.

Visuals and Movement

Here are a few simple suggestions on how to manage your movements in the room while working with visuals.

- While working with traditional visuals, stay close to the screen but do not block people's view of the projected image. (Figures 14-1 through 14-5 show acceptable positions at the screen for different room arrangements.)
- While working with computer slide shows, work either at the screen (e.g., for explaining sections of a process flow chart) or use a remote control to highlight the part of interest. In the latter case, *be careful not to spend long periods with your back to the audience!*
- If a projected visual is still of active interest to the audience even though you are not discussing it at the moment, *keep on the move* so you don't continuously block the *same person's* view of the screen!
- When not using a visual, get as close to the audience as possible, and move so you can be in contact with different audience members.
- Do not turn your back on anybody for more than a few seconds.

AVOIDING DISTRACTIONS

Visuals present many opportunities for annoying distractions that break the audience connection. Here are some areas to watch out for.

Pointer Fiddling

If you are a "pointer fiddler," your best approach is to *pick up the pointer only when you need it* and then immediately put it down. (If you are tall, you may not need a pointer at all.) Get enthused about your message, and your hands will soon find something better to do than torturing that pointer.

Moving Shadows

Moving images or shadows attract a lot of attention, and some people dislike them intensely. This means you should avoid pointing at the transparency on the projector (especially if you're shaky — the projector will magnify that tremor dramatically!). Point at the screen instead. Similarly, don't cover up parts of a transparency to reveal points one by one (a technique called "stepwise revelation"). It tends to annoy people — perhaps because it puts you in an obnoxious I-know-more-than-you position reminiscent of high school teachers.

What about writing on a transparency as you speak? In every audience, we find at least one person who hates it with a passion (although quite a few people seem to view it *favorably*). Therefore, think carefully before you do this. Are you using it as a genuine tool for *interaction?* Then it's justified. Or are you just writing down your own points? Then a flip chart or a properly prepared visual is more appropriate.

Demo Objects or Samples

Demo objects can be a great addition to a presentation, but they create major distractions that you need to minimize. For instance, many people will stop listening to you until they have seen the "thing." But will they *ever* see it? In many cases, the object gets stuck somewhere in the middle, leaving half the audience resentful!

Here is a case in point. Your demo object has made it nicely through the left side of the room and now passes to C and D at the end of the table. The setup there is as shown in Figure 14-9.

Now, will D pass the object on to E, who is separated from him by *two empty chairs?* In our experience, chances are not all that great, especially if D is a considerate or shy sort who feels bad about creating a commotion. In the meantime — unless you have stepped in to retrieve the stuck object — the entire right half of the room may not have a clue of what you are talking about, and even if they do, they may be tormented by the wistful thought, *"Oh, if I could only see and hold the OBJECT the people over there have seen!"*

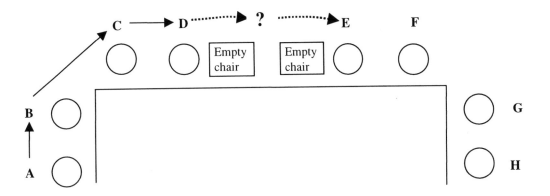

Figure 14-9. One of the complications you may run into when using demo objects: people having to pass the object on over substantial gaps. Will they do it?

So, first, decide whether you must really pass the object around. Can you just hold it up? For instance, relative brightness of a paper is easily demonstrated with two sheets of different brightness held up side by side; even at a distance, the difference is usually striking. Or if you have some small objects you want to show, they may be much more effectively and quickly demonstrated with a *magnified photograph* you can project.

Sometimes it is best to walk from table to table and show people exactly what you want them to see. It may take no more than half a minute, and it keeps the whole process tightly under your control.

If you do decide to pass the object around, **keep track of it.** Make sure everybody sees it within a reasonable time, and plan your talk in such a way that those who are waiting for the object can still follow you.

SPECIAL ISSUES WITH OVERHEAD PROJECTORS

Overhead projectors have a number of limitations that you should be aware of. We'll look at three of these:

1. The projected image may not be square but much wider at the top.
2. Transparencies may slide around or fall off.
3. Transparencies may curl from the heat and perhaps fall off.

With a little skill, you can work around these minor problems and use this standard presentation and training device to good effect. Old-fashioned though it is, it has some advantages over computer slide shows, especially simplicity.

The Keystone Effect

Originally, overhead projectors were intended for projection of images *up*, over the speaker's head, onto a tilt screen mounted near a high ceiling. Such a tilt screen has two advantages:

1. It is visible at all times to every audience member, since people are not blocking each other's view.
2. It shows a reasonably *square* image of the slides.

In most presentation rooms today, there is no such high-mounted tilt screen. In fact, the ceiling usually would be too low for such a screen. The common result is a screen image annoyingly shaped like a keystone:

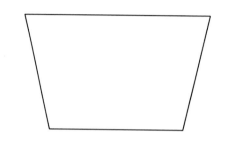

Not surprisingly, this bothersome phenomenon is called the *keystone effect.* You can often cure it simply by *improvising a tilt screen,* provided the screen is suspended from the ceiling, with its bottom free to move. If so, attach a few strips of masking tape to the bottom of the screen and then to the wall, so the screen tilts at an angle to the wall (see Figure 14-10). This will avoid or minimize the keystoning so that your slides will project without distortion of text and graphics.

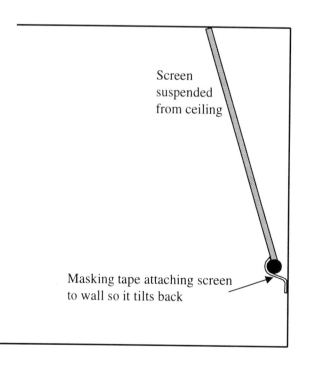

Screen
suspended
from ceiling

Masking tape attaching screen
to wall so it tilts back

Figure 14-10. A simple solution to the keystoning problem: an improvised tilt screen

Transparencies Sliding Around or Falling Off

Transparencies have a tendency to shift on the projector stage, or even float off altogether, especially if the projector is not set up totally straight (it almost never is). One solution to this is a professional transparency frame made of heavy plastic, with an exact 8 ½" × 11" opening for the transparencies. Once you set up this frame on the projector, all your transparencies will automatically be in the proper place — and *stay* there (unless they *curl* — but that's another problem). The main price you pay for this solution is that you'll have to lug yet another heavy accessory along.

A solution that is simpler, cheaper, and lighter, but not quite as neat, is to place a few strips of masking tape on top of each other in the proper place on the projector stage (see Figure 14-11). Provided the projector is not slanted in some other direction, they will act as a guiding edge for your transparencies and stop them from sliding off. If you make the strips long enough, they will form a solid cutoff line all across the bottom of the screen.

Transparencies Curling and Floating Off the Projector

The heat of the projector stage may cause transparencies to curl. You may not notice it for a while, because it takes time for the heat to build up. But then, just as you're ready to delve into a detailed discussion of your visual, you find that its sides have curled up so far that the visual is no longer even readable or recognizable. One step further, it may have lifted off like a hot-air balloon and sailed into the audience.

We once had this problem with a whole batch of visuals. Since we'd used expensive transparencies that should not have done such a vile thing, we complained to the manufacturer, who sent us a replacement. We then reprinted the whole lot — only to find that it acted just like the previous one! In the end, it turned out that the problem lay not with the transparencies but with our color printer, which had applied color in an uneven, improper way that induced curl.

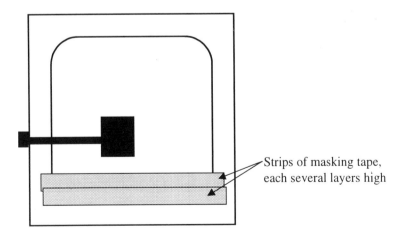

Strips of masking tape, each several layers high

Figure 14-11. The "masking tape trick" to stop transparencies from sliding around

The solution to the curling problem is simple but not very elegant. Simply put a *blank transparency on top of the slide* you are showing. The weight of the extra transparency will keep your slide flat. However, changing slides will become a bit more laborious. If you hurry that part too much, you'll probably lose that blank transparency, and then the hunt will be on for another blank, and more and more blanks as you proceed. There's a lesson in that, too, of course: don't hurry, or it will take you a lot longer!

EXERCISES AND DISCUSSION

Exercise 14-1. Is there some spot, *other* than next to the projection screen, where you can stay *throughout your presentation* without blocking somebody's view of the visuals? If so, show that position on the diagrams in Figures 14-1 through 14-5.

Exercise 14-2. Suppose you are pointing at sections of a flow diagram directly on an overhead transparency. Can you do this without blocking a single person's view of the visual? How? If not, does it matter that just one person cannot see the visual you are discussing, as long as you make sure it's not always the *same* person?

Discussion 14-1. How many people in the group dislike "stepwise revelation" of a transparency (placing a piece of paper over the transparency and sliding it down a step at a time to reveal the next points on the slide)? Why? How many dislike the equivalent approach in a computer slide show: a "build" slide with bullets appearing one at a time, and old bullet points perhaps dimming? What practical consequences does this have, in your view?

15

Handling Questions

Often, the question-and-answer period is your key to getting audience commitment, because it lets you respond to any doubts about your ideas. Unfortunately, it's also the time when you can lose credibility. To succeed, you need preparation, the right attitude, and a few specific techniques for stimulating and controlling the discussion.

REDUCING SURPRISES THROUGH PREPARATION

If you followed our advice on preparing a presentation, you will have begun the whole process by *considering all major audience questions and objections* (see Chapter 1). Therefore, you already have a list of detailed audience questions about your message. For those questions not addressed directly in your talk, you need to prepare answers. This should include

- The "simple answer" (see the discussion later in this chapter)
- Backup details: explanations, support numbers, relevant examples or quotes
- Charts or other visuals, if helpful
- Handout pages, if appropriate

Be sure to anticipate all the *tough* questions, including those about costs, benefits, feasibility, possible problems introduced by your proposals, relevance to listeners' special situation, and the solidity of your evidence — your data and their interpretation. (Handling tough questions is discussed in more detail below.) If you feel at all unsure that you have covered all likely ground, ask a colleague to help you with feedback — others may see obvious questions and gaps where you see none.

If you come across some important question to which you just do *not* have the answer now, you can still prepare to some extent simply by making a note on

- How to find out the answer
- By when you can reasonably find out

175

That way, if the question comes up, you won't be groping around with embarrassment for a "way out."

DECIDING WHEN TO TAKE QUESTIONS

If you haven't done so during your initial audience and needs analysis, decide on the best format and timing for question-and-answer. In most situations, aim for the least formal and most interactive format that is accepted by the organization and appropriate for the occasion.

Make sure you understand what the audience needs and how individual audience members tend to behave. This should have the greatest influence on the format you choose. The other factor you need to consider is how well you deal with interruptions.

If you're worried about the time limit and expect lengthy digressions, consider leaving questions to the end. However, if you want a lot of audience input and your subject is complex, taking questions throughout or after each major section is more effective. That way, people will still remember the issues clearly, and the discussion will be more to the point. Also, there will then be less need to repeat your points in order to sharpen the questions.

Here are some of the questions you might ask in making your decisions:

- Will they hold questions if you ask them to?
- If you let them interrupt freely, will chaos result?
- If you reserve questions for the end and this is a technical talk, will they be able to remember technical details long enough to ask useful questions?

Figure 15-1 summarizes these and other factors to consider in the timing of questions.

SETTING AND USING Q&A RULES

Establishing rules for question-and-answer is extremely important to help you deal with excessive interruptions, repetitive or lengthy questions, questions that stray off the subject, or people who monopolize the discussion. It's a simple two-step process:

1. Spell out the Q&A rules for your presentation when you start. (The best place usually is at the end of your "Plan" section of the *R-A-M-P* introduction.) For example, you might say:

   I will allow two minutes for questions at the end of each section; let's deal with remaining questions at the end. Also, to make sure everybody has a chance to give his or her input on the project, I'll take only one question from each person. Then if there is time left at the end, we can have additional questions.

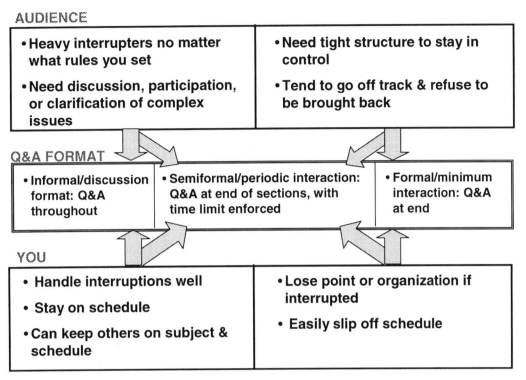

AUDIENCE

• **Heavy interrupters no matter what rules you set** • **Need discussion, participation, or clarification of complex issues**	• **Need tight structure to stay in control** • **Tend to go off track & refuse to be brought back**

Q&A FORMAT

• **Informal/discussion format: Q&A throughout**	• **Semiformal/periodic interaction: Q&A at end of sections, with time limit enforced**	• **Formal/minimum interaction: Q&A at end**

YOU

• **Handle interruptions well** • **Stay on schedule** • **Can keep others on subject & schedule**	• **Lose point or organization if interrupted** • **Easily slip off schedule**

Figure 15-1. Factors influencing your choice of question-and-answer timing and format

2. Invoke the rules when necessary to cut a question short, postpone discussion, or move on to other people's questions:

Sorry to have to interrupt you, but we agreed we'd keep questions and comments to under a minute. You asked whether we'd looked into X. We did, and we found that Y… Yes, Linda, you were next with a question?

The main mistake most speakers make is to set no Q&A rules at all or simply to announce that they'd like questions held to the end — which the average business audience promptly ignores. Then, as interruptions and off-track questions derail their talk, they scramble to make up the rules on the fly.

Unfortunately, making up rules on the spot *lacks authority* and tends to sound *arbitrary* or even personal. For instance, warding a questioner off with the sudden news, "Please, let's have only one question from each person" may seem like a frantic, arbitrary attempt to shut up one inconveniently critical audience member.

BASIC QUESTION-HANDLING SKILLS

Questions show interest, and you should *appreciate that interest,* no matter how it is expressed. First, get in the habit of *truly inviting* questions. Don't say "That's all, I guess" or "Questions?" but something of the order of "And now I'd be glad to answer any questions you may have." If your listeners look blank, you can prime their thinking: "For instance, you may be concerned about details of the three vendor proposals."

With that proper attitude of appreciation in place, you'll find it easier to do everything else right, from basic body language to smooth handling of hostile questions or comments.

Controlling Your Body Language While Dealing with Questions

Many speakers who are energetic and expressive do a terrible job of controlling their body language while dealing with questions. They fidget with their hands, play with their eyeglasses, slouch or shuffle, and make sad, supercilious, or weird faces.

The problem, of course, is that while you are *listening* to questions, you have nothing much to do: you're just waiting for the questioner to finish talking. So what *do* you do?

The answer is: *not much.* Clearly, it would be silly to act all charged up when most of the attention is on the person who is asking a question. Think about it: what's your job while you're listening? It's really fourfold:

1. Appreciate the interest.
2. Relax.
3. Pay attention.
4. Keep an open mind.

Now think about the body language that goes along with these four jobs.

Appreciate the Interest: Smile; move closer to the person; make eye contact; nod.

Relax: Keep your arms and hands relaxed, since you're not talking; stand quietly, without shuffling or fidgeting. (See the *athletic stance* described in Chapter 10 for a relaxed position that nonetheless maintains reasonable energy.)

Pay Attention: Maintain full eye contact; stand with enough energy to reflect attentiveness (don't slouch, hang onto tables or chairs, or fidget). Positive "attention" gestures such as rubbing your chin are O.K. and don't interfere.

Keep an Open Mind: Even if you disagree, smile or keep at least a straight face. Don't raise your eyebrows, scratch your head, break into a lopsided sardonic grin, or otherwise show disdain or superiority. Also, avoid crossing your arms, especially if you're upset or anxious — the combination of facial expression and upper body will transmit clear signals of defensiveness or even aggressiveness that will work against you.

Above all, it pays to be in touch with your facial expressions. Many people have extreme "listening faces" that they're not at all aware of. For example, while listening thoughtfully, one client did a good imitation of a wild boar. It looked something like the grimace in Figure 15-2.

Figure 15-2. Many people are unaware that they make extreme "listening faces" such as this "boar face."

Your Key Skill: "Simple Answer First"

Over and over, we have found that what the audience most appreciates is a *direct, simple answer* to any question. Giving that kind of answer on short notice requires practice and some good, focused thinking. It's basically the same challenge as in an impromptu talk, where you have extremely little preparation time and are expected to keep the exposition very brief. In fact, if basic question handling proves to be a problem for you, you would profit greatly from studying the guidelines on impromptu talks in Chapter 16 in detail and doing the exercises relating to impromptus.

Here is how the whole process of "simple answer first" works.

First of all, *pause and think.* What's the question all about, in the simplest terms? Is it about money, timing, method, alternatives, or quality? Make sure you get it right and keep it simple. Some presenters seem to feel the audience does not have a second to spare, so they rush right into answering. It's more important not to waste whole *minutes* by giving a misleading answer or going off on tangents.

Second, if there is any chance that some people in the audience didn't hear the question, or if the question seemed longwinded or muddled, *rephrase it clearly* before answering. There's no need to acknowledge every question with a teacher-like "That's a good question." In fact, quite a few people are put off by that. A preface such as "OK," "I see," "Right," or "Yes, of course" has the same positive impact without the annoying quality.

Third, decide what is the *simplest acceptable answer* to that question — say, "Quality is good overall; customers are not complaining." If you got the question down to simple terms, finding a simple answer will be that much easier. However, many presenters routinely have a very hard time giving a simple answer. It just will not cross their lips. This is especially true for scientifically trained people, who are keenly aware of all the imperfections or inaccuracies of "simplistic" statements.

If you have this problem, remember that you can "take it back" to some extent in the rest of your answer. Your up-front answer is just something you're putting on the table to get the process of understanding started. To help yourself make that leap into temporary inaccuracy, put the following little preamble in your mind:

"To simplify this brutally…"

Most people find that such a phrase steers them into the right direction, despite their instincts for perfection and accuracy.

Fourth, *expand on your answer* — but no more than absolutely needed. This is where you can put your qualifications, corrections, examples, explanations, and support — numbers or other data, visuals, etc.

Here's an example to illustrate what we mean. One presenter in one of our seminars gave an excellent talk on gardening. In the question period, one audience member asked: "When do you think is the best time to plant?" Now this presenter, being aware of all the details, qualifications, and complications affecting this momentous decision, embarked on a four-minute discourse. "Well, it depends, of course, on *what* you're planting…" (He went through what seemed a pretty exhaustive list of the major kinds of flowers and bushes you might want to plant.) "And then, of course, it also depends a lot on what *climate zone* you're in." (Here, he gave us the complete list of all the zones — there being many more, one could see from the listeners' faces, than most of the audience had imagined.) At this point he'd pretty much lost most of the audience. Then, as an afterthought — perhaps feeling that something essential was missing — he added: *"Well, basically, you want to get the stuff in as soon as possible after the last frost."*

Four Basic Steps for Handling Questions

Step 1: **Stop and think!** Do you really understand the question? Do you know the basic answer? Rushing into a response helps neither you nor the audience.

Step 2: **Acknowledge and rephrase the question if necessary.** This is helpful if some people couldn't hear the question or if the question was longwinded or unclear.

Step 3: **Give the *simple answer* first.** It may be all that is needed — and it's what the audience is most waiting for!

Step 4: **Expand on your answer no more than absolutely necessary.** If more detail is needed, the audience will let you know. Above all, avoid repeating your points.

That last statement was the *simple answer.* In fact, everybody woke up and took note. They all knew that they'd heard what they *needed — the real answer they could remember and flesh out as needed.*

So, instead of doing the same and first running through all the details and complications in your answers, *pause* long enough to

- Grasp the essence of the question
- Dredge up the simple — even oversimplified — answer to that question

Then, if you're bothered by the inaccuracies of the answer, simply add the qualifications and corrections *after* you've given the simple answer. You'll find you don't need half the details you would have mentioned if you followed the typical rambling method. For instance, *one or two* climate zones would probably be enough to illustrate what "after the last frost" means.

What To Do When You Don't Know the Answer

Even with the best preparation, there will be times — perhaps many more than you'd like — when you don't have the answer to a question. Unfortunately, each time this happens, there is at least a threat to your authority, even when the question obviously doesn't relate to the main subject of your talk. So, it's not surprising that many speakers resort to solutions that don't involve the dreaded "I don't know":

- Fudge the answer.
- Play a favorite politician's game: simply answer a *different* question on which they do have the facts.

If you are tempted to try one of these old tricks, ask yourself this: Have *you* ever been deceived by them? We haven't found one person who said yes, so it's silly even to think about it as an option. It would only damage your credibility as a whole. Instead, just come out with the truth: "I don't know."

The main dangers in this situation are that you may seem (1) flustered or guilty, (2) unhelpful, (3) unprepared (if the question related to your subject), or (4) generally not very knowledgeable (if the question was not strictly on the topic but at least vaguely related).

There's not much you can do about problems (3) and (4). They really relate to your preparation and the general depth of your knowledge. If it's a serious issue, then your audience has just given you notice that you need to improve in these two areas. Hopefully, you'll do better next time around. However, there's plenty you can do about the first two issues. Here are some suggestions:

Avoiding Guilt Signals
> Smile.
> Nod.
> Stand erect.
> Maintain eye contact.
> Speak loud and clear.

Being Perceived As Helpful
> If possible, promise the answer for later.
> Show that you mean it by giving a *definite time* ("by this afternoon") and *means* ("by e-mail").
> Reinforce this by *writing down* the question in front of everybody.

Handling Multiple Questions

Some speakers get thrown off somewhat by multiple questions — usually because they lose track of the component questions. The solution is simple: once you realize that you are facing a multiple question, make a note of the questions, either privately or on a flip chart. Before plunging into your answers, take a moment to decide if it's better to handle them in *another sequence* than the one in which they were presented.

Here is an example.

Question: *I have three questions.* [This is your cue for taking notes in case you miss any of the three.] *One, what's the best approach to watering if you have sandy soil? Two, why is it so bad to water during full sunshine? And three, what are your thoughts on mulching?*

Answer: *O.K., let's start with mulching.* [You decided to make question 3 the first to answer.] *"A good mulch helps to keep plant roots cool and retains some moisture so you don't have to water as often as you do without mulch.*

That already gives you some partial answers to your other questions. First, what's the best overall approach to watering if you have **sandy soil***? Clearly, you need to water* **more frequently** *with sandy soil because the soil doesn't hold the water well. However, the* **mulch** *holds it, so if you use a good mulch, you can water less often.*

Second, why is watering in full sunshine bad? Because the sun may burn the rootlets when they start to dry out. However, the mulch will keep the rootlets both moist and cool, so this is less of a problem. Still, it's generally best to water early in the morning or late in the day. And if you do water in full sunshine — say, because things got too parched — then make sure you really soak the soil.

Handling Complex Questions

Many complex questions are really a lecture with one or more implied or buried questions. The main challenge is to extract those buried questions, then answer them in the simplest possible way. A second challenge is to deal with the "lecture" portion. Perhaps you basically agree with it; in that case, there's no problem. Otherwise, you may refute the relevant statements *as you back up your simple initial answer.*

As with multiple questions, you may also find it advisable to make some public notes once you realize that you're being handed a lengthy, complex affair. Even if you can keep things straight (since you are presumably familiar with most of the issues), the audience often can't, and having the public notes there will help them follow the discussion.

Let's take an example of such a complex lecture/question:

In 1992, there was a survey on various ethical aspects of the Human Genome Project. Interestingly, it showed X, Y, and Z. [Lengthy details follow, suggesting that X, Y, and Z are eminently reasonable findings.] It seems to me that your survey comes up with quite different results.

Your first challenge is to extract the implied questions. In this case, there seem to be three questions:

1. *Do* the findings differ?
2. Why?
3. How exactly, or at least roughly?

Your simple answer might then be something like

Yes, our survey results differ, because our survey population consisted of recombinant DNA researchers, whereas the one you're referring to targeted a mix of the general public and academicians from the biological fields. We found X', Y', and Z'. [Brief summaries] These are what you might expect from people who are both more knowledgeable and involved.

Postponing Questions

Remember what we said earlier about establishing your Q&A rules. Once these rules are in place, it's easy for you to go back to them and defer questions without seeming arbitrary or unreasonable.

Suppose you said at the beginning: "I will allow two minutes for questions at the end of each section; let's deal with remaining questions at the end." Then if questions begin to go over the two minutes, you can ward off the next ones with a statement like

I'm delighted there are more questions, but our two minutes are up, and we need to move through the rest of the presentation. Could you please make a note of your questions, and if we have time at the end, we'll take them up then? Thanks. So, we have seen that... [Recap main point of section and transition to the next one.]

You may also want to *postpone all questions during a specific period* — say, while you explain something intricate that would suffer from any interruption. Even heavy interrupters may comply with a clear, limited request such as: "For the next two minutes, I'd be grateful if you could hold your questions while I show you just how this process works." Again, this is infinitely more realistic than trying to stop questions ad hoc when you find yourself unable to cope with interruptions.

One word of warning on the issue of postponing questions or answers: *think twice before trying it with high-level managers* unless you know the person to be modest and reasonable. Otherwise, the scene will run something like this:

You: *Thank you for the question. With your indulgence, I'd like to take this up at the end* [or *during the next section of my talk*].

Manager: *Your indulgence my foot! I asked you a question, and I want an answer —* NOW! [*Or you're fired!* is understood — no need to say it.]

Diverting Off-Track Questions

If a question is off the subject, postpone it politely but firmly: "Right. That's a complex issue in itself. I'd be glad to discuss that after the meeting." Sometimes a *quick, simplified answer* will avoid arguments and resentments.

More often than not, those asking off-track questions are also *persistent*. In that case, you need to move quickly to *stop major time theft*. If necessary, cut into the question as soon as it becomes clear that it's a repeat or variant of the earlier off-track question and throw the ball to somebody else:

As I said, I'll be happy to discuss this after the talk. Yes, please, you had a question? [Take the next question.]

Stopping People From Monopolizing the Discussion

Nothing can glaze the eyes of the audience quite as much as the monopolizer who drones on and on, creating a presentation opportunity for himself. Unfortunately, most presenters are totally unable to stop such people. Keep in mind that monopolizers usually are (1) under the illusion that everybody admires them for their cleverness and (2) impervious to correction or criticism by "hint." In other words, you'd need to hit them right between the eyes with a very heavy two-by-four before they'd even blink. (And even then, they'd probably resume their contribution as soon as they regained consciousness.)

The *only* way to deal with such people is, again, by falling back on your pre-established Q&A rules and enforcing them crisply:

Thanks — as I said, we're going to have just one question per person for now. Yes, you had a question?

Closing the Session with Style and Focus

The question-and-answer session may have raised many side issues and complex details. Consequently, at the end of everything, your main message may have totally escaped the audience. So, as you thank them, they may be scratching their heads and thinking, "Well, we sure had a lot of interesting questions, and she answered them pretty well, but what on earth was the whole thing about?"

The problem can be remedied very simply with a *focused summary* at the end of the question period. Hardly any business presenter does this, yet there is such an obvious need for it. Here is an example:

Thank you for your helpful questions. I hope you agree that we should implement the new XYZ system as quickly as possible, in view of the $400,000 in annual operational savings and the improvement in customer satisfaction we can expect.

With such a two-sentence summary, you can be sure the audience leaves with your main message still clearly in their mind.

HANDLING HOSTILE QUESTIONS

Tip

In handling tough questions, follow two simple laws:

- Stay *calm and friendly*, no matter how negative the questions.
- Go into question sessions with a *positive attitude:* view all questions as an *expression of interest.*

When it comes to hostile questions or comments, a *sense of humor* definitely helps. Above all, don't take aggressive remarks personally — realize that presentation settings simply bring out extreme behaviors in some people.

Remember what we said earlier about the proper attitude toward questions: questions show interest, and you should *appreciate that interest,* no matter how it is expressed.

Here are three big problems with hostile questions that any effective strategy must take into account:

1. The attack tends to rattle you, especially if it is unexpected, and makes it hard to think of an effective reply.
2. The negative flavor of the question or comment lingers and spoils the effect of your reply.
3. Often, the attack is renewed in follow-up questions.

Let's see what you can do about these problems.

Problem #1: The Unsettling Effect of a Surprise Attack

A positive attitude, as we noted at the beginning of this section, is a big help with problem #1. However, an even more effective remedy is to *minimize surprises* through proper preparation. In a business presentation, there is really no excuse for not having answers to *common tough questions* — and those are exactly the ones that tend to be delivered by managers in caustic ways.

Typical tough questions to expect include those about

- Costs
- Benefits
- Feasibility
- Relevance to a listener's special situation
- Solidity of your evidence — your data and their interpretation
- Your qualifications — why the audience should take you seriously

Of course, you cannot anticipate every question. Therefore, you must be able to handle surprises — even extremely upsetting ones — without losing composure. The main tools for this are *buying time* and *neutralizing abrasive questions.* Simply learn not to rush into your answer — especially not to a hostile question. Instead, think about what this question is really all about. Those three or four seconds of thinking time may seem like an eternity to you, but to the audience, they seem perfectly natural and reasonable. The second tool, neutralizing caustic questions, is dealt with next, because it's also the solution to Problem #2.

Problem #2: The Lingering Effect of the Caustic Question or Remark

A caustic question leaves a bad echo in the room that colors your answer. To erase that echo, you can insert a simple positive phrase such as "Right," "Yes, of course," or "OK" before your answer. If you are evidently not thrown by the question and can maintain a smile, and your answer is immediate and confident, then this is all that is needed.

Many times, however, you *are* rattled, or need time to formulate a good answer. In that case, you need more ammunition. Look at it this way. The attacker typically implies that you are an *idiot.* This is what the audience hears just before you answer. If you then stumble insecurely into your answer, the thing that goes through people's mind, whether or not they realize this, is: "Here's the idiot trying to answer that one." You need to erase that thought with an *objective restatement of the question* — for instance: "OK. You're understandably concerned about feasibility...." That way, the audience hears you *confidently answering a reasonable question.*

So, just think for a few seconds: *What is this question all about in simplest terms?* Then rephrase it without the sting and prepare to answer it.

Things that will *not* erase the damaging echo include "Well," "Uhm," or convulsive throat-clearing. Less obviously, a *sarcastic comeback* also doesn't work. It just *prolongs the negative vibrations* and gives the questioner control over the tone of the discussion. As presenter, you are supposedly in charge of keeping the tone of discussion civilized; by stooping to the questioner's level, you give up control and thereby lose face.

Exercise 15-1 gives you an opportunity to develop this skill of objective rephrasing. We recommend that you do it — and keep in mind that in real life, you don't have several minutes to sit down and figure out how to get it right!

Handling Hostile Questions: The Four Cardinal Steps

1. Make eye contact and listen fully; maintain positive body language.

2. Rephrase the hostile question to make it as clear and objective as possible and to prepare a more positive ground for your answer.*
   If necessary, ask clarifying questions to uncover the exact objection or question.

3. Answer the question briefly, *turning to others* in the audience.

4. Immediately take questions from other people in the audience.

* Rephrasing is *not* necessary if (a) the room is small, so that everybody heard the question *and* (b) you are not at all rattled by the hostility but are able to answer the question *immediately* and in a *friendly manner*. In that case, simply preface your answer with a *positive acknowledgment* such as "O.K.," "All right," or "Yes, I see…" Note that these preambles do not mean "I agree" but simply "I see your point." ***Do not ever preface your question with aggressive expressions such as "I disagree," "I couldn't disagree more," "That's utter nonsense," "You're just plain wrong there,"* etc.**

Problem #3: The Tendency for the Attack To Continue

Caustic people, unfortunately, also tend to be members of the class of *persistent* people. No sooner have you answered a hostile question than the follow-up is delivered.

If you established sensible rules for Q&A, the problem may be solved easily by referring to them — in particular, "one question per person." For many occasions, that rule is not feasible, however; for instance, high-level managers may insist on asking as many questions as they like to satisfy themselves that a project makes sense. Even in such situations, however, you can often forestall further questions by

- Avoiding eye contact with the questioner as you come to the end of your answer
- Immediately taking a question from another audience member

It may not work if the attack came from a high-level audience member who is determined to press on with his cause, but it's a good strategy when the attacker is some other lower-level pest.

Handling a Hostile Question: An Example

At the end of your presentation, an influential manager in the audience bursts out:

"This is all nonsense. We don't have time or money for this."

Question rephrased by you:
"Does this project make sense? Should we devote valuable time and money to it? Obviously, those are the basic questions we need to decide."

Your answer:
"Let me summarize the main *benefits* first …
"Now, the *costs* of doing it are …
"I think that when you weigh those costs against the benefits, it's a good investment that will pay for itself in two years and open up a whole class of new opportunities that wouldn't be available to us otherwise.
"Yes, Bob, you had a question?" [Taking a question from another audience member]

EXERCISES

Exercise 15-1. Handling Tough Questions

Consider the following tough or caustic questions (all of which, incidentally, are on subjects that should be predictable in a business presentation, such as cost or method). In the second column, quickly restate the question in a neutral, reasonable way so you can answer it calmly and effectively. In the third column, outline how you would answer the question briefly.

Exercise 15-1. Handling Tough Questions *(continued)*

Caustic Question	Question Rephrased in a Neutral Way To Allow Effective Answer	Outline a Brief Possible Answer
Attack on practicality or cost: "Let's just suppose everything you say is true. Now, if we tried to actually put this thing you're proposing into our mills, do you have any idea what it would *cost?* It would blow us right out of the water!"		
Attack on experimental method: "I have no doubt you got the data you say you did. The problem is, those data all result from a totally inappropriate methodology. The proper method you should have used for such an experiment is..."		
Attack on interpretation method: "I've been looking at those data you presented, and I don't think they show anything like what you claim. With the kinds of variables you were studying, the only statistical method that would give you meaningful results would be the Mandelbrot two-tailed beta-square chaos test."		
Attack on goals: "I'm sure we all enjoyed your little presentation. But I don't see how it relates to the *real problem* we set out to tackle. If you remember, we were trying to ... But you only told us how to..."		

Exercise 15-1. Handling Tough Questions *(continued)*

Caustic Question	Question Rephrased in a Neutral Way To Allow Effective Answer	Outline a Brief Possible Answer
Attack on persuasiveness: "You say X is Y. But why should we *believe* you? Can you *prove* it? I may have missed something, but I don't recall hearing any *evidence*."		
Attack on results: "I'm sorry, but I just can't believe those data. I remember two recent studies that showed that the trend is just the other way round. How do you explain *that*?"		
Attack on your authority: "You talked at great length about XYZ. I just wonder: Have you ever actually been *involved* in a real XYZ? [Then, when speaker admits he hasn't : "So it's all just a *theory* you've been presenting. Thanks. That's all I wanted to know." [Audience laughs]		
Attack on relevance: "This is all very interesting. But what's it got to do with our operational realities? Our processes are totally different from the one you discussed. They don't even use the same *chemistry!*"		

Exercise 15-2. Handling Negative Comments

You have started giving a slick presentation to a bunch of current customers, explaining your company's philosophy of "Customer First." (Assume you are a vice president who is intimately involved with the entire "Customer First" strategic issue.) Your zippy introduction contained your main message, and you have just embarked on developing your theme in the body. Your plan was to answer questions at the end of your talk. At this point, one audience member remarks:

*All this stuff about 'Customer First' sure **sounds** great, but I don't believe a word of it. I don't think you're giving us anything — you just do whatever is convenient and profitable for **you**. In fact, I'm just about ready to switch supplier.*

You observe that some other audience members nod their heads and look at each other as if they agree.

How would you handle this situation? Consider all aspects of the task:

- Initial response
  - Would you **acknowledge** this comment? How?
  - Would you **rephrase** it before responding? How?
  - Would you ask any **clarifying questions** before answering? Which?
  - Exactly **what words** would you use to lead into your response?
- Overall strategy of response:
  - What are your **goals** at this point?
  - How can you **achieve** them?
  - What **points** would you make? (Base these on your knowledge of your own company.)
- Closing
  - Would a **summary statement** be helpful? How would you phrase it?
  - Is **follow-up** needed? What kind? What words would you use to announce or describe it?
- Should you have been **prepared** for such a comment or question? Why?
- **What traits and/or skills** does it take to handle such a comment **without preparation**?
  - Do you have those traits or skills?
  - If not, how can you develop them?

Hint: The original goal of this talk to customers presumably is to cement good relationships. The customer comment, however, seems to indicate that relationships are all but positive. Is there any chance that the audience is ready to take in the PR message of "Customer First" at all, at this point? If not, what is the *new goal* of the presentation? And how can you best achieve it?

In our view, this is an extreme situation (imminent customer loss) calling for a *radical response,* not for a bit of rephrasing and clever answering. Put yourself in the audience's position and think about what *you* would consider an honest, radical response from the presenter.

Exercise 15-3. Assess your attitudes, habits, and skills relating to handling of questions in a presentation. Use a simple verbal scale of *always, usually, rarely, never.*

Preparing for Questions:
Consider all major audience questions and objections beforehand _____
Prepare reasonably for these questions:

    The "simple answer" _____

    Backup details: explanations, support numbers, relevant examples or
       quotes_____

    Charts or other visuals, if helpful_____

    Handout pages, if appropriate_____

Anticipate all *tough* questions_____

Deciding on Timing and Format of Q&A:
Decide beforehand on timing and format of Q&_____
Choose the least formal, most interactive format appropriate for the occasion_____
Take into account audience needs and likely behavior of key audience members_____
Take into account how well I deal with interruptions_____

Setting and Using Q&A Rules:
Spell out Q&A rules at the end of my introduction_____
Invoke the rules to cut a question short, postpone discussion, or move on to other
    people's questions_____

Basic Question-Handling Skills:
Invite questions with an appreciative phrase_____
If necessary, prime people's thinking in order to generate good questions_____
Control body language while dealing with questions:

    Smile_____

    Move closer to the person asking the question_____

    Make eye contact_____

    Nod_____

    Keep arms and hands relaxed (avoid crossing arms or fidgeting) _____

    Stand quietly, without shuffling _____

    Stand straight, without slouching or holding onto things_____

    Control signals of disagreement or displeasure (raised eyebrows, superior grin, etc.)
    _____

    Avoid strange "thinking faces" while listening_____

Follow the *Four Basic Steps for Handling Questions:*

    Step 1: Stop and think _____

    Step 2: Acknowledge and rephrase the question if necessary_____

    Step 3: Give the simple answer first_____

    Step 4: Expand on the answer no more than absolutely necessary_____

Am good at handling "I don't know":

    Straightforward admission without signals of guilt_____

    Authoritative and positive in promising answer for later, when appropriate_____

Assertive but positive in postponing questions when necessary_____

Exercise 15-3 *(continued)*

Effective in handling multiple or complex questions_____
Assertive yet friendly in handling off-track questions_____
Firm but friendly in cutting off persistent questioners_____
Good at *closing* the Q& A session with a final summary of the main message_____
Effective in handling *hostile* questions:

    Maintain sense of humor _____
    Stay calm and friendly, no matter how negative the questions_____
    Make eye contact and listen fully_____
    Maintain positive body language_____
    Rephrase the hostile question to make it objective and civil_____
    If necessary, ask clarifying questions to uncover the exact objection or question_____
    Avoid aggressive preambles to my answer, such as "I disagree" _____
    Avoid prolonged dialogue by quickly taking questions from others_____

Review all your answers in this exercise. Note where you answered "never" or "rarely." In the light of this, what are the biggest changes you should make in this area of preparing for and handling questions?

_____
_____
_____
_____
_____
_____

16

Dealing with Unpleasant Surprises

We'd like to pass on to you a simple philosophy that will allow you to handle any unpleasant surprises at delivery time. This is important, because you can't always be prepared for everything: sometimes you'll run into unexpected problems, and you'll need to respond quickly and flexibly.

This philosophy or attitude says:

> **Anything may happen — but it won't be the end of the world, and *it won't stop me from giving the audience my message.***

Why does this work? Because it will keep you focused on your main goal instead of the "trouble." When you obsess about the problem, fear, guilt, or anger will unsettle you and make it hard to do the right thing. By contrast, when you concentrate on your goal, you will find creative ways to work around the obstacle.

Let's see now how this philosophy of message focus can help you through some typical problems.

EQUIPMENT TROUBLES

Lots of things can go wrong with equipment. We'll take just one common example: a burned-out projector bulb. Of course, you should have checked beforehand that there was a working spare — but perhaps this was the one time you forgot, and it turns out the spare is also dead. Never mind, you know how to contact the person who can help you — *right?* Or perhaps you carry a spare bulb?

Let's say you were human and took none of these precautions. What's the worst that can happen? You can't project your visuals. You could dwell on that problem and collapse with guilt and shame, or perhaps blame the people responsible for the setup. *Or you could remember that this isn't the end of the world and channel your energy into finding alternative ways to get your message across.*

Can you switch to a flip chart? If so, how much time will it cost you, and what supporting details or minor points can you skip to compensate? Or can you do *without* visuals? What *examples* could you substitute as persuasive or explanatory support? If the talk is truly dependent on your transparencies, can you give a much abbreviated version of it and follow up with a *written summary,* including your charts?

The point is: there are always *some* options — and keeping your mind firmly on your message will allow you to think of those options, whereas obsessing about the problem will tie you into knots of frustration.

Seeing Surprises as Challenge and Opportunity

How you deal with unwelcome surprises tells the audience a lot about you. In particular, it shows how secure, flexible, and clear-thinking you are. So remember: *by making the message-focus philosophy a part of your outlook, you can turn potential disasters into an impressive show of strength.*

THE "SHRINKING TIME" PROBLEM

It's upsetting and deflating when you're suddenly asked to give your talk in half the time. (Actually, it's so common that you should *always* be prepared for it!) Again, focusing on the time problem commonly leads to pathetic solutions, such as talking at double speed. Instead, ask: "What parts of the talk are indispensable for *getting my main message across?*" Then your options will immediately become clear:

- Cut extra examples.
- Simplify complex points.
- Skip any points that are not needed to prove your case or make your main concepts understandable.

In many cases, you could again combine these options with *written follow-up* and achieve all the results you wanted and look like one cool presenter!

BORED OR TURNED-OFF AUDIENCE

People can give you worse problems than equipment, because they have *feelings* you have to consider as you try to "fix" things. Also, they are a lot more important than your presentation machines. After all, you're not trying to persuade the projector of your point of view, but you *are* trying to influence the people in the audience.

One of the biggest challenges is perhaps a generally *bored* audience. It's easy to feel like a loser and fall apart. But if you do have a message that ties to the audience's needs, refocusing on that message may turn things around.

How To Be Prepared for Surprises

If you in the least suspect that your presentation time may be shortened at the last moment (as often happens in any conference-like setting), or that your audience may be uninterested, easily confused, or resistant to your ideas, then be ready with *two or three presentation plans* (see also the discussion in Chapter 7):

- **Plan A** — the full talk, taking the allotted time, with no details or arguments added or deleted
- **Plan B** — a shortened version if your time gets cut or the audience appears bored with your details or examples (note what examples, visuals, details, or subpoints to skip)
- **Plan C** — a version with extra explanations or arguments if the audience appears confused or unconvinced (note what examples, data, visuals, explanations, or arguments you could add and what to drop to make room for the additions)

The first thing to do is to find out the *source* of the boredom. Are you giving unnecessary explanations? Then cut them. Have you lost them with abstract generalities? Then think of concrete examples that make your points clear. Or have you simply gone on too long? Then shorten your talk, as discussed earlier. The main point is not to give up on your message but to find out what is getting in the way and correcting that as well as you can.

The audience may also seem *confused*. This is one of the easier problems to solve. To begin with, you can simply ask a question to check if confusion is the issue: "Let me ask a question: Has everybody understood why we …?" Then, if indeed there was confusion, add the necessary explanations. (That's where having prepared Plan C comes in handy. See the box above.)

Finally, the audience may be resistant or even hostile to your ideas. Again, <u>insofar as it's possible to reconcile your position with the audience's</u>, you may be able to turn the situation around by

- Adding persuasive arguments from your Plan C, perhaps complete with visuals
- Interspersing a few minutes of intensive audience interaction to bring objections to the surface and address them

However, note the underlined condition in the preceding paragraph. If your message intrinsically conflicts with important values, beliefs, or desires of the audience, then no amount of creative argument or discussion may change that resistance. Again, the trick is to fall back on that basic philosophy with which we started this chapter: *Anything may happen — but it won't be the end of the world....* All you can do is to deliver your message to the best of your ability; the results, ultimately, are not up to you. You have to be able to live with that simple fact.

SLEEPERS

You're going along fine — but all of a sudden, you realize that one of your listeners has gone to sleep. He may even snore. It can happen to any speaker, and it doesn't mean that your presentation is poor. It's just part of life.

The real problem is that the *audience stops listening* to you when there is a sleeper in the room. All they can think is: "Joe's asleep. Doesn't he look like a perfect angel? Now what's Martha going to *do about it?*" It's a glaring break in your connection with the audience that you have to try to repair.

In a smaller audience, this is more important — and, fortunately, also easier to handle. To wake up the sleeper, try moving a little closer to him while maintaining or very slightly raising your volume. This may induce a nightmare in the sleeper — say, of a freight train approaching him.

The trick is to do all this in such a way that *nobody in the audience is tempted to laugh* as the sleeper comes to. That means, first of all, that *you* should not lapse into a grin of satisfaction if you succeed. Also, you may want to fix the audience with a serious look before, during, and after the "wakeup call." They'll get the message that you mean to be tactful about the whole thing. Needless to say, these cautions are doubly important when the sleeper is your boss or some other high-up audience member!

In a larger audience, such as a conference, the problem is less disturbing, but it's also harder to solve. One possibility is to pause or drastically change your volume, either up or down. The sleeper may again react to the sudden change in surroundings and wake up.

SIDE SHOWS

People talking to others in the audience during your presentation can be very unsettling — not only to you, but also to the audience. Even if it involves higher-up audience members, you need to address the problem.

Here is a workable incremental approach:

1. Smile and stop for a few seconds.
2. Ask in a *positive*, nonabrasive way whether the talkers have some thought or question to contribute: "Yes — did you have a thought or question on this?"
3. Involve them by asking a substantive question, if that is feasible. (It's always an option in a training session or a meeting, which are the most likely settings to produce these kinds of interruptions.)
4. Stop, look, stay silent (with a *smile* on your face, not a furious scowl) until they stop. (They usually will — this is quite an assertive step.)

If the interrupter is a "power person," a relatively safe option is to walk closer to him or her while continuing to talk. It's a subtle threat, and it *may* just work, simply because it hooks into basic instincts of aggression and dominance. However, many of your upper-management interrupters play games of domination much better than you ever could, and they'll enjoy seeing you squirm and struggle. Your options in that case are really nil, unless you want to maneuver yourself out of a job!

IMPROMPTU PRESENTATIONS

Impromptu talks of any kind are the most dreaded challenge for many people. The best way to overcome the dread is, of course, to practice impromptus as much as you can. (Joining *Toastmasters* is one great way to do that.) The other thing that helps greatly is to have a *structured approach* to such talks. This is what you will learn in this section.

Prepared "Impromptu" Speeches

The best way to handle an impromptu presentation is to *be prepared* for it. Winston Churchill, for instance, was known to rehearse all his important "impromptu remarks" to parliament. The main problem is to recognize "presentation-prone" situations. Here are some of them:

- Weekly or monthly meetings with management (in fact, almost *any* meeting with management)
- Meetings or social occasions with customers
- Social occasions at conferences
- Award ceremonies
- Weddings, anniversaries, birthdays, etc.

When one of these situations is coming up, always make sure you're prepared with succinct statements of your work, ideas, or other items that may come up.

Dealing with True Surprises

You can't *always* be prepared, so you have to learn how to handle truly spontaneous talks or mini-presentations.

Above all, *don't respond in a panic.* Rather, buy time with some gracious phrases of appreciation. ("Yes, thank you, I'll be happy to do that. I'm glad you're interested in...") While you're uttering these pleasantries, think quickly, using the following *structured approach.*

- Think of *one aspect* of your assigned topic that will *interest this audience.*
- Turn that aspect into your *main message.*
- Expand that message with *two or three key points.*
- If you have the facts available, illustrate each key point with an *example,* relevant numbers, etc.; otherwise, simply expand it by explaining the point in more detail.

Example 16-1

Impromptu Topic: Talk about your work over the last month.

Fact: Not much was accomplished because of certain frustrating problems that turned out almost impossible to solve.

Angle: Audience may be interested in those problems and ways you have found to solve them.

Message: Last month was a time of *learning* some interesting things.

Key Points:

1. There are some company-internal problems (communication/cooperation among different departments) that I was never really aware of.
2. I learned first-hand how important it is to overcome these problems if we want to respond quickly to customer concerns.
3. I have found that there *are* ways to improve cooperation, and you may be interested in hearing about them: …

Example 16-2

Impromptu Topic: Introduce a colleague who is to be honored.

Angle: What has this person done that is of interest to the audience?

Message: I want to introduce a person who has made a few "ripples" in almost everybody's life here.

Key Points:

1. She improved some important things at the workplace: …
2. She has taken a personal interest in many of the people present and helped them in small and big ways: …
3. She made a *big* ripple at the last company rafting trip by falling into the river.

Effective Structure for a Very Brief Impromptu Contribution: Head & Body

- Think of *one aspect* of your assigned topic that will *interest this audience.*
- Turn that aspect into your *main message.*
- Back up that message with a simple example, numbers, or some other detail.

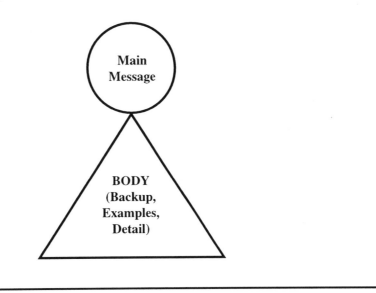

EXERCISES

Exercise 16-1. Evaluate your attitude and skills in dealing with unpleasant surprises and emergencies at delivery time. Use a verbal scale of *always, often, sometimes, rarely, never.*

Attitude:
Am able to keep perspective when things go wrong ("It's not the end of the world")
_____

Shortening a Talk on the Spot:
Am prepared for on-the-spot shortening with "Plan B" (cutting details and minor points)_____
Am able to make up for lost details with *written follow-up*_____

Exercise 16-1 *(continued)*

Adjusting a Talk To Deal with Confused or Resistant Audience:

Am prepared with "Plan C" — extra explanations, arguments, data, visuals_____
Am able to get to the *source* of confusion or resistance by asking questions_____

Sleepers and Side Shows:

Am able to wake up sleepers without causing embarrassment_____
Am able to stop side conversations in subtle, positive ways_____

Review all your answers in this exercise. Considering answers of "rarely" or "never," what are the biggest changes you should make in this area of handling unpleasant surprises?

_____
_____
_____
_____
_____
_____
_____

Exercise 16-2. Practice impromptu talks, picking topics from the following list. Remember to follow the structured approach outlined in this chapter. For each topic, *decide who the audience is* (unless the audience is already described) and try to address their interests.

Topics:
- Highlights of my work this month.
- A person who had a profound influence on my thinking.
- Some ways to make work more pleasant and productive.
- Safety at work or at home.
- How to deal with road rage — other people's and your own.
- What to do when a cop pulls you over for speeding.
- How to get peace of mind.
- Introduce your boss, professor, or colleague to a conference audience.
- Your best friend is finally getting married (or getting married again). Describe to the wedding audience just what kind of a person the lucky new spouse is getting.
- Angry hunters are confronting angry animal protectionists at a town meeting. Somebody realizes that you are the only reasonable person in the room who is able to understand both sides and talk about a "way of tolerance."
- Any other topics you like.

17

Moderating a Conference Session

It's an honor to chair an interactive panel or a conference session. On the other hand, it's also a great responsibility, because the moderator can make the difference between a successful session and one that appears pointless, disorganized, or, because of people's uncivilized behavior, thoroughly upsetting.

COMMON COMPLAINTS ABOUT CONFERENCE SESSIONS

Here are some frequent complaints about interactive or conference sessions:

1. The moderator makes no real contribution beyond announcing speakers and talk titles.
2. Worse, the moderator makes a *negative* contribution by giving wrong biographical information or misstating the topic or content of a talk.
3. Time limits are not enforced, so that some speakers are unfairly cut short or even skipped.
4. There is no real interaction between panelists when the audience expected lively discussion.
5. Speakers seem poorly prepared — everything looks like a last-minute job.
6. There is no common theme to hold contributions together.
7. A few people dominate the discussion, often in ways that are of no interest to the audience.
8. Discussions have an overly aggressive tone.
9. People often can't hear the questions and so don't understand half the answers.
10. There are few good questions, and neither moderator nor speakers make enough of an effort to encourage them.

Of these, problem 2 is perhaps the most damaging to your reputation. Unfortunately, it's not at all rare. Apparently, moderators often feel compelled to make some contribution (to avoid complaint 1), yet they haven't *prepared* for it; the solution they embrace is to wing it with a quick guess — which more often turns out to be a *bad* guess!

Tip

To avoid common problems with conference sessions, do what out-standing moderators do: prepare early, use superb questioning and summariz-ing skills, and take responsibility for all aspects of the session.

While most speakers have no trouble correcting a wrong name or affiliation, quite a few make desperate moves to recover from a "wrong topic" announcement by their moderator. For instance, some are too shy to correct the moderator and simply delve into their talk, startling the audience with the discrepancy between what the moderator announced and what they are saying. Others are so unnerved, they actually try to shift their talk on the spur of the moment just to accommodate the bungled introduction! Many others do, of course, correct the moderator, using the scheme *"Actually, I'm going to be talking about* basic color theory *rather than* recent color developments in the coating area." But even if the correction is presented with elegant, low-key humor, the damage to the session is irreversible.

LEARNING YOUR ABC — OR PQR

Consider the ten complaints. What are the keys to avoiding them? It seems to us there are just three. You might call them the Moderator's Virtues:

1. *Preparation:* Start *early* to prepare yourself and to get participants to prepare.
2. *Questioning and summarizing skills:* Keep discussions moving with focused questions and timely summaries that reestablish common themes.
3. *Responsibility:* Make it your job to attend to all aspects of the session — from coordinating content to setting rules to maintaining a professional tone.

Clearly, complaints 1, 2, and 6 (and even 5, as we will see below) can be overcome with proper preparation; 4 and 10, with good questioning/summarizing skills; and the others, by taking charge. In the following pages, we will focus on the tree Moderator's Virtues and show their role in each phase of an interactive or conference session.

THE POWER OF EARLY PREPARATION

Let's take a closer look at the benefits of good preparation. Specifically, let's see how early preparation can help you

- Influence speakers to prepare top-quality contributions.
- Tie together separate contributions with a meaningful session theme and helpful summaries.
- Introduce speakers and their talks correctly.
- Lay the ground for interesting questions and interactions.

The Challenging Tasks of a Moderator

Outstanding moderators understand that there is more to the job than introducing speakers and making a few futile attempts at enforcing time limits. Here are the major challenges they set for themselves:

- Plan ahead, and motivate speakers to prepare early, despite busy schedules.
- Coordinate the parts into a cohesive whole.
- Get agreement on fair, smooth procedures, including timing and turn taking.
- Motivate speakers to do their best.
- Set a positive, productive tone for the session.
- Give focus to the session with concise overviews and summaries — yet remain more in the background than your speakers.
- Involve the audience.
- Stay in control of the session: enforce timing, turn taking, and civilized tone.
- Ask good questions that move the session along.
- Clear up misunderstandings and ambiguities.
- Redirect discussions that stray from the subject.
- Protect speakers from abuse.
- Make the whole occasion special.

Motivating Speakers To Prepare Well and Early

A common complaint about conference papers or panel contributions is that they seem poorly prepared. You might say you have no control over that — you're there to moderate, not to produce papers or ideas. But are you really so powerless?

Imagine you're a conference speaker. One month before the conference, you get a phone call, letter, or e-mail outlining the moderator's view of the session, inviting your thoughts on the session theme, and asking for biographical information and a preliminary draft of your paper as soon as possible. Isn't this likely to make you think a little earlier about your paper than you would otherwise?

The truth is that many speakers are not disciplined enough to prepare early without some such reminder. Even though you may feel you are pestering them, you are doing them a service, because you're saving them from the disaster of last-minute preparation.

In fact, it's flattering to be attended by a moderator who takes a real interest in you and the session. It sets high expectations and pushes speakers to give their best. Perhaps the conference as a whole won't be memorable, but your session will stand out as special!

Getting a Head Start on Your Own Contributions

A friend of ours is very good at assembling expert panels of people from industry and academia for exciting symposia at a major university. However, because he is very busy with so many simultaneous projects, he sometimes forgets to follow up on preparations until it's too late. Recently, for instance, he left the preparation of his own overview until the day before the symposium. Then, when he tried to reach the panelists by phone, half of them were out of the office. He felt very bad about having to wing his introductions the next day!

Most conferences, of course, require speakers to submit an abstract well in advance of the occasion. Why not just develop the overview and summaries for your session from those abstracts?

For an answer, think back to some talks you've given. When did you submit the abstract? One week before the deadline? One day? And how much did it have to do with the final talk you delivered? If you are like most people, there wasn't much similarity between abstract and paper. So what happens to moderators who base their contributions on early abstracts? They embarrass themselves and their speakers with inaccurate introductions!

The solution is to get your own information, closer to the time of the conference. Then you'll be sure that your biographical data are up to date and that you're summarizing facts, not abandoned plans.

One of your most important tasks, especially for truly interactive panels, is to *tie separate contributions to a main theme,* which is also the subject of your overview. Listeners want to take away a few coherent thoughts on a single issue, not just a collection of unrelated ideas. How can you get speakers to adjust their content so a coherent session results? Only by communicating early and, if necessary, repeatedly. If you have strong ideas on the subject, you may be able to give gentle guidance; otherwise, you can inform speakers what others in the session are planning to contribute and thereby spark some thoughts for change.

Making the Most of Early Preparation

Here are the key steps for you to complete *one month to one week* before the session:

1. Get content and biographical information from presenters. This pushes speakers to start preparing early and therefore gives you more time to do a thorough job.
2. Ask presenters to prepare 2-5 questions for the audience to consider, so you can develop a plan for stimulating discussion.
3. Summarize all the information you got into an overview of the whole session; try to find some unifying theme that will set a thoughtful tone and lead to a unifying discussion involving the audience as well as the panelists.

Laying the Groundwork for Interesting Questions

Here is a simple way to raise everybody's appreciation of the importance of the question-and-answer sessions. Ask presenters to *prepare 2-5 questions the audience might find useful to ask.* This has several benefits:

- It will make presenters more sensitive to the audience, and therefore may make their contributions more interesting.
- It will focus speakers more on essential interaction rather than just lecture that may be less interesting to the audience.
- It will allow you to prepare your moderating plan.

ON THE SCENE: MAKING YOUR CONTRACT WITH THE SPEAKERS

If you were lucky, most of your speakers responded to your prodding and supplied you with the material you requested. Realistically, however, there are always a few people who just can't be motivated. When you arrive at the conference, you have one more chance to fill in the gaps and also to agree on basic rules for the session.

If you can do this the *day before* your session, it's all for the better. Sometimes, of course, that just isn't possible, and you'll have to settle for a brief meeting sometime before the session. In any case, give some thought to *how to reach your speakers.* Perhaps you can arrange a meeting by e-mail a few days earlier. It's a lot less risky than assuming that everybody will be staying in the same hotel and relying on voice mail.

Here are the main things you need to accomplish:

1. Meet with presenters to review your overview and their questions.
2. Listen to their concerns about the subject, the session, technical details, etc.
3. Establish time-keeping rules:
   - What signals will you give speakers?
   - Let them understand that you will enforce the time limits strictly.
4. Agree on the format for question-and-answer sessions.

You might also use some of your conference time before your session to get in touch with some of the audience members. For instance, there may be some people you know who could make interesting contributions to the discussion — but they may not be planning to attend your session. Talking to them may change their mind. Also, just discussing the content of the session may get people's mind into gear for thinking about key issues and asking the kinds of questions that put spark into the discussion. This is not to say that you should plant *questions;* rather, plant *ideas* that lead to spontaneous questions.

GETTING OFF TO A STRONG START

You have seen how to use early preparation to secure top-notch contributions that form part of a coherent picture. That preparation also gives you the material for a strong start that introduces the theme, sets a positive tone, and focuses everybody on interaction rather than individual stardom.

Here are the detailed steps for that strong start:

1. Welcome the audience and invite participation.
2. Give a *very brief* overview of the whole session; mention how each talk relates to the session theme.
3. Involve the audience from the start:
   - Tell them that you'll mention some possible questions before each paper.
   - Invite them to note their questions and pass them in or ask them.
   - Announce that there will be only *x* questions from any audience member unless time permits more. (This will help cut down on people heckling or dominating the discussion.) Also, state that you are committed to maintaining a *civil* discussion at all times.
   - Tell them *when* to ask questions. (Note: This may *differ* for different talks in the session.)
4. Introduce the first speaker:
   - State name, title, and other information relevant to the presentation or contribution.
   - Give the title (and an idea of the substance, if helpful) of the talk.
   - Mention sample questions or topics for the audience to consider, so people may listen more purposefully.

KEEPING THE SESSION LIVELY BUT UNDER CONTROL

Now let's see how to keep up the momentum and fulfill the promise of your strong start. In the main part of the session, your job is fourfold:

1. Support each speaker:
   - Introduce each.
   - Help with setup changes, lighting adjustments, etc.
   - Assist in handling emergencies such as equipment trouble.

2. Organize and control Q&A sessions at the end of each talk and/or at the end of the entire session:
   - Tell the audience when to ask questions, especially if the rules are different for the next talk.
   - Make sure everybody can hear every question and answer.
   - Direct the question to the appropriate speaker.
   - Rephrase or exclude uncivilized or off-subject questions.
   - Enforce all Q& A rules, such as the limit on number of questions per person.

3. Stimulate the discussion:
   - Ask focused questions, if necessary, to get things moving or revive them.
   - Call on people if necessary.
   - Suggest ranges of questions to ask.
   - Relate and interpret comments to bring out important themes.

4. Enforce timing rules:
   - Inform speakers about remaining time, using prearranged signals.
   - Bring the talk to an end if the speaker doesn't manage to end on time. (Don't keep on asking "Could you wrap it up, please?" if the speaker has been unable to do so after two such invitations!)

The fourth task, enforcing timing rules, is the most visible — everybody notices when you don't do that job properly. It also takes some "mental muscle": don't kid yourself, speakers who go over their time rarely stop unless you basically carry them off stage. So prepare yourself to be tough and don't get into prolonged begging.

The other tasks are more subtle. Yes, people will miss it if you don't introduce the speakers, but otherwise, they'll just have some vague sense that the session isn't high-class. On the other hand, if you've seen a few outstanding moderators at work stimulating the discussion and pulling together scattered points into a coherent picture, you know what a difference this can make to a session.

Most of the items on the task list are obvious and need no further explanation. Two of them, however, deserve more detailed discussion. These are (1) the art of asking questions to move the discussion along and (2) handling uncivil, off-subject, or otherwise troublesome questions. We will take these up in separate sections at the end of this chapter.

CLOSING THE SESSION IN STYLE

Your last job is to close the session in such a way that people feel as good as possible about it. This is your last chance to pull together disparate strands of the discussion so the common threads emerge.

Presumably, you came prepared with notes on the talks, based on what the presenters provided before the conference. To these, you'll have added notes on important points added by the speakers as well as by audience members in the discussion. Out of all these notes, you need to fashion a brief summary that will stay in the audience's mind.

Most moderators fall short on this job. Having gone overtime in any case, they do no more than rush out some phrase of thanks — say:

> *Well, great. Thanks to everybody — especially our last speaker, who had to condense her talk from 20 to 5 minutes on a moment's notice! See you all next year!*

Compare the value of this to what the audience can get out of a proper closing along the lines of the following example:

> *Thank you. We've heard three very different positions on the issue of patenting the results of recombinant DNA research. From the bio-ethics perspective, ... [mention highlights] From the industry perspective, ... [highlights] And from the perspective of academic research, ... [highlights] As the questions and discussion brought out, reconciling these perspectives is not easy but necessary for sensible*

legislation and government policies. And it should be possible if we take a few concrete steps: ... [list them] Again, many thanks to our presenters, and to the audience for participating so constructively!

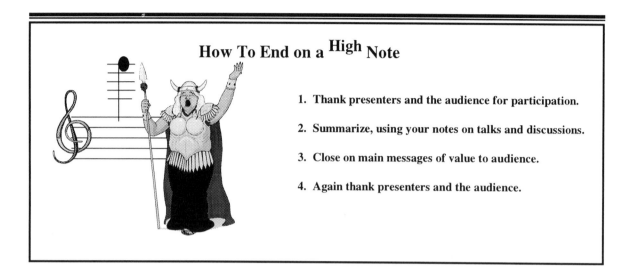

THE ART OF STIMULATING DISCUSSION THROUGH GOOD QUESTIONS

When the discussion stalls (or never gets off the ground), or heads into a fruitless direction, good moderators jump in with helpful questions. This is one of the more difficult skills to learn. In particular, you need to develop the knack of asking *focused questions* that have a good chance of producing useful responses.

Using Focused Questions

Focused questions are opposed to *closed* (or *yes-no*) questions and *open* questions. Here are some examples of the three question types:

Open: What can you tell us about your company?
Closed: Is your company fully committed to solid waste reduction?
Focused: Where is your company headed in the area of solid waste reduction?

Open questions are likely to produce an uncontrolled stream of information. Closed questions may yield a very meager response ("yes," "no," "pretty much," etc.). Focused questions combine the virtues of both open and closed questions: they get the discussion going, but in a structured, more predictable way.

Obviously, you will always need a mix of open, closed, and focused questions. However, focused questions are the hardest to formulate, and therefore much more rarely used by unskilled moderators or interviewers. Practicing them will make it easier for you to use them when they would be helpful.

Specific Use of Focused Questions in Panel Discussions

In a panel discussion, the moderator can often profit from the formula

Background statement + Focused question

to get the discussion started or move it along.

Example:

> [**Background:**] "Over the last few years, we've seen widespread implementation of chlorine-free bleaching in order to reduce the discharge or mission of chlorinated compounds. [**Focused question:**] What are the two or three biggest technical and economic challenges you see in moving to totally chlorine-free bleaching, which excludes not only elementary chlorine but also chlorine dioxide?"

Contrasting Examples:

1. *Open question:*
   "What do you think about Totally Chlorine Free bleaching, or TCF?" [Does not give enough direction to the contribution]

2. *Closed question:*
   "In your view, is it feasible for the industry as a whole to move to totally chlorine-free bleaching?" [Restricts the contribution too much and may get no more than "Yes!" or "Absolutely!"]

CONTROLLING UNCIVILIZED OR OTHERWISE OUT-OF-LINE QUESTIONS

As a moderator, you have considerably more authority over the question-and-answer session than most speakers. Partly, this is because you occupy an *official position* that entails keeping order. But partly, it also is because you are at a moral advantage: any rules you impose or enforce are not in your own interest (as they are when a speaker does the same) but in your speakers' interest.

Tip

Here are two qualities that will get you far as a moderator: *gracious* yet *firm*.

For instance, it's one thing for a speaker to say, "I'm just not going to answer that question" when presented with an uncivil remark; it's another for a moderator to say:

> *Please, let's keep to the rules we established at the beginning. I am committed to maintaining a civil tone of discussion. [To the speaker:] You heard the question — you don't need to answer unless you want to.*

Chapter 15 contained advice on *rephrasing hostile questions.* As a moderator, you'll do well to study that section carefully and apply it in all your sessions. Also, study the advice given there on warding off persistent or off-track questions.

Finally, don't forget the power of *well-meaning humor* in moderating questions. Sometimes it is better to laugh off a hot-headed remark rather than get severe about it, as long as you protect the speaker by offering her a rephrased, civil version of the question to answer.

Exercise 17-1 gives you an opportunity to practice these skills in peace on paper. If you find that it takes you a long time to deal with some of the problem questions in this exercise, that's a good indication that you need additional study and practice. Remember, in real life, your response has to come within seconds.

EXERCISES

Exercise 17-1. Controlling Inappropriate Questions
Instructions: Decide how the moderator should handle the following questions. Aim at firmness without insulting the questioner. In some cases, you may want to give the speaker the *option* of replying (though perhaps to an appropriately *rephrased* question).

Inappropriate Question	How To Control/Redirect/Rephrase
"I'm sick and tired of all these academics coming along and telling us what to do. Obviously, you've never seen the inside of a factory, or you wouldn't be telling us this stuff about all this fancy new chemistry. Do you have any *idea* what's involved in changing basic chemistry between production runs?"	
"I don't know what the *point* of all this is. Who cares if the bonds between those fibers are because of hydrogen or Van der Waltz or whatever you call him, or subatomic forces, or gravity, or the moon, or whatever! We all know they stick together, or we wouldn't have paper. Why don't you start telling us how to *make better paper* — that's all we care about! We don't want to hear about these age-old theoretical battles between structuralists and hydrogenists and all the rest of you!"	

Exercise 17-1. Controlling Inappropriate Questions *(continued)*

Inappropriate Question	How To Control/Redirect/Rephrase
"This is all very interesting. But what's it got to do with our operational realities? Our processes are totally different from the one you discussed. They don't even use the same *chemistry!*"	
"I think this whole thing was totally biased. You obviously have some special interest that leads you to choose or twist your data and interpretations. I don't trust any of it."	
"I have no doubt you got the data you say you did. The problem is, those data all result from a totally inappropriate methodology. The proper experimental method you should have used for this is a double-blind randomized noise-controlled XYZ method…"	
"I don't know about anybody else, but I find all this incredibly boring. What's the point of it?"	
"I'm sorry, but I just can't believe those data. I remember some recent studies that showed that the trend was just the other way round."	

Exercise 17-1. Controlling Inappropriate Questions *(continued)*

Inappropriate Question	How To Control/Redirect/Rephrase
Question that goes on for more than 3 minutes and really is a show-off mini-lecture.	
"I'm sorry, I just can't believe any of this. It all seems totally far-fetched."	
Question that shows that person slept through part of the presentation	
Question that is clearly *off the subject*	
Persistent question	
No questions	

Exercise 17-2. Evaluate your own moderating skills. If you have experience moderating conference sessions, base your evaluation on that experience. If you do not, reflect on your attitudes, habits, and skills (especially question-handling skills as shown in your own presentations). Use a verbal scale of *always, often, sometimes, rarely, never* to answer the following questions.

Plan ahead and contact speakers way in advance _____

Able to motivate speakers to prepare early and to give thought to the session theme_____

Prepare an overview based on material from speakers _____

Get agreement on fair procedures, including timing and turn-taking _____

Introduce speakers and their subjects properly _____

Set a positive, productive tone for the session _____

Give focus to the session with concise overviews and summaries, yet remain more in the background than the speakers _____

Involve the audience _____

Make sure people can hear all questions and answers _____

Stay in control of the session: enforce timing, turn taking, and civilized tone _____

Ask good questions that move the session along _____

Clear up misunderstandings and ambiguities _____

Redirect discussions that stray from the subject _____

Protect speakers from abuse by excluding or rephrasing questions etc. _____

Good at using *focused questions* to get discussions moving or back on track _____

Close the session with a final summary of contributions and discussion _____

Review all your answers in this exercise. Considering answers of "never" or "rarely," what are the biggest changes you should make to improve your effectiveness as a moderator?

_____

_____

_____

_____

_____

_____

PART 3

MAKING THE MOST OF
PRESENTATION TECHNOLOGY

18   **Making the Transition to Electronic Slide Shows 219**

19   **Using Presentation Software Intelligently 227**

20   **Practicing and Delivering Slide Shows 255**

21   **Web Presentations and Web Meetings 275**

18

Making the Transition to Electronic Slide Shows

"Dazzle them with your next presentation!" the commercials order us. And they show us how to do it: with lots of cutting-edge equipment, from power-packed laptop computers to high-resolution portable LCD projectors. All you need to do is to push the buttons....

It's a tantalizing promise. But is it realistic? Let's look at some scenarios.

SCENARIO 1: GONE WITH THE WIND II

The conference room is gently darkened in front so your equipment recedes into a dignified techno half-shade. That equipment includes: a laptop (with more horsepower than a Ferrari); remote control with ten number buttons, a trackball, a cute little color LCD screen, and a built-in laser pointer; a superbright LCD projector of the latest design, with 20 million colors and inputs for any conceivable multimedia equipment; a huge projection screen covering the entire front wall; a VCR controlled by the same remote you're using to control your computer; a theatre surround stereo sound system; and a lavalier mike clipped to your stylish lapel (you're wearing a Dior suit, freshly pressed).

Setup was a breeze. You just popped the LCD projector onto the table, parked the laptop next to it, and put the VCR player on a side table. All the units communicate smoothly by infrared.

There is enough light to show the confident gleam in your eyes as you face your hushed audience, sleek remote control in your hand. You greet your listeners graciously, then relax them with a humorous-yet-professional apropos remark (ripples of appreciative laughter).

The first slide explodes onto the screen in brilliant color, electrifying the audience into oohs and aahs. The sound system gives a rich color to your voice, adding a subtle vibrato. Click — next slide. You draw effortlessly on the projected slide with the remote's trackball to guide your listeners' attention.

Click — another slide: a 3-D graph, rich in color and bursting with persuasive power. A bullet point floats onto it from the left, another follows from the right, another from the bottom. The audience is alert, waiting for "bullet attacks" from eight directions. Who would dare to sleep? Who would dare to question points made with such efficient power?

Click — a slide with a movie "object." You click on the object; the VCR springs to life, showing the flawed production process you are discussing. The image is projected through the LCD panel onto the large screen, leaving some listeners open-mouthed. Click — the VCR stops; more slides come up.

Click — the VCR resumes, showing the much improved production process you are proposing. Summary slide. Questions?

Yes, there are lots of keen questions, some requiring detailed answers. You branch to an optional section of your computer slide show to illustrate technical details of the new procedure.

Applause, applause! It's the biggest hit since *Gone with the Wind.* They are dazzled indeed: the word "wow" is written on everybody's lips. Later, they all surround you and ask: "How did you do it? Can you teach us?" Wow!

Is it just a dream? Not necessarily — but it's not what we usually see. For more common scenarios, read on....

SCENARIO 2: HOT UNDER THE COLLAR

The speaker before you used grungy black-and-white transparencies, so the audience will really appreciate the computer slide show you've prepared for them. For the occasion, you've borrowed a nice (you hope) LCD projector from another department. Your notebook is a little slow, with its outdated processor and poky display — but what's the rush? You've tested the slide show several times on the computer at home, and it looks great. And to make things even better, the manager who lent you the projector also gave you a handy remote control to zip through your slide show!

The audience knows something's up, because they can see you running around with cables and equipment. In fact, one fellow has the indecency to laugh as you trip over a cable and spill coffee all over your suit. It seems the room is getting a little hot — or is it just all the exercise?

There seem to be so many cables. And so few electric outlets! And the only room for your trusty old laptop seems to be on the floor, next to the projector table. But with patience and help from some of the audience members, you eventually get everything plugged in.

You're finally ready. Your computer is going through power-up and the Windows start-up screens. For some reason, nothing much seems to be showing on the projection screen (a dingy affair on a three-leg stand). Perhaps too much light in the room? Well, you'll just have to dim the front lights a bit. However, there seems to be no switch for the front lights. It's either lights or no lights! You plunge the room into darkness and pray for an image.

And there it is! A little dim and fuzzy, with strange colors, but nonetheless, it's certainly the Windows main screen! Now where is that remote? Hit PowerPoint! But wait — how do you hit PowerPoint? There isn't a trackball or other pointing device on that remote control! You adjust the projector focus (no great change apparent) while you rethink your strategy. There seems to be only one answer: squat by the laptop and work directly from it until you manage to load your PowerPoint presentation. From that point on, the remote "forward" and "backward" buttons should be enough.

Finally, your title slide comes on, and you scramble to your feet to address your audience, still a little shaky from all the exertion and excitement. There's no way of telling whether anybody is listening — it's too dark for that. But at least you manage to remember most of your talk, and the slides are all there, more or less. The projected colors seem to bear little relation to those on your laptop screen, though. As a result, it's sometimes hard to see where one pie slice stops and another starts, or where intersecting curves on a line chart continue. And sometimes, images seem to blend pretty much with the background....

Also, the remote takes getting used to, in the dark: it's always a toss-up whether you hit the "forward" or "backward" button. Some slides pop back so often, they become like old friends and are greeted by cheers from the audience.

The biggest problem occurs when you try to skip over an optional branch of hidden slides in your show. You try several times, first with the remote, then directly with the laptop. The program keeps going straight into the branch instead of skipping over it. In the end, you move quickly through all 20 slides of this branch with the remote. Unfortunately, after showing the first slide beyond the optional block, you hit the wrong button, and instead of advancing, the show returns to the slide just before the optional branch! Another round of attempts to jump over that branch — but in the end, you have to go through all 20 optional slides again....

Fortunately, there's no time left for questions, so you just gather up all your notes, machines, and cables. Everybody — including you — seems busy avoiding eye contact as you sit down quietly.

Wake me up from this nightmare, you say? Unfortunately, it may not be a dream. At this very moment, it's probably happening all over the world, in countless conference rooms!

In fact, one of the most common problems is that nothing works at all. This was the case at a recent university-hosted industry conference. An impressive crowd of corporate top honchos had showed up with their latest-model, power-packed laptops, ready to present. The doors opened at 9 a.m., and the conference was under way five minutes later, with no time for such niceties as testing of setup. However, as speaker after speaker stepped up to the podium, they all had the same deflating experience: their computers did not work with the university's projector, and no amount of fiddling helped.

Now, had even one brought backup transparencies? Of course not — what an old-fashioned idea! So they started without any visuals whatsoever, making lots of apologies and remarks such as: "Well, this is where I would have liked to show you just how we're going to set up the new process..." One even held up his computer and turned it so the audience could see his tiny "visuals." There were few questions for these speakers — confusion was too complete to be cleared up by a few extra impromptu explanations.

Only the last speaker succeeded — because he'd brought his own projector, which he could be sure would work with his laptop. Of course, he knew better than to mention the existence of this up-to-date projector until it was his turn: he wasn't going to risk any disaster such as a burned-out bulb before his own turn came up!

Or consider this example. A speaker was all set to give a talk to a group of technical editors for a journal. However, the presenter before him had been unable to get her computer and LCD projector to work together (she wanted to illustrate Internet procedures relating to the magazine). The second speaker therefore had to give his entire talk from the wrong end of the room while the first one was fiddling with her equipment at the head of the table, where all the power and phone connections were. In that case, by a miracle, the electronic slide show finally did work — but only after upsetting the schedule and thoroughly spoiling the second speaker's talk.

IS IT WORTH GETTING INVOLVED?

If problems and embarrassment are so common, is it worth getting involved at all? Yes, for two reasons. One, the new technology, though far from perfect, does offer tremendous advantages; you just need to spend a little time getting familiar with it *and take traditional backup*. Two, audiences are becoming spoiled by the successful high-tech presentations they see. Already, color is so common that your old black-and-white visuals look dangerously quaint. Soon, transparencies will seem equally outmoded as electronic slide shows become the norm. So, you really don't have the option of staying out of trouble.

One of the greatest promises of the new technology is quick, inexpensive access to multimedia, especially photographs and video. This can be of great value in illustrating technical facts — yet it's rarely used by presenters today. In these chapters on presentation technology, we will show you how to strengthen your presentations by taking advantage of these multimedia options — not in order to "dazzle the audience," as Scenario 1 implies, but to *help them get your message*.

Another benefit of modern equipment is powerful remote control over slides, which allows you to stay in contact with your audience throughout the presentation. Again, most presenters don't exploit this strength; instead, they let the equipment take them into isolation. This is another area we will explore.

Finally, today's software does make it possible to produce well-balanced visuals in a reasonable time — if you know how to steer around some common weaknesses. We will therefore discuss quick ways of getting the most out of your presentation software.

A PAINLESS MIGRATION PATH VIA COLOR TRANSPARENCIES

If you are nervous about getting involved with all the complicated new technology, color transparencies are a good starting point because they are easy to produce and pose fewer challenges at delivery time than LCD projectors. While they don't offer slide transitions, animation, and build-up slides, they do allow you to practice integration of color photographs — a key skill you can exploit and extend in electronic slide shows.

Color printers range from inexpensive ink jet and bubble jet printers to thermal transfer color printers, dye sublimation printers, and color laser printers. For most presentation purposes, a good color ink jet printer should be perfectly acceptable.

Most of the popular color printers are easy to operate, and your presentation software should work smoothly with them. Your main task will be to use color to be helpful rather than overwhelming. (See Chapter 7 for more guidance on color.) Here are a few suggestions (we will discuss software issues in more detail in Chapter 19).

- Work with only a few colors at a time. One color for the background and two or three colors for your chart elements is a good (though usually difficult) goal. If you need extra colors, try dark and light shades of the same color.
- Start with the preset color schemes your software offers you. Most of these schemes are well balanced and attractive.
- Use contrasting colors for curves, and label each curve directly in the same color as the curve.
- Give your presentation a consistent look by keeping the same background color and slide headers.
- Print proofs on regular paper at reduced size (to save on expensive transparencies and ink). When you are satisfied with the output, change the paper type to "transparency" and print full size.

INCORPORATING COLOR PHOTOGRAPHS

One great advantage of the new technology is the ease with which you can incorporate photographs into your presentations. Often, a good photo can illustrate technical facts or procedures much better than abstract diagrams or engineering drawings — especially for a nontechnical or mixed audience. In the past, this called for 35mm slides, which meant several days' development time, uncertainty of results, and the need to handle temperamental 35mm slide projectors. Today, it is easy to put photographs on convenient transparencies, with no development time, or to project them directly from your computer via an LCD projector, without any need to print. (However, there is the matter of *backup transparencies* if you opt for an electronic slide show. Unless you think problems are highly likely, you could simply use *black-and-white laser-printed* transparencies as your backup.)

The key skill you need for integrating photography is electronic processing of photographs and video. It's the one skill that will truly move you into the multimedia-presentation world — and you can practice it very effectively at this simple level of color transparencies produced on a color printer. (The same skills and equipment will allow you to project photos and video through an LCD projector.)

You have three basic options for capturing photographic material: (1) transfer printed images to your computer with a scanner, (2) use a video frame grabber to pull still "frames" from a videotape, or (3) take original photos (or movies) with a digital (filmless) camera.

Scanners. Scanning is the least interesting option in our context, because it requires development time and doesn't do much to teach you basic multimedia skills. However, if you have ready-made photographs or material from magazines or books, scanning is the simplest solution. Once you've brought the scanned image into your presentation software, select it and *crop* it to exclude any parts you don't want. (See the help section of your software for details on the crop tool.)

Video Frame Grabbers. Videotaping has many advantages: it's cheap; there is no development time; you can instantly check the result and re-tape, if necessary; and the equipment is available everywhere. Video frame grabbers let you pull single images off videotape or TV. They used to be expensive and technically complex (high-end models still are); however, a new generation of inexpensive, high-quality, external models makes it possible for anybody to use this technology. In most instances, their resolution is more than adequate — in fact, much finer than that of your original videotape. Usually, you simply plug it into a parallel or USB (universal serial bus) port on your computer and connect its video cables to your VCR. Software for modifying the captured images is typically included.

A higher-powered alternative is video editing hardware, which can also produce still images from a video source. There are inexpensive external versions available, again with software included, that produce acceptable results and are just as easy to use as the video frame grabbers.

Digital Cameras. These are cameras that store their images in electronic form rather than on film. This saves you the time and effort of printing photos and then scanning them. Furthermore, some of these cameras, including inexpensive models, produce not only still pictures but also digital video clips that can be played through an LCD projector. Therefore, once you learn how to use such a camera to bring photos into your presentation, you basically also know how to add video clips and play them as part of an electronic slide show.

Inexpensive models that produce digital video clips usually must be connected to a computer while you shoot pictures. Obviously, this is cumbersome unless you are dealing with very limited movement (such as a person talking). If you have to move around a lot to take video footage, shoot it with a good VCR and then extract digital clips from it with video editing hardware and software, as described above. Digital still cameras, on the other hand, are available as freestanding units (without the need for a computer) at many price and quality levels, and transferring your digital photos to the computer is quick and simple, either through cables or various disk media.

We recommend highly that you begin experimenting with both video frame grabbers and digital cameras. They not only give you more helpful and interesting visuals today but also offer you an inexpensive and painless way to get ready for the more advanced facets of multimedia presentations.

MOVING TO ELECTRONIC SLIDE SHOWS

Electronic slide shows offer several advantages over traditional color transparencies, including elegant transitions between slides, "builds" (sequential highlighting) of bullet points, and animation of chart elements. If you have a good remote control, slide shows also free you from the projector, so you can stay in touch with the audience while changing slides. Today's presentation software even allows you to draw on your slides during delivery, using a high-level remote control with a trackball. (Obviously, you

---

Tip

Always make *backup transparencies* for any electronic slide show, at least of your key visuals — even if they're just black and white. And don't forget to arrange for a standby overhead projector!

can also draw from the laptop, but then you'll be blocking some people's view of the screen, as is the case when you draw on overhead transparencies.) Finally, as mentioned before, video sequences can be integrated directly into the show, without any need for a VCR.

All this comes at a cost, though: you need to test and practice — and even with that, you must be prepared for something to go wrong. So, you're not going to save on printing cost and time, because you absolutely must have backup transparencies. Also, unless you are truly comfortable with the equipment and the software, you may get overwhelmed by the technical aspects of your show and therefore lose touch with your listeners rather than get closer to them.

Typical Equipment

Electronic slide shows use an LCD or similar projector instead of acetate transparencies and an overhead projector. Your presentation is controlled either from your computer or with a remote control device. Here are the main things you need:

Laptop computer. The computer must be powerful enough to run today's demanding presentations software at a decent speed.

LCD Projector. The projector should have at least Super VGA resolution for reasonably crisp screen images, and at least 1,000 lumens brightness to allow you to leave lights on in the room.

Wireless Remote Control. There are remote controls available that control your computer; others come with the projector. Without a remote control, you will be tied to the computer for changing slides, which means giving up one of the greatest strengths of the new technology. However, many remotes (especially the ones that come with the projector) give you only primitive control — say, "next slide," "previous slide," plus perhaps a few number keys that can be programmed. Upscale devices that control your computer come with a full set of number keys and a trackball or other drawing and pointing device so you can control all aspects of your presentation. If you present often, consider buying your own remote for your computer. That way, your setup is more predictable and you can practice smooth changing of slides even if you don't have access to the projector until delivery time.

Up-to-Date Presentation Software. All the modern packages are designed to produce slide shows with a wide choice of slide transitions and text and graphics animation. Chapter 19 offers guidelines on working effectively with your software.

Audio and Video Integration

If your projector has speakers, you can use it to transmit sound as well as video. There are two basic options:

Option 1: A VCR connected to the projector with standard video and audio cables. Make sure the projector you'll find at the presentation site does indeed have audio and video capacity and the proper input terminals as well as cables.

Option 2: Video and sound stored as digital files on the computer. This saves you the hassle of arranging for a VCR and then setting it up and controlling it during the presentation. However, there are some possible problems:

- You must still have an audio connection from computer to projector. You may well find those cables missing on the projector, especially if it is provided by a hotel. Smart presenters *carry a set of basic audio and video cables* with them in their computer case.
- Sound files can be quite large. Alternatively, if you use high compression to save space, sound fidelity may be terrible.
- Video files can be extremely large. If you opt for lower resolution or fewer frames per second, you may get poor-quality, choppy video.

We suggest using a regular VCR for longer sequences or when video quality is important. Similarly, consider integrated computer sound only for short recordings; otherwise, use a VCR (if video is involved) or a tape recorder.

19

Using Presentation Software Intelligently

Whether you use electronic slide shows or traditional transparencies, your visuals must be easily readable, instantly understandable, and reasonably consistent and attractive. (See Chapter 6 for the general principles of effective visuals.) Fortunately, you can meet these goals without spending much time or reading every page of your software manuals. We'll discuss some helpful strategies that work for most presentation programs. Finally, we'll offer guidelines specifically for preparing electronic slide shows.

MAKING VISUALS EASY TO SEE AND UNDERSTAND

Unreadable visuals are still the most common complaint. To make key elements easy to see, you need large (at least 18 points) bold type and thick, contrasting lines. Most software templates encourage large type, as long as you don't get involved in sub-sub-bullets; however, default lines in a line chart are still often too thin. Unless you plan to read exact values from a chart (which you don't in a presentation), you don't need the precision offered by thin lines. (If you want to read out exact values, just put them on the figure as data labels — an option available in all programs.) One of your tasks, then, is to learn how to make your lines thicker and change their style and color for best contrast.

To make visuals easy to understand at a glance, you must avoid clutter and label curves and pie slices directly whenever feasible. This means deleting unnecessary grid lines, line markers, and legends.

Exactly how you make these adjustments differs from program to program. The appropriate commands may be hidden under several menus, including *Format, View, Chart, Edit,* and even *Insert.* Here are some time-saving tips (see your program's on-line help or manual for more detailed instructions).

- Experiment with clicking, double-clicking, and right-clicking on slide regions or elements. Double-clicking tends to activate formatting screens, whereas simple clicking selects elements or regions so you can move, resize, or delete them or apply menu choices to them.

- Once you've selected an item or region on a chart, try clicking the right mouse button; this often displays special menus for the selected items.

- To change the appearance of a chart on a slide, double-click on it to get into chart editing mode. Then click, double-click or right-click on lines, labels, legends, etc. to bring up the format options for them. Alternatively, try the obvious menus from the main menu bar — say, *Chart, Edit, Page,* etc.

- To add labels for curves, type them with the *Textbox* or *Text* tool, adjust the size and style as needed, and push them into place. Delete the legend only after that, so you can verify easily that you've labeled things correctly. After deleting the legend, you may have to move the labels again because the chart may have increased in size as it incorporates the place of the deleted legend.

- To return to the slide containing the chart, click outside the chart.

Some programs let you save a customized chart style with your preferences of line colors and thickness, legend treatment, grid choices, etc. so you can apply it to other charts. (This was true in early versions of PowerPoint, but was dropped as of the 2002 version; Corel Presentations, on the other hand, offered the feature in its 2000 version.) You can achieve the same result in any case simply by **copying a chart** with your favorite options into any new presentation and then editing the data sheet as needed. If the target chart is reasonably close in character to your model, this may save you time.

Customizing Charts by Ungrouping: A Last Resort

As a last resort, if you cannot get the line thickness or style you want, select the chart and ungroup it. Usually, you can then change each element from the program's main menu and tools, such as the line-thickness tool on the main tool bar. *However, the chart is then no longer connected to the underlying data table,* so you cannot make any data changes and have them automatically reflected in the chart.

The safest way to proceed is to *make a duplicate slide* of your chart, then ungroup and change only one of them. If you need to change data later, you can use the backup slide to access the data table and produce an updated chart. When you've finished updating, you can customize (after backing up once more!) the new chart again.

In the following pages, we will illustrate general procedures for customizing charts, including the most radical option, ungrouping (see box). Details such as menu choices and commands may differ for your software, but the general principles will be the same.

Let's start with a simple line chart (Figure 19-1) produced with typical default options, which include a grid, thin lines, and a legend. We'll delete the grid, make the lines thick and label them directly by hand, and delete the legend.

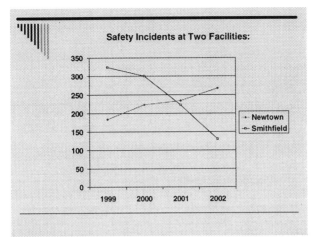

Figure 19-1. Typical line chart produced with default options. Note the legend, grid, and thin lines.

First, we must *select* the chart for editing (Figure 19-2). Double-clicking may get you directly into chart editing mode; alternatively, you can click on it, then choose the appropriate chart-edit command from the *Format, Edit,* or other menu. In editing mode, the data sheet for the chart should open to allow changes, and submenus should become available either directly from the chart-editing menu or by clicking on chart regions (see the example in Figure 19-2).

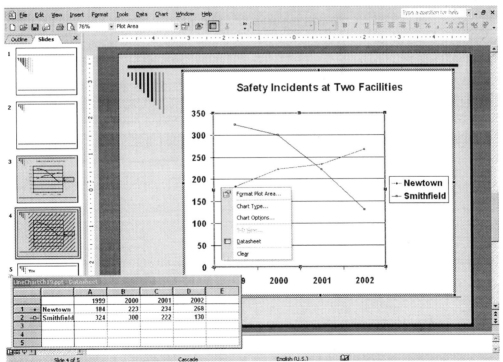

Figure 19-2. Double-clicking on the chart area puts it into editing mode, with the data sheet open to make changes. Subsequently left- or right-clicking on different areas of the chart opens different menus for changing the overall chart options or specific parts of the chart, such as the series (*lines*). Here, a menu opened (*lower left portion of the chart*) to allow changes to the plot area or to the overall chart.

In the example, we want to delete the grid and the legend. Therefore, we choose *Chart Options* from the pop-up menu, which gives us access to these features as well as axes, titles, and data labels (for displaying data values at each data point). Figure 19-3 shows a typical example of such a *Chart Options* dialogue box with several tabbed sections for making changes.

After deleting the grid and the legend, the chart appears as in Figure 19-4. That figure also illustrates the next step: selecting the data series (the different lines in the chart) in order to change their style. Notice the "selection points" on the descending curve in the figure. Right-clicking or choosing a command from the *Format, Edit,* or similar menu should give you access to a dialogue box for changing the format for the series (see Figure 19-5).

We chose the thickest line style available for the data series and added text labels to the curves from the main program screen (usually, adding text is not possible from the chart-editing mode). The result is shown in Figure 19-6. Notice that even the thickest line style available in our program is skimpy for a presentation, especially if the lighting is not optimal. Therefore, we chose to produce thicker lines by ungrouping the chart (see Figure 19-7). As we mentioned earlier, it's advisable to make a ***backup copy of your chart*** before ungrouping so you still have access to your data sheet in case you need to add or change data later.

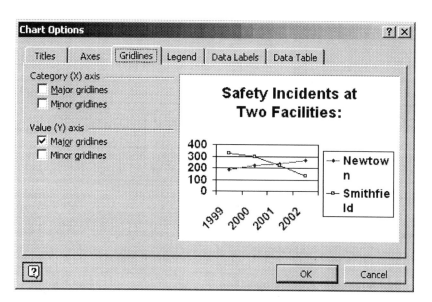

Figure 19-3. Choosing *Chart Options* from the pop-up menu shown in Figure 19-2 allows you to change gridlines (here, uncheck the Y axis "Major gridlines" box), legend (uncheck "Show legend"), data labels, etc.

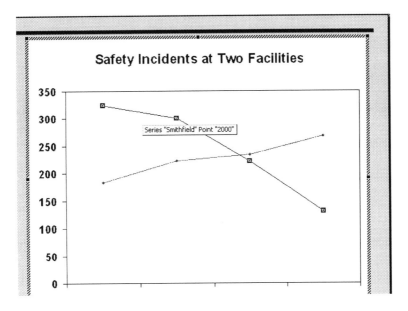

Figure 19-4. Appearance of the chart after deleting grid and legend. Now the *data series* (*lines*) must be selected and formatted one by one. Here, the first series has been selected, and right-clicking brings up the formatting menu in Figure 19-5.

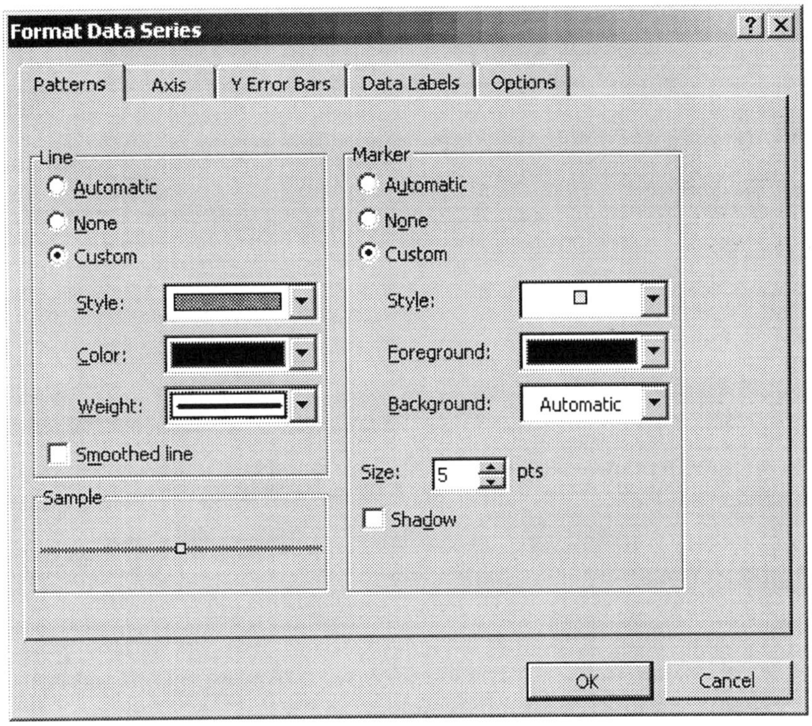

Figure 19-5. Typical formatting menu for a data series, with tabbed sections. Here, we selected the thickest line style available, then repeated the process for the second data series.

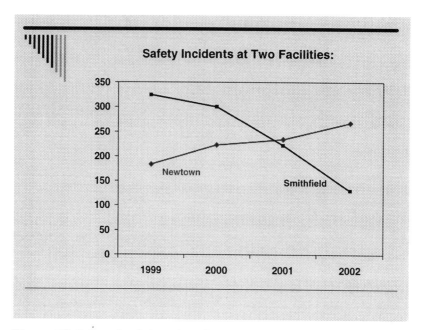

Figure 19-6. Result of changing chart options, including line style for the two data series, and adding labels for the curves. Notice that the data lines are still thin, even though we chose the thickest style available. Further changes must therefore be done via ungrouping, shown in the next steps.

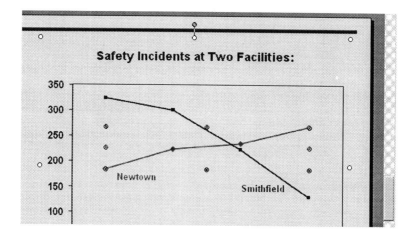

Figure 19-7. From the program's main screen, the chart is ungrouped so each chart element can be changed freely. We want to change the data lines, so we select those one at a time (notice the selection points around the "Newtown" curve) and change them in the appropriate menu (see Figure 19-8). Note that from an ungrouped chart, your **_data are no longer accessible_** for changing. Therefore, it's essential that you make a **_backup copy of the original chart_** in case you need to add or change data.

Ungrouping is done from the program's main screen. First, select the chart, then choose *Ungroup* from the *Draw* menu on the drawing tool bar, or from some appropriate menu such as *Object*. Once the chart is ungrouped, you can select any of its elements and delete or change it. In our case, we select the data lines (see Figure 19-7) and change them from an appropriate menu or tool-bar item (here, the *Format Autoshape* menu, shown in Figure 19-8). The final customized chart is shown in Figure 19-9.

ACHIEVING CONSISTENCY AND BALANCE THROUGH SLIDE MASTERS

The easiest way to give your slide show a unified appearance is to work with a *slide master*, or common background and layout for all slides. You can adjust the look of that master by adding text and graphics and changing the color scheme or presentation template. To make the changes, select *Master* from PowerPoint's *View* menu. (In Corel Presentations, invoke *Background* or *Layout* from the *Edit* menu; in Lotus Freelance, use the *Presentation* menu, then pick *Edit Backdrop*. In general, each program will employ different terms and menus for this task, but all major packages will offer some way of producing a uniform background easily.) Any changes you make to the slide master apply to all your slides unless you specifically override them for some slides.

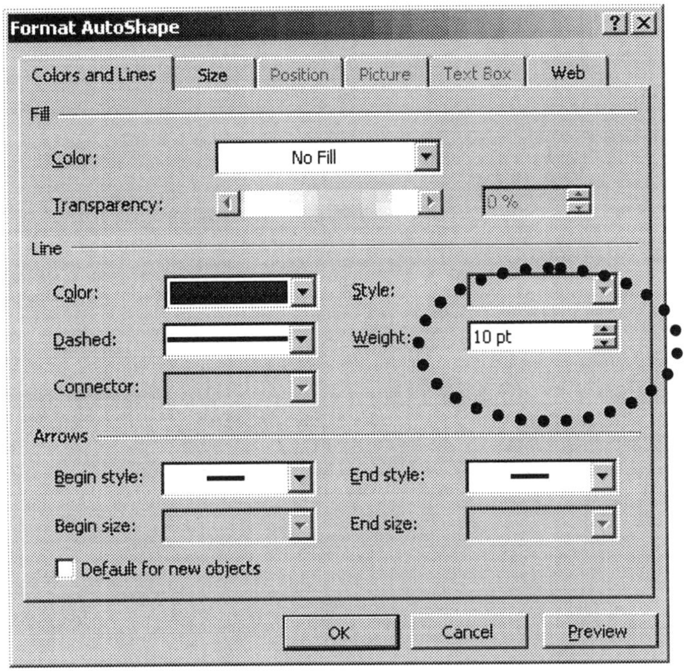

Figure 19-8. In our program, the line-thickness tool on the main tool bar did not allow for lines thicker than 6 pt — still not enough for our purposes. However, going into the *Format Autoshape* submenu under the *Format* menu allowed us to specify much thicker lines. Here, we chose 10 pt lines. The result is shown in Figure 19-9.

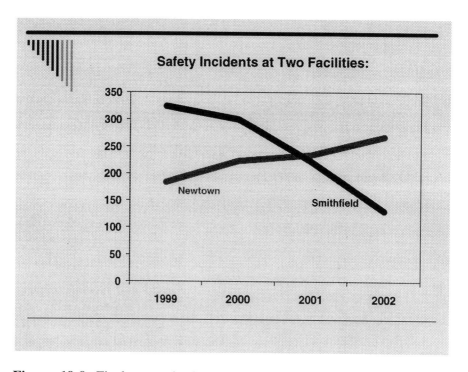

Figure 19-9. Final customized chart after ungrouping and changing line thickness to 10 pt. from the program's main screen

Programs such as Lotus Freelance, Microsoft PowerPoint, and Corel Presentations come with well-balanced color schemes and design templates that make it easy to achieve an attractive look. You can apply these to the master slide/background layer or even directly to the entire presentation (the simplest solution if you have no common text or graphics you want to place on every slide). Problems arise when you add or change colors: the balance may be lost, and a garish look might result. The obvious solution is to be very conservative in making changes to colors. (See the discussion of color in Chapter 6.)

USING CONTENT TEMPLATES

Content wizards are, on the surface, an attractive automation feature. However, in the end, they may only cost you time — and lead you astray as well. Typically, you'll end up with a canned presentation structure that is not tailored to specific audience needs and encourages you to use too many bullet charts. In other words, the Wizard still isn't smart enough to write the whole presentation for you — you'll have to do some of the thinking yourself!

These content templates come under many (continuously changing) names, such as Auto Content Wizard or SmartMasters. Figure 19-10 shows a typical example, produced by PowerPoint's Auto Content Wizard. The main elements of the presentation are quite acceptable, but notice that the *order* in which things are presented makes for a very weak talk — with real-life examples withheld until near the end, and your own main message postponed even further.

For more examples of outlines produced by such content templates, see the exercises at the end of this chapter. Finally, see Appendix D, which not only discusses typical commercial templates but also offers our own suggestions for specific types of presentations. You can easily produce your own templates based on our outlines. In the case of the basic presentation template or outline, you can also contact us directly by e-mail (perccom@aol.com); we'll be glad to send you a file that's usable in PowerPoint or Lotus Freelance.

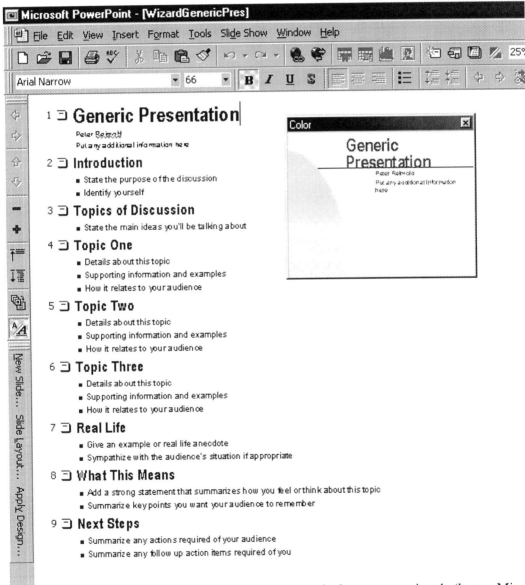

Figure 19-10. Content outline provided by a typical content wizard (here, Microsoft PowerPoint's Auto Content Wizard for a "Generic Presentation"). Note the weak introduction and the delayed main message. The view shown is "Outline View," from which you can easily change the titles and bullet text on all slides and also apply global font changes.

USING AND CUSTOMIZING
ELECTRONIC CLIP ART

No matter how large your collection of electronic clip art, chances are that you can't find exactly the image you need for your presentation. Often, however, there are some that are close to what you want. To use such "near fits," you must learn how to change parts of clip art.

The main techniques required are (1) ungrouping and grouping drawings or elements, (2) editing points, and (3) bringing elements forward or backward for editing and correct final overlap or layering. To add extra elements, you also need some basic drawing skills with line and shape tools.

Here are some extra tips:

- Make frequent backup copies of slides or drawings so you can recover easily if things go wrong (they always do).

- Group elements before moving them so parts don't get left behind; also, resizing is easier with grouped images.

- When drawing, moving, or resizing in PowerPoint, avoid grid snap-to (which pushes things into unwanted positions) by holding down the ALT button.

- To cut off unwanted outer portions of an imported clip art image or photo, use the *crop tool.*

- If some element is not accessible for selecting and editing, try moving interfering elements (such as larger elements that are layered on top of the one you want to edit) backward (usually an option under the *Order* submenu of the *Draw* menu). You can change the layers back to their proper final order after you've finished your editing.

Figures 19-11 – 19-15 illustrate some of these techniques. First, a clip art image of a jolly trimmer is inserted from file and ungrouped (Figure 19-11). Let's say we want to change his mouth to a nasty snarl, enlarge his nose, and put the logo "Budget Force" on his sweater sleeve.

In the first step, the mouth area is selected (Figure 19-12), deleted, and redrawn. Then the words "Budget" and "Force" are added with the text tool, moved into position, and rotated to follow the direction of the sweater sleeve (Figure 19-13).

Finally, the nose outline is selected for "point editing" (Figure 19-14) and changed to give a bigger nose (Figure 19-15).

Figure 19-11. Clip art placed on a slide and selected for "ungrouping" (one of the commands under the *Draw* menu).

Figure 19-12. After ungrouping, it's possible to select the mouth area and simply delete it so you can draw a new mouth with the expression you want.

Figure 19-13. A new mouth has been added with the irregular polygon drawing tool, and the words "Budget" and "Force" have been added and rotated into proper position. This is a good point at which to make a *backup copy* of your efforts in case the next steps ruin the image.

Figure 19-14. Nose outline selected for editing with the *Point Edit* command. Note that each point of the nose outline is visible; you can delete points, add new ones for finer control, and drag any point to a new position.

Figure 19-15. The final result of the editing. Drag a rectangle around the entire image and *group* it so it can be moved and resized easily.

PREPARING SLIDE SHOWS

Electronic slide shows let you do some things you can't do with color transparencies. For example, build-up (or "progressive disclosure") slides and transitions alert the audience to changes in your story through dynamic visual effects. Video and audio clips can provide extra explanatory power. And hidden slides, available in some programs, let you either skip or show one or several consecutive slides, depending on your needs at delivery time.

Unfortunately, slide shows are becoming like competitive fireworks: every few months, somebody adds a supernova, and everybody else has to scramble to catch up. We don't imagine this trend to reverse soon. So, let's see how you can live with it without getting burned out.

The Triple Challenge

Most serious presenters with whom we have talked share three valid concerns about presentation technology:

1. They don't want to stand out as "techno-dorks" — the only ones who don't know how to make things jump, wiggle, and spin on the screen.
2. They want to use the available tools for some solid purposes: to explain concepts better, make ideas more memorable, keep the audience focused on the essential parts of a slide, or even add some low-key touches of entertainment or humor.
3. They don't want to spend a lot of time learning or using the technology.

The secret to meeting these challenges lies in a simple principle of balance:

Get attention without causing distraction.

To appreciate the importance of this principle, think about how a good water colorist will render a brick building. She certainly won't paint every brick — just a few to suggest the rest! This saves her a ton of work, yet improves the picture by avoiding perceptual overload.

You can follow the same philosophy: ***do less to achieve more.*** You'll have less to learn and less to prepare, yet the audience will appreciate your efforts more. And nobody will doubt your technology know-how just because you apply it sparingly!

Transitions

A transition is a gradual replacement of a slide by a new slide. Its big advantage (besides showing that you know how to do it) is that it announces the arrival of the new slide. This is important with electronic slides because people don't see you changing slides as they do with transparencies; therefore, if the new slide is similar to its predecessor, they may miss the change and get very confused.

Tip

If a slide is very similar to its predecessor, make sure to use a noticeable transition so people don't think they're still looking at the same slide.

The best way to set transitions is from Slide Sorter View for your entire presentation. Then, if you want special transitions for a few selected slides, you can set those separately. Again, it's the water colorist's way to save time and avoid overload. Set the speed of transitions to "fast" or at most "medium" and test the result to make sure the transition is noticeable yet not so slow as to keep the audience waiting impatiently.

This is one area in which the fireworks competition is really heating up. There are various add-on products you can buy to spice up your slide show with TV style transitions. However, even the standard transitions provided with newer presentation software include all kinds of high-powered effects that can impress the most hard-boiled audience.

Remember "attention without distraction." Any change that takes too long is distracting; so is any transition that mangles, decomposes, or otherwise manipulates text. Quick spinning of an entire image, or one simple vertical rotation, is in fact less distracting than a dissolve, blinds, bars, or checkerboard. Wipe, split, cover/uncover, box in/out, and newsflash are examples of transitions that don't cause distraction, but the list grows every year, so you have plenty of choices.

Text Animation, or Build-Up Slides

Build-up slides are an elegant way to keep the audience on track with your story by adding bullet points to a basic slide as you talk about them. For instance, if the first build-up shows the title BENEFITS OF NEW SYSTEM, the next three might add ♦ SPEED INCREASED 40%, ♦ COSTS DECREASED 10%, AND ♦ ACCURACY IMPROVED 25%. You prepare all this as just one slide but set it up as an animated bullet-list slide that will be displayed one step at a time.

This tool has some obvious advantages. First, it prevents the audience from reading ahead of you and perhaps tuning you out. (You could achieve the same with transparencies by covering up the body of the slide and revealing it point by point. Unfortunately, this is a big turn-off for many listeners, whereas nobody seems offended by the electronic equivalent.) Another advantage is a more rapid "screen refresh rate." The MTV multi-generation (that's all of us!) hates staring at the same image more than a few seconds, and build-ups keep things moving. Finally, build-ups save you a lot of clumsy pointing: when the next bullet item floats on, everybody understands that you've moved to the next point.

Tip

Like a great water colorist, use your brush sparingly. Keep transitions and animations simple, and reserve the most dramatic ones for your key slides.

However, there are also dangers. Above all, this feature encourages you to ramble without ever giving the audience a preview of your key points. Before clicking on the "build-up" or animation option, ask yourself if the audience would gain more by seeing the big picture at a glance; if so, build-ups may be more appropriate at the next stage, when you discuss each point in more detail.

Another danger is overuse. Some speakers seem to think that build-ups are major entertainment. They're not. Word charts are boring, no matter how much the words in them wiggle, jump, or flash. Which brings us to the last danger: distracting effects, such as dissolves or blinds, for each new bullet point.

Tip

As much as possible, set up transitions and animations once for the entire slide show. It's less work and yields a more consistent look.

Text Animation and "Attention Without Distraction"

What does "get attention without causing distraction" mean for bullet-list animation? Basically, give items enough movement so they "point at themselves" (that way you don't have to point at them but instead can stay in touch with the audience); on the other hand, don't prolong the movement, and don't allow strange things to happen to letters of the text. This leaves you with such options as ascend, fly, box out, wipe, spiral, or stretch but excludes crawl, swivel, dissolve, blinds, and checkerboard.

To speed preparation and produce a more consistent effect, we suggest selecting all slides from the Slide Sorter view, then picking an animation such as wipe right, ascend, or camera. (Unlike drive or fly, these will work for *all* your bullet slides, because movement is strictly local rather than across the screen and through any graphics or text that happen to be in the way.) Test your slide show; if your global animation scheme does not work well for a few specific slides, then choose a different scheme just for those.

Animating Graphics

No matter how the technology changes, animation of graphics will involve certain basic techniques. First, you must split the graphic image into parts you can move separately. Second, you need to combine parts with any text you want to appear together with them. Third, you must define sequence and type of movement.

Say you imported an image of a four-piece puzzle, and you want to introduce it one piece at a time with appropriate text. Figure 19-16 shows an example.

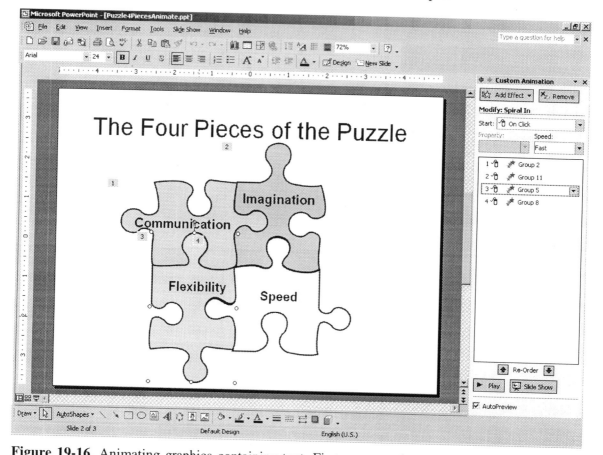

Figure 19-16. Animating graphics containing text. First ungroup the graphic (here, into its four pieces.) Add text to each piece, then group the text with its graphic piece. Then choose custom animation for the four pieces (here, Spiral In). In the box on the right, you can change the effects, animation speed, and sequence in which the elements appear.

First, you need to *ungroup* the image. Next, type text labels for each piece, move them into place, and group each puzzle piece with its text label. Finally, apply a *custom animation* (see Figure 19-17 for an example) to define order of appearance and effect for each piece. It's time-consuming, so you can see why restraint helps: use this just for your key visuals, not every graphic.

One useful type of graphic animation is *sequential presentation of chart elements*, such as the different curves in a line chart. Some packages, including PowerPoint, let you do this directly from the chart-editing mode. However, options tend to be limited (thin lines, legend, etc.). An alternative is to ungroup the chart as illustrated in our earlier example, then set custom animation so that the curves come on after everything else, and one at a time.

Hidden Slides

When you mark one or several consecutive slides as hidden (available in PowerPoint but not in all other programs), they will not show unless you give a special command (H). This can be very useful if you are not sure how much time you will be allowed or just what your audience's interests are. In principle, it's much easier to manage hidden electronic slides than to handle optional transparencies. However, in practice, many speakers get hopelessly confused at delivery time and end up showing most of what they didn't want to or never finding slides they really wanted. Another danger is the temptation not to time your talk but just rely on the built-in flexibility of hidden slides. Impromptu cutting is never as effective as planned cutting that is based on a timed rehearsal.

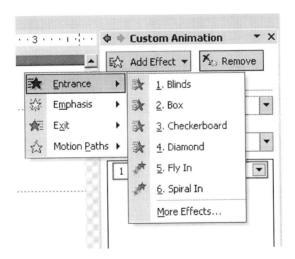

Figure 19-17. A sample Custom Animation menu for animating selected graphic elements (including text produced with the text tool rather than from the bullet-list layout template).

To mark a slide as hidden, pick "Hide Slide" from the *Slide Show, Tools,* or similar menu, either from Slide View or from Slide Sorter View. (To unhide it, just click "Hide Slide" again.) When you've finished, test and practice. Here are some things to pay attention to:

- How do you show a hidden slide? (Type H or its number.)
- If you show the first hidden slide, will the next hidden slide show automatically? (Yes.)
- Is there a command for "Show the next nonhidden slide"? (No — you have to type its number followed by ENTER.)

Be sure you know where all your hidden slides are. In fact, if you have many, print out a list of your slides; it may save you from embarrassment at delivery time! If hidden slides are not allowed in your software, simply put all your optional slides at the end of the show, after a black slide. Alternatively, use *embedded presentations* (covered next) if those are available.

Optional Branches to Embedded Presentations

Microsoft PowerPoint and Lotus Freelance allow you to insert a special kind of "object" into a slide, namely, an embedded presentation. (Corel Presentations, as of this writing, allowed neither embedded presentations nor hidden slides — or, more precisely, allowed only *permanently* hidden slides that you can't access in a show.) This allows you to put optional branches into your presentation. At delivery time, you activate such a branch , if necessary, by clicking on its icon or image on the slide on which it is embedded.

Know How To Exit From an Embedded Presentation!

What do you do if you want to exit from an embedded presentation before its last slide? In PowerPoint, *push the ESC button.* If you use this feature, it's important for you to find out how your program handles this task — you don't want to be frozen into having to show all optional slides just because you don't know how to exit!

In the case of PowerPoint, many presenters would be afraid to press ESC because they are aware that this is the same key that exits them from the main slide show. However, in the version we used when writing this book, this was not the case — ESC just terminated the *embedded* show. In Lotus Freelance, ESC *never* exits a show directly but instead brings up an exit menu that lets you return to the show.

To embed a presentation on a slide, choose *Object* from the *Insert* or other appropriate menu, then specify the file name of the presentation you want to include. In PowerPoint, the presentation will automatically play as a slide show; in Lotus Freelance, you may have to open the embedded presentation and specifically set it to play as a slide show, and only then place it as an object on the appropriate slide. To prevent unnecessarily large files, you may want to check the option to "link to file" rather than save a copy of the embedded presentation in the main presentation file.

Black Slides

Black slides are useful when you want a blank screen. Put one at the end of your show, to prevent the program's main screen from appearing if you should advance past the last slide. Also, if you keep extra slides for the question-and-answer session at the end of the show, you can separate related groups with black slides. Finally, you may want to insert black slides at certain points of your show when you want a blank screen, without distraction from the last visual discussed. (You can achieve the same effect at delivery time by typing "B" in PowerPoint.)

Embedding Video, Sound, and Other Applications in Your Show

Most software lets you embed various "objects" in a slide — for instance, a video or audio clip, a spreadsheet, or a word processing document. (PowerPoint also allows embedded *presentations* — covered above.) To activate the object during the show, you click its icon or placeholder on the slide. This opens the program that created the object, with the object in the active window.

One advantage of this approach is that you can manipulate the object with the program that created it. For instance, you can change values in a spreadsheet in response to audience questions and explore the effects of the changes. When you are finished, the program will return you to the correct point in your slide show.

The most interesting application is perhaps video. If you have managed to create a digital movie, you can launch it from your screen show and project it like your regular slides. Does this replace traditional videotape? Not yet. If you have a longer movie to show or need high quality, the digital version is inconvenient or inferior. However, for short, simple applications such as illustrating a procedure or showing people in action, embedded video avoids extra equipment and gives you uninterrupted remote control over your presentation.

To embed a video clip, look for an *Insert Object* or *Insert Movies Or Sounds* command under the *Insert* or similar menu. Browse to find your video file and specify the *play settings* you want — automatic or on mouse click.

Typically, after embedding, your slide will show an image of your movie's first frame. Now enlarge this image proportionally by dragging a handle so it will play full size. During playback, you have access to control buttons so you can freeze a frame and even copy it and paste it onto another slide if that is helpful for the discussion.

Video is a complex topic, and there are several video formats available. What this means in practice is that plenty of things can go wrong. The PowerPoint Help section includes extensive troubleshooting tips, as do other programs. If tests show a problem, consult these sources.

Even if you currently have no need for embedded video, you can practice the relevant skills by inserting one of the video clips that come with Windows and learn how to troubleshoot as well as control the video at delivery time.

Audio clips are handled in a similar manner. You would rarely want independent audio during a live presentation, other than as part of a movie clip. However, *narrated presentations* can be useful when some people cannot attend your live talk. Chapter 21 describes how to produce such an audio-oriented presentation.

EXERCISES

Exercise 19-1. Critique the following presentation outline, which is based on a Lotus Freelance SmartMaster for the presentation category "Project Status Report."

Assumptions
- The audience is familiar with the project.
- The audience is busy and distracted.
- The audience includes decision makers who tend to fire questions throughout and like to have a substantial "working discussion."

**Title: Jam-Free High-Brightness Multipurpose Paper: Project Status
March 15, 2000**

Agenda
- Review project background, objectives, and benefits
- Team changes
- Project constraints
- Current status
  - Schedule
  - Action items
  - Budget status & forecast
- Going forward
  - Milestones, risks, opportunities
  - Next steps

Project overview: Brief description of project
- Started Oct. 1999
- Pressures to match competition
- High priority
- Limited budget due to corporate R&D cuts
- Several technological challenges related to coating, filler, sizing, and base sheet structure

Exercise 19-1: Project Status Report *(continued)*

Objectives of project
- Fill obvious gap in product line
- Exploit significant market opportunity

Benefits of the project
- Higher margin than single-use papers if production costs can be kept low
- Large, growing market of convenience users
- Our unique technological strengths will allow us to surpass competition in this area

Team (organization chart)
- One new member, to tackle filler issues that have emerged
- Lost key member in coating; need assistance in filling gap

Constraints
- Final product must be priced < $x/ton
- Development costs must be < $1 million
- Paper must pass acceptance criteria for all uses (laser, copier, inkjet)

CURRENT STATUS (section title slide with clip art)
Current status: Schedule
- Generally on schedule; ahead in base sheet issues
- Exception: 2-3 weeks behind on coating issues due to loss of key team member

Current status: Technical issues
- Performance for laser acceptable on all criteria
- Performance for copier: need 10% improvement in jamming
- Performance on inkjet: dot density 15% lower than acceptable limit
- Brightness: 2 points below target
- Estimated product cost: $45/ton higher than target

Current status: Action items
- Assign new team member to solve coating issues; may require new hire
- Test three promising new coating formulas to improve jamming and brightness
- Test sizing change to improve dot density on inkjet
- Explore lower-cost filler; expected to improve brightness as well

Current status: Budget status
- 60% of budget used — on target
- Details

Exercise 19-1: Project Status Report *(continued)*

Current status: Budget forecast
- Details if results as expected
- If performance and product-cost targets not reached with next changes in coating, sizing and filler, extra 6 months of development may be required, at estimated cost of $300,000

GOING FORWARD (section title slide with clip art)
Milestones and Completion Dates
- Assign or hire coating expert and bring into project - March 30
- Lab and pilot tests on new coating formulations - May 1
- Test sizing formula and lower-cost filler - June 1
- Mill trials of top choices of coating, size, and filler - August 1

Risks
- With competition heating up in this market, there is price pressure on specialty coating suppliers
- Pilot plant has been experiencing scheduling problems — delays in that phase possible; alternative pilot facility may have to be explored

Opportunities
- Coating formula Y, though not successful for copier, gave superior brightness and dot density for inkjet and should be pursued in separate project
- Base sheet as last modified performed exceptionally in laser printer and may be good choice for low-cost single-purpose paper

Next steps
- Bring team up to full strength
- Run scheduled trials and present results by June 10

Summary
- Project close to technical targets
- If remaining performance gaps can be closed with next trials, budget and schedule will be on target
- Risks inherent in complex project: overruns of cost and time if technical issues not resolved
- Need to decide how much to commit if targets not reached; large opportunity at stake

Exercise 19-2. Critique the following outline, which is based on a Lotus Freelance SmartMaster for the presentation category "Project Proposal."

Assumptions

- You are addressing the management team of a large training organization.
- You are proposing a major push into Distance Learning.
- The company is basically conservative.
- There has been a history of failures with investments in new technology, such as multimedia training courses on CD-ROM.
- Senior managers are neither keen on the Internet nor comfortable with it.

Title Slide: Expanding Into Distance Learning, Madeleine Lajeune, March 2, 2000

Agenda

- Objectives and background of project
- Key issues to address
- Proposal overview
- Benefits and risks
- Alternatives
- Scope and deliverables; milestones
- Project team
- Cost/benefit
- Additional considerations and next steps

Proposal Objectives

- Help company become a leader in this new market and training technology
- Increase customer base
- Reach new market segments

Background

- Definition of Distance Learning; growing trend
- Potential for high profit margins if well done
- Major competitors moving in

Key Issues

- Establish strong presence on the web; make program highly visible and high quality
- Keep technology risks low; avoid uncontrolled "scope crawl" through clear goals and plan

Exercise 19-2: Project Proposal *(continued)*

Proposal Overview

- Select key courses suitable for Distance Learning
- Develop a powerful interactive web site to deliver such training
- Do it quickly to avoid being left behind by competitors
- Make programs high-quality and glitch-free to attract and retain customers

Benefits

- Costs are low for customers; also for us after initial investment in technology
- Attract customers we would not reach otherwise, because of greater convenience

Risks

- Technology "seductive" — must avoid using features just because they are available
- Complex development prone to delays (must use experienced personnel)
- Failure possible if appropriate expertise not used

Possible Alternatives

- Do nothing — forgo market opportunity
- Scale down to inexpensive "expanded web page" approach; don't match competitors
- Step up more traditional "multimedia" — e.g., video courses with e-mail access to instructors

Project Scope

- Begin with four key courses identified as suitable for Distance Learning/Internet delivery
- All development in-house
- External web hosting, using our own dedicated web server and software for maximum control

Deliverables

- Redesigned courses for web presentation
- Redesigned/upgraded web site
- Negotiated agreements with selected web host
- Dedicated web server and software ready to go to web host

Project Milestones: Tasks & Completion Date

- Redesign selected four courses; redesign web site: June 1, 2000
- Select web host; test redesigned web site: June 15, 2000
- Marketing studies: June 1, 2000
- Server and software tested and ready to go to web host: Sept. 1, 2000
- Full-scale site development; start advertising and promotion: Sept. 1, 2000

Exercise 19-2, *continued* **(Project Proposal)**

Project Team
- Much of the expertise available in-house (organization chart)
- Hire four people with strong web-site design, training software and Internet marketing experience

Cost/Benefit Analysis
- Costs: web site development; hosting; software; hardware (dedicated server); personnel
- Projected market share and revenues: charts
- Projected spillover increase in share of traditional training programs (based on experience of other companies)
- Side benefit: improvement in traditional training programs resulting from redesign of key courses

Additional Considerations
- Speed is of the essence: latecomers will have a hard time being visible
- "Incremental development" ("baby interactive web site") is unrealistic and dangerous from a marketing point of view: customers will perceive "poor quality"/amateurish programs and not return to web site
- Learn from our past technology failures rather than be defeated by them!

Summary
- Proposal in brief; benefits; costs; risks

Next Steps
- Decide; allocate funds; hire people and form team

Exercise 19-3. You are giving a presentation to potential recruits at a top-notch college or university. Evaluate the usefulness of the following two general outline schemes and develop an outline that would be more useful to your situation.

A. PowerPoint Auto Content Wizard for "Company Overview"

> **Title Slide:** Company Name, "Company Overview," Author
>
> Executive Office
> Finance
> Sales/Marketing
> Legal
> Computer Services
> Human Resources
> Operations
> Research / Development

B. Lotus Freelance Smart Master for "Corporate Overview"

Title Slide: Company Name, "Company Overview," Author

Agenda
Company Overview
Business Definition
Product Line Description
Competitive Advantage
Significant Events
Financial Performance
Additional Performance Measures
Stock Price Performance
Segment Overview
Segment Structure
Segment Definition
Sales by Segment
Profitability by Segment
Outlook by Segment
Industry Overview
Industry Landscape
Industry Size and Growth
Industry Trends
Impact of Industry Trends
Competitor Landscape
Market Share
Strengths and Weaknesses
Summary and Outlook
Corporate Outlook
Recommendations

Exercise 19-4. Analyze the usefulness of the following outline for "Company Meeting," which was generated by PowerPoint's Auto Content Wizard. Change the outline to fit the needs of the situation.

Assumptions
• You are a mill manager addressing employees at the yearly meeting.
• Competition and markets are tough.
• Downsizing is overloading employees and making them fearful and resentful; morale is low.
• The company needs technological breakthroughs and 10% gains in productivity to get out of profit/stock decline and avoid further layoffs.

Exercise 19-4: Company Meeting *(continued)*

Title Slide: Theme, Author, Date

Agenda

Review of Key Objectives and Critical Success Factors
- What makes company unique
- What makes company successful
- Shared vision
- Review key undertakings of past year

How Did We Do?
- Brief overview of performance against each objective

Organizational Overview
- Introduction and broad goals of each organization
- Any changes
- Organization chart might be effective here

Top Issues Facing Company
- Address any high-profile issues

Review of Prior Goals
- Financial
- Competitive
- Progress

Progress Against Goals
- Summary of key financial results
- Revenue
- Profit
- Key spending areas
- Headcount

Revenue and Profit
- Forecast vs. actual
- Gross Margin
- Important trends
- Compare company to rest of market
- Use multiple slides to break out meaningful detail

Exercise 19-4: Company Meeting *(continued)*

Key Spending Areas
- R&D
- Sales and Marketing
- General and Administration
- Areas of improvement
- Areas needing attention/caution

Headcount
- Goals
- Results

Goals for Next Period
- Strategic undertakings
- Financial goals
- Other key efforts

Summary
- Summarize key successes/challenges
- Reiterate key goals
- Thanks

Exercise 19-5. Find clip art expressing concepts of interest to you for your presentations, then *customize* it by deleting, adding, or changing parts and adding words as needed.

Exercise 19-6. Select some charts you have previously produced and optimize them, using the principles discussed in this chapter. If you have no suitable old charts, make up new ones, using default options for line, bar, or pie charts.

Chapter 20

Practicing and Delivering Slide Shows

Many presenters (including, in our experience, technically savvy engineers!) seem to have trouble just finding the power switch on an overhead projector, let alone the focus knob. The new multimedia-generation technology is many times more complex and troublesome than that old projector, so don't just show up and hope for the best. Instead, minimize risks with an intelligent *four-step approach:*

1. Practice everything that can be practiced with what's available to you during rehearsal.
2. Set up and check the equipment and the room, including lighting.
3. Troubleshoot common problems quickly. (You learn that as part of step 1, practice!)
4. Be prepared with low-tech backup — and set yourself a time limit for switching to it if problems cannot be fixed quickly.

THE RADICAL APPROACH TO PRACTICING

It's amazing how many things can be practiced without an LCD projector, but few presenters seem to take advantage of that fact. They just run through their slides a few times on the computer, doing no more than advancing from one to the next, and then sweat out a truckload of problems at delivery time. Let's see how you can do it differently.

Tip

The more complex your equipment and the software options you are using, the more important it is to *test and practice* and *take low-tech backup.*

Of course, if you have access to the equipment you'll be using during delivery, then by all means test and practice thoroughly on that equipment. For now, though, we'll assume that you have no access to a projector, or only to a projector that may be quite different from what you'll face at delivery.

Here are some important things you can practice in these circumstances:

- Changing slides from the keyboard and with the remote control (if you have a remote that controls your computer rather than the projector)
- Pointing to slide elements with the software's pointer or arrow tool, either from the computer or with the remote control
- Annotating or drawing on slides with the software's pen or annotation tool, either from the computer or with the remote
- Activating or skipping hidden slides or embedded presentations
- Jumping directly to a specific slide
- Exiting from an embedded presentation (or a series of hidden slides) before its last slide
- Activating embedded video or audio
- Turning the screen blank or black
- Returning the screen to normal slide show mode from a blank or black slide
- Recording notes or action items on the computer during the slide show
- Recovering from mistakes, such as prematurely exiting via ESC
- Activating the video out port on your laptop computer in case your computer does not automatically enable that port if a projector is connected to it
- Identifying all relevant ports on your laptop, such as the video out (VGA), audio out, PS/2 mouse, and USB port
- Connecting appropriate cables to those ports
- Changing the video resolution on your computer to a lower one in case this is needed for compatibility with the projector, and changing it back to its original setting

---

A Lesson in Resolution Matching

Some years ago, somebody came to our office to demonstrate the newest, brightest, sharpest LCD projector. At the end, we brought out an old VGA 640×480 laptop and asked the expert if he thought we could set it to output SVGA 800×600 video to the projector (the manufacturer had once told us we probably couldn't). The sales rep's answer was yes: he'd done just that with the laptop he was using. So we made the change — and our laptop promptly refused to boot Windows, complaining about an error in its video system. By the time we had laboriously reset our Windows video resolution from DOS, the sales rep had packed up and left, forgetting a few cables in his hurry to get away.

What are the lessons? One, *resolution mismatch is a major headache*. Two, unless you have lots of time for testing and fixing, *don't even think about raising the resolution of your laptop*. (If we'd tried to make this change five minutes before a presentation, there would have been no electronic slides, because we couldn't even get into Windows.) Three, *be ready for anything*. For instance, our rep told us that the bulb used in that projector "technically never dies"; it only deteriorates in quality. Well, only the day before, an associate of ours had such a bulb dying at the beginning of his university seminar — and no one had a spare bulb (not surprising, at $175 per bulb). So, be ready, be early — and make sure you have ***backup transparencies!***

A SAMPLE PRACTICE SESSION WITHOUT PROJECTOR

Let's run through a quick practice session that allows you to check your slide show thoroughly while also teaching you some hardware and troubleshooting skills. This includes steps (such as simulated mistakes and recovery) that add to your presentation time, so it's not useful for checking your timing. Rehearse your presentation properly first, then add this practice session to become familiar with most aspects of a slide show.

Practicing Setup

We'll assume for this that you located a small conference room for this practice session. If it's just your office, then certain steps, such as setting up the screen and determining the proper position for the projector, are not applicable — you'll have to learn them theoretically (or practice them separately another time) and execute them smoothly at delivery time.

1. ***Set up the projection screen,*** or lower it from the ceiling (usually with an electric switch). See Chapter 14 for common room layouts and screen positions.

2. ***Determine the best position for the projector.*** Here are some considerations:

   - How big is the screen: 5' × 5'? 6' × 6'? 7' × 7'? 8' × 8'? Or even bigger?
   - How much of that screen would you like to fill, ideally? That's your target image size.
   - Projectors differ in the size of the image they throw at a given distance; also, most let you adjust the size somewhat with a zoom control. However, the following table gives a rough idea of the *range* of image sizes you can expect.

Distance to Screen (Feet)	Image Width (Feet)	Image Height (Feet)
5	2 – 3	1.5 – 2.5
8	3 – 5	2.5 – 4
12	4 – 8	3.5 – 6
16	6 – 10	5 – 8
20	8 – 13	6 – 9.5
30	11 – 20	9 – 15

   - Suppose you want an 8' × 8' image. Can you find a spot for the projector table that is 12 – 16 feet away from the screen? If you can't, what will you do? Set up the projector closer to the screen and live with a smaller image? Or move the projector table inside the U of a U-shaped room, as in this scheme:

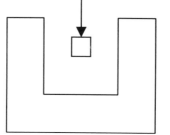

The latter choice will restrict your mobility drastically. Can you live with that, or is it better to accept a smaller image size?

- In an arrangement where you have just one large combined "boardroom" table, the projector may have to sit toward the middle of that table:

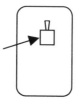

In a very small setup, you may even have a table-top screen set up at the head of the table, and the projector set up in the middle of the table.

3. **Determine the best place for your computer and other equipment, such as a VCR.** A VCR can be stored on the floor or a low shelf of a projector table — but that's not a good choice for your laptop! Even if you are using a remote control, you need easy access to your laptop in case you must give commands that are possible only from the keyboard (such as "show hidden slide" or "go to slide #x").

4. **Connect your laptop to the projector.** You can't do this fully, since you don't have a projector, but you can practice the computer end of it. First, locate the VGA (or video out) port on your laptop. It looks like this:

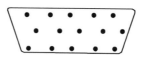

If you have a VGA cable (and we suggest you buy one — it beats hoping the projector awaiting you will have one!), connect it to that port. The other end will be connected to the projector (more on that later). Both connectors on the VGA cable should look something like this, with three rows of five pins to match the VGA port on the computer:

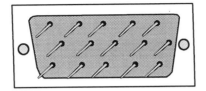

5. *Connect (imaginary) projector, other equipment, and computer to power.* Use an extension cord and power strip (items you should own and bring to the presentation) to do this. If power cables end up where people, including you, may be walking around, tape the cables down with duct tape to avoid accidents.

6. *Power up all the equipment in the proper order.* This means powering up the imaginary projector first, then all other equipment, with the computer being last.

Useful Items To Bring to High-Tech Presentations

Here are some useful things to keep ready in a bag for your next high-tech presentation:

- Power strip and extension cord
- VGA cable
- Standard RCA video and audio cable
- Audio cable with stereo mini plugs
- USB cable
- Remote control for your computer (if you present often)
- Duct tape, masking tape, and cellophane tape
- Scissors

Practicing Troubleshooting Image and Sound Problems

Many image and sound problems are in fact *computer* problems, which you can learn to solve without access to a projector. Here are such items (others that must be solved by adjusting the projector are discussed later).

1. No slide image is projected. SOLUTION: *Activate the computer's video out (VGA) port.* Pretend the projector's startup screen displayed, but your slides did not. This may be caused by no signal going to the computer's external video out port. (Some computers send a signal automatically if a projector or monitor is connected; others don't.) Unfortunately, each computer tends to have a different code combination for activating this port, so you really need your hardware manual (or on-disk documentation) to find the correct key combination.

If you don't have that documentation handy, study your laptop's function keys. Does one of them bear the following symbol?

If so, try pressing the Fn key (between the CTRL and ALT keys) and at the same time the key with this symbol. For instance, one of our laptops has the F5 key marked with this symbol, and pressing Fn + F5 indeed brings up a small menu for choosing among LCD, CRT, and TV. In other cases, there may be no menu, but you just cycle through the two or three video options when you press the correct keys.

Other possible key combinations include (among many others) Fn + F4, CTRL + ALT + <, CTRL + ALT + F10, Fn + F3, Fn + F7, Fn + END, and CTRL + ALT + END. As you can see, there are enough of those to make on-the-spot trial-and error troubleshooting a hopeless game! This is exactly why you should practice these aspects *now,* when you have the time to look up your documentation or do a little intelligent experimentation.

Once you've found the correct activation code, ***write it on a label and stick it to the bottom of your laptop.*** You may need that information at delivery time — soon or in the distant future!

2. *Only part of your slide is displayed, or text is distorted.* SOLUTION: ***Adjust your computer's screen resolution*** to match that of the projector. Pretend that the projector's startup screen was displayed fully, in proper size, and without distortion, which fingers resolution mismatch as the most likely source of the problem. Laptop resolutions tend to be at least one step ahead of middle-of-the-road projectors (the kind usually provided for you). Therefore, to project properly, bring your computer's resolution down to the projector's level.

The easiest and quickest way to do this is to right-click on an empty area of the Windows main screen, which pops up a short menu including Properties. Choosing this brings up a Display Properties menu. Click on its Settings tab, and you should see a screen as in Figure 20-1. To lower the screen resolution, you move the slider to the left and click the "OK" button.

3. *The image is noisy or streaked.* SOLUTION: ***Deactivate the screen saver on your laptop.*** There are also various projector adjustments that may solve this problem, but screen savers are a common source of trouble. To turn the screen saver off, follow the same procedure as for changing the screen resolution, but instead of choosing the *Settings* tab in the *Display Properties* menu, pick the *Screen Saver* tab and choose "None."

4. *The screen suddenly turns blank after a few minutes of showing the same slide, or a promotional logo for the projector pops up.* SOLUTION: ***Turn off power saving mode in the computer's power management program.*** This is usually a special program provided by the computer manufacturer and not part of Windows.

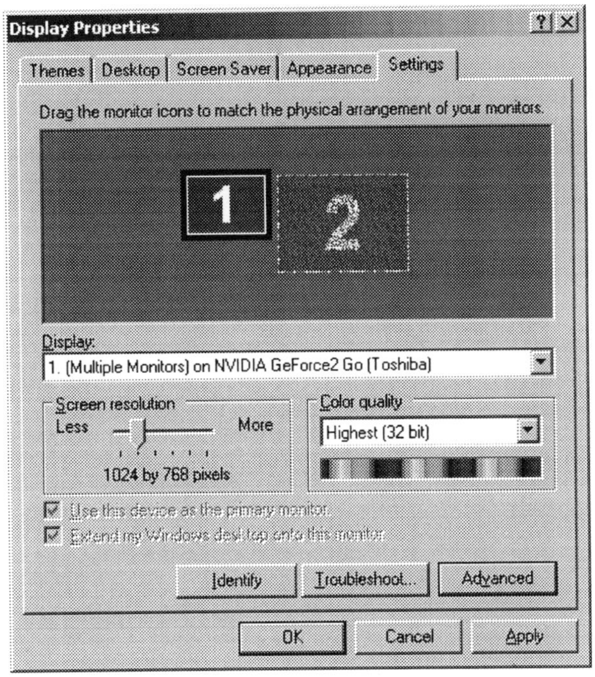

Figure 20-1. The Windows *Display Properties* menu, which lets you adjust screen resolution and color settings (shown here) as well as turn off the screen saver.

The problem occurs most frequently when presenters choose to run their laptop on battery rather than AC power. In battery mode, most laptops are by default set to go into "sleep" mode after a few minutes of inactivity. Running the laptop on AC usually avoids the problem, because sleep mode is invoked much later — say, after 30 minutes. Still, even in this case, you would be wise to check your settings and adjust them to higher values for any upcoming presentation.

If you must run on battery, learn how to choose "presentation mode" or some other power mode that does not send your computer to sleep periodically. Again — it's much better to do this *now* rather than after a few embarrassing moments during your presentation!

To find the power management program, let your mouse hover over the items on the Windows Task Bar at the bottom of the screen (or wherever you chose to place it). When you find something telling you about Power, *right-click* it, then open the program mentioned. A screen similar to the one in Figure 20-2 should open.

In the example, clicking on the "Details" button for the highlighted "Full Power" option under the "Plugged In" section brings up a further menu that lets you adjust the settings for that mode, as shown in Figure 20-3. You can do the same for any of the modes in the "Running on batteries" section.

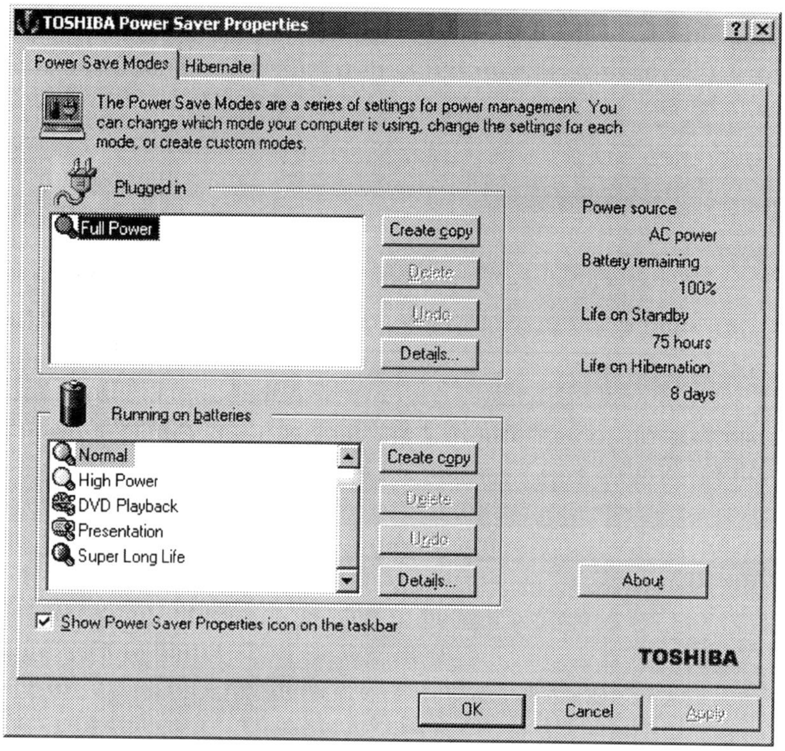

Figure 20-2. Typical power management menu that allows you to choose different power modes. If you have to run the laptop on battery power, for instance, choose "Presentation," which prevents screen blanking.

5. The sound does not work, or the volume is too low. SOLUTION: *Adjust the sound on the computer and then on the projector.* Projector adjustments will be discussed later, but you can practice the three computer-related steps:

    a. Uncheck the *Mute* box in the software sound control, if necessary.

    b. Set the software-level volume control toward high.

    c. If your laptop has a hardware volume control, set it, too, toward high.

Practicing Slide Show Control

Almost every software aspect of an electronic slide show can of course be practiced on the computer, without a projector. The only qualification relates to the issue of *keyboard control vs. remote control.*

    Hopefully, you'll have access to a remote control at delivery time. If so, but you don't know what kind of remote it will be, the safest assumption is that it will offer no more than a way to advance to the next slide. Be prepared to do everything else (blank the screen, annotate slides, jump to a specific slide, show a hidden slide or embedded presentation, etc.) from the computer.

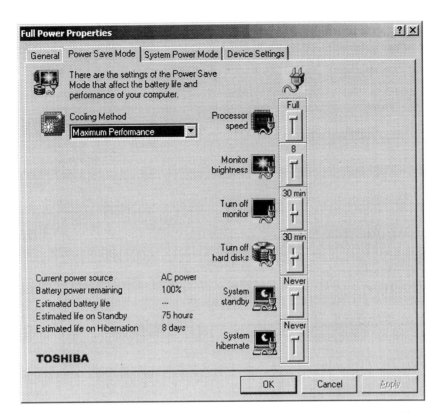

Figure 20-3. Clicking the "Details" button on any of the power modes in Figure 20-2 brings up a menu such as this one, which lets you set longer times before monitor and hard disk shut down after inactivity. Even if you run the computer on AC, you should check these settings and choose safe ones. (The default settings here, 30 minutes, should be safe even for a long presentation.)

Let's look at some common slide show tasks and see how best to practice them. To begin with, Table 20-1 shows a typical example (PowerPoint) of keyboard controls during a slide show. *Make sure that you know the corresponding commands (insofar as they exist) in your presentation program, and practice them.*

Navigating through the slides. ENTER and BACKSPACE are the most common commands for "go to next slide" and "return to previous slide." If you are using a remote control, there may be just one button for advancing to the next slide, two buttons for "forward" and "backward," or a left and a right mouse button. In the last case, you can customize PowerPoint, for example, to use the right mouse button for returning to the previous slide (see the box below).

Other common keys for "forward" that may function in your software are the right and down arrow keys and the space bar. Similarly, to move backward, the left or up arrow key may work. Make sure you know the proper keys in your software and practice to use them smoothly even with the lights halfway dimmed.

TABLE 20-1. Some PowerPoint Commands You Can Use While Running a Slide Show in Full-Screen Mode

Desired Action	**Command**
Next slide	ENTER or left mouse click
Previous slide	BACKSPACE (or right mouse click, if "popup menu on right mouse click" has been disabled)
Go to slide <number>	<number>+ENTER
Black screen, or undo black screen	B
White screen, or undo white screen	W
End a slide show	ESC
Exit from embedded presentation to main presentation	ESC
Erase on-screen annotations	E
Go to next hidden slide	H
Change pointer to pen	CTRL+P
Change pen to pointer	CTRL+A
Show the shortcut menu	SHIFT+F10 (or right-click)
Help: Show a list of controls	**F1**

You also need to know how to go to a *specific slide.* For instance, if you want to review a slide during Q&A, it's nice to be able to go to that slide directly rather than reverse through the whole show. Similarly, if you accidentally exit from the show in the middle by pressing the ESC key, you'll save a lot of time if you can go directly back to the current slide after restarting the screen show.

In PowerPoint, the command for going to slide number n is to enter the number n *and then press ENTER.* It's important to remember the "ENTER" part, because most other commands don't require it. Again, make sure you know what the proper command in your software is and practice it a few times.

Using hidden slides. As discussed in Chapter 19, not all programs allow hidden slides or embedded presentations for optional branches. In PowerPoint, hidden slides are skipped unless you type the command H before the first hidden slide.

Letting the Remote Control's Right Mouse Button
Return the Show to the Previous Slide

If the projector has a remote control with left and right mouse button, you may be able to use the right mouse button to return to the previous slide. To do this in PowerPoint, you need to reconfigure the program slightly to disable popup menus from appearing on a right mouse click during a slide show. In our version, this meant choosing Options from the Tools menu, clicking on the View tab, and de-selecting the option "Popup Menu on Right Mouse Click" in the Slide Show section. In a slide show, a left mouse click then advances you to the next slide, and a right click returns you to the previous slide.

Unfortunately, the disabled popup menu is rather important. To make it easily accessible, one needs to specify on the same menu to "show popup menu button," which one can click with the mouse pointer. Otherwise, the only way to access the menu (which includes the handy "Meeting Minder" for writing notes, minutes, and action items) would be to press SHIFT + F10 — a hard-to-remember combination not even mentioned in PowerPoint's slide show help menu (activated via F1).

Lots of problems and confusing questions can arise with hidden slides.

1. You may forget exactly where you have hidden them, so finding them becomes a guessing game unless you exit the screen show and find them in slide or slide sorter view. If you are using several hidden slides, perhaps in several locations, print out a thumbnail view of your entire slide show and keep it ready for trouble-shooting, right with your notes.
2. You have shown the first hidden slide by typing H. What happens if you press ENTER to go forward? Answer: you'll see the next slide in your show — no matter whether it is normal or hidden.
3. You may show one of a series of hidden slides and then want to skip the rest to return to the normal slide show — but pressing ENTER only gets you the next hidden slide. Really, you want a command for "show next non-hidden slide," but there is no such command in PowerPoint. Instead, you must type the number of the non-hidden slide you want, + ENTER.
4. You have shown a series of eight hidden slides, then the next normal slide — but now someone wants to see the previous "normal" slide again. Will BACKSPACE get you there directly, or will it go through all the hidden slides? The answer (which may of course change with each software version) is: BACKSPACE will go through all the hidden slides that you have shown. Therefore, to go directly to the previous "normal" slide, you would have to type its number + ENTER.
5. You want to show a hidden slide directly during Q&A. Can you just type its number to display it? Yes — in PowerPoint, this works.

Using Embedded Presentations. To activate an embedded presentation, click on its icon or placeholder on the slide. (If the remote control doesn't have a pointing device, you'll need to do this from the keyboard.) In PowerPoint, to *exit* from an embedded presentation before reaching its last slide, *press ESC.* This gets you back to the main show.

Activating Video Clips and Other Embedded Objects. As with embedded presentations, click on the placeholder on the slide. This will start the video, open your word processing program with a specific document in its main window, etc. Each embedded application tends to have its own way of controlling what you display and also of exiting to your main show. *Make sure you know how to exit properly, and practice it.*

Activating the Popup Menu for Changing Pointer/Pen Options, Opening the Meeting Minder, Etc. In PowerPoint, click on the menu button in the lower left screen corner. If the button is not visible, move the mouse; this should make the button appear. *Check what the procedures are in your software, and practice them thoroughly, both with the keyboard and, if you have it available, a remote control.*

Pointing to Objects on the Screen. Choose the pointer/arrow rather than the pen, by pressing CTRL + P in PowerPoint. Then move the pointer where you want it with the mouse.

Annotating the Screen with the Software's "Pen." In PowerPoint, CTRL + P switches from a pointer/arrow to a pen. You can change the color of the pen from the popup menu. To draw, hold down the left mouse button while moving the mouse. *To erase drawings, type E.*

Recording Speaker Notes, Meeting Minutes, Or Action Items. In PowerPoint, use the Meeting Minder for any of these tasks. See above, "Activating the popup menu...," to learn how to open the Meeting Minder. A small window pops up that lets you type your notes (which get attached to the active slide), minutes, or action items. Action items in PowerPoint are conveniently grouped at the end of the slide show so you can print them out easily or transfer them to a word processing document and e-mail to participants after the presentation.

Getting Help. In PowerPoint, pressing F1 during a slide show displays a help screen of keyboard commands for slide shows. It may not be the most elegant way of controlling the show, but it beats going madly through 20 slides, for instance, to find what you want.

Displaying a Black Or White Screen. In PowerPoint, type B for a black screen, W for a white screen. To return to a normal screen,, type B or W again, or just ENTER. *Make sure you know the corresponding commands in your program, and practice them.*

PRACTICING WITH A PROJECTOR

Now let's assume you have access to a projector for rehearsal. In that case, there are some additional things you can practice. Above all, you can become comfortable with "working the room" and interacting with the projected image. Also, if the projector comes with a remote control, you can practice using it efficiently.

First, let's consider the case where you can practice on the *same projector* you'll be using for delivery. In that case, you can *test and adjust* all the things discussed in detail in the next section, "Delivering Your Electronic Slide Show." What's even better, you can take your time and do everything thoroughly, without the pressures of delivery.

In particular, check for **resolution mismatch** between your computer and the projector. (See the earlier discussion in this chapter for details.) If you need to adjust your computer to a lower resolution, then do it now and ***leave it adjusted*** for delivery.

Also, check whether the ***image is sharp and bright.*** If not, can you get a brighter projector? If none is available, how much do you need to darken the room to get good visibility? Can you live with that? If the equipment available to you gives you unacceptable color quality, brightness, or sharpness, go for high-quality color transparencies instead; they will be more helpful and classy than a dim, fuzzy slide show. But even if everything looks great, remember Murphy's Law and ***take backup slides!***

What if the projector is *not* the same you'll be using at delivery time? In that case, you won't be able to make time-saving adjustments now, or practice the exact tasks you'll be facing at delivery. However, many techniques are similar for most of the newer projectors, so you can develop valuable skills by practicing. That way, if you have to adjust things or troubleshoot at delivery, it will take you a fraction of the time it would if you had no practice.

DELIVERING YOUR ELECTRONIC PRESENTATION

At delivery time, you'll need to deal with three major tasks: (1) setting up quickly for optimal viewing and interaction, (2) troubleshooting, and (3) presenting the show without losing audience contact or getting overwhelmed by the technology. If you have practiced as described earlier in this chapter, you'll be surprised how quickly you can move through the first two tasks. And if things are set up properly and tested, you'll have a much easier time concentrating on the audience in the actual presentation.

Basic Setup

In many cases, others will have done the setup for you, and you only need to check that it meets your requirements and test that everything works. On the other hand, you may also have to do everything yourself. In the following discussion, we'll assume that this is the case; if it's not, be grateful for anything on the list that you don't have to do!

1. Set up the screen; if necessary, improvise a "tilt screen" for a distortion-free image without "keystone" effect. See Chapter 14 for an explanation of room and screen arrangements.

2. Determine the best position for the projector. See the earlier section "A Sample Practice Session Without Projector," subsection "Practicing Setup," for guidance on this. Unfortunately, for a big image, you often have to give up some mobility or comfort. If you have practiced this step, even theoretically, you'll get through it in no time; if you haven't, you'll be running around a lot with that projector, plugging and trying and moving and retrying!

3. Determine the best place for your computer and other equipment, such as a VCR. Again, you have already practiced that (see "A Sample Practice Session Without Projector," subsection "Practicing Setup").

4. Connect the projector to your laptop and to any other equipment. You practiced the *computer* end of this, namely, finding the VGA video out port on your computer and connecting the VGA cable to it. Now connect the other end of the VGA cable to the projector. Also connect RCA video and audio cables from any VCR or similar equipment to the RCA jacks on the projector. Some projectors do not allow any direct connection to equipment;, instead, everything is plugged into a *cable hub*, which is then connected to the projector with a special cable.

Ideally, the projector should arrive neatly with its case, complete with a lucid manual and a full set of cables. Invariably, though, someone has walked off with the projector manual, and someone else with half the cables, leaving it to your ingenuity to figure out the mysterious buttons and where to connect those missing cables. As we discussed earlier, one way to minimize cable trouble is to *bring the essential cables yourself.* This includes the VGA cable to connect computer and projector, RCA audio and video cables, and one or two cables with stereo mini plugs at both ends. Of course, if the projector needs a special cable hub that has gone missing, you can stop right there and switch to your backup transparencies!

5. Connect the projector, other equipment, and computer to power. As discussed, use an extension cord and power strip to do this, and tape down with duct tape any loose cables that might be in people's way.

6. Power up all the equipment in the proper order: projector first, then extra equipment, then the computer.

7. Make sure you've turned off your computer's screen saver to prevent transmission interruptions or unwanted side shows. As discussed, it's best to run the laptop on AC power to avoid periodic screen blanking. If you must run from battery, *switch off the computer's power management system.* (See the earlier section "A Sample Practice Session Without Projector," subsection "Practicing Setup" for details.)

Projector Setup

Here are the basic steps involved in getting most projectors set up and adjusted for your show.

1. Remove the lens cap. It's a simple step — but without it, you may be hunting for mysterious causes of a "no image" problem!

2. Raise the leg(s) on the projector and tilt it so it is at a 90° angle to the screen. This eliminates "keystone" distortion of the projected image (see the discussion of overhead projectors in Chapter 14), especially if you also improvised a tilt screen.

3. Check for a complete, distortion-free image. At this point, what is projected may be only the projector's startup screen, showing perhaps a logo or promotional message. If the image doesn't display completely, raise or lower the legs of the projector, or adjust the *zoom control* on the projector (often, a large ring around the projector lens) to make the image smaller. If the image is too small, turn the zoom control in the other direction to enlarge the image. *If the image remains too large or too small after adjusting with the zoom control, move the projector forward or back and start again with step 2.*

4. Adjust the focus to get a sharp image. Usually, this means turning the focus ring on the front of the lens.

5. Check if your computer screen is projected properly. If it is not, then go to the Troubleshooting section below.

Troubleshooting

If you are dealing with a newer projector and your computer is reasonably up to date but not hyper-powered, then chances are that at this point, you have an acceptable image — brightness, tint, and contrast may be all you have to fine-tune. If you are not so lucky, then this section offers some tips that may solve your problem.

Above all, have a general plan. The worst thing is for a presenter to fiddle around for ten minutes, keeping the audience waiting, and then rush through her talk in a red-hot sweat. Under those circumstances, nobody is going to be impressed by the electronic fireworks — much better to give up at the appointed starting time and switch to backup transparencies.

Here is a sample outline of such a plan. Adapt it to your own taste — and *follow it!*

- If the remote can only handle "next slide," do everything else from the computer.
- If the remote fails, control the show from the computer.
- If nothing works by presentation time, use the **backup transparencies** or handouts! (Transparencies are useless if all you have available is an LCD projector — so make sure you request a backup overhead projector!)

- If the program freezes, restart the computer and use the waiting time in a productive way, such as question and answer on the parts you have already presented.

Below are some common problems and steps that may solve them. As noted, many of these can be practiced before the presentation if you have access to a projector.

Several of the remedies discussed involve changing settings on the projector, using its *menu.* If there is no manual with the projector explaining details, look for a *Menu* button on its top or sides; then push it and see if a screen with obvious choices is displayed. To move around the menu, you need to push appropriate navigation buttons, which should be near the *Menu* button or on the remote control. Finally, to make choices, you may need to push a designated button, or something that functions like a left mouse button.

No image — not even the projector's startup screen. Remove the lens cap. Is power plugged in? Is the bulb securely in its socket? Is the power strip on? Is the projector switched on?

No image of your slides (but the projector's startup screen displays OK). Check all cable connections. Check for bent pins in the connector plugs. Choose the proper input source for the projector, if there is a choice (video vs. computer): to project slides, the source must be set to *computer.* Make sure your laptop's external video port is turned on (see the earlier section "A Sample Practice Session Without Projector," subsection "Practicing Setup"). Turn everything off and then on again in the proper order (computer last).

Incomplete image of your slides even after adjusting the projector image (e.g., the startup screen or video from a VCR) to proper size and focus. Adjust the horizontal and/or vertical position of the image with the projector's *Image* (or similar) menu or any appropriate manual controls. Adjust the computer's screen resolution to match the projector's (see the explanation in the earlier section "A Sample Practice Session Without Projector," subsection "Practicing Setup").

The "Bring a Spare Bulb" Myth

Not so many years ago, it might have made sense to bring a spare bulb for a standard overhead projector, in case there wasn't a live spare in the projector for on-the-spot switching. These days, with LCD projectors, bringing that bulb will probably not save the day even when you're dealing with your own projector.

Why? Because typically, you'll have to wait 15 – 30 minutes *to let the bulb cool down* before you can change it. By then, your presentation is probably over! So, instead of relying on spare bulbs and other dubious rescue schemes, switch to your *backup transparencies.* (What do you mean, you didn't bring any?)

Streaks in the image. From the projector's *Image* or other menu, try switching *Auto Image* off, then on again, as this may reset things properly. If it does not, try adjusting *sync* and *tracking* manually until you get a clear image. Check that you have deactivated the screen saver on your laptop.

Fuzzy image. Try cleaning the lens or adjusting the focus knob.

Image reversed from left to right or in some other way. Check if the projector has been set for *rear projection* or *ceiling projection.* If so, set it to normal mode.

Screen suddenly turning blank. Check if you have hit the *standby button* (push it again to see if the projector comes back to life). With many projectors, pushing this button blanks the screen for some minutes (which you can often adjust), after which time the lamp may turn off.

Screen turns blank or a promotional message for the projector pops up. Check if your laptop is running on battery, in power-saving mode. Either plug in the AC power supply or switch off the power-saving mode (see the earlier section "A Sample Practice Session Without Projector," subsection "Practicing Setup").

Display keeps changing between your slide and a message such as "perfecting the image." Check the projector's *Controls* or similar menu to see if "Plug and Play" is set to on. Setting it to off may solve this problem.

Lamp suddenly shuts off. There may have been a power surge. Switch the projector off, then on again.

No sound. Check your computer's sound settings for "mute" setting or low volume (see the earlier section "A Sample Practice Session Without Projector," subsection "Practicing Setup"). Adjust the projector's sound volume. Some projectors have sound buttons on the remote.

You suddenly forget the commands for controlling the screen show. In PowerPoint, the answer lies in your good friend, the F1 key, which pops up a help screen for slide-show controls.

Issues with Remote Controls

In the best of worlds, the projector comes with a remote control. Alternatively, you perhaps own a remote that controls your computer. The latter alternative has three great advantages: (1) it lets you make sure you can use remote control for your show, even if the projector lacks a remote; (2) it lets you practice with the exact accessory you'll be using at delivery time.

The minimum any remote control will offer you is a button to advance to the next slide. If that's all you find, then simply control everything else from the computer.

The most common additional features in a remote are a right mouse button, a trackball or similar pointing device, and special function keys, which may be programmable. Of these, you're most interested in the right mouse button and the pointing device. The function keys may allow you to switch between computer and video source and perhaps blank the screen by invoking the projector's standby mode. In higher-end models, there may also be buttons that you can figure out only after studying the documentation at great length — so if it's not your own remote, forget about those fancy extras.

If you have access before the presentation to a remote control with a pointing device, take the time to practice both choosing from menus and drawing annotations. Some models are quite difficult to control until you get used to them. Also, be aware that some *hide the left mouse button* in rather surprising places. For instance, our projector comes with a remote whose left mouse button is on the control's ***underside,*** arranged like a trigger. It took us quite some frustrating moments to figure this out.

Show Time!

With electronic slide shows, it is especially important to remember your presentation purpose, because it's so easy to get overwhelmed and lose perspective. That purpose is to make your message understood and accepted, not to dazzle the audience. You can achieve that even if there are glitches, as long as you stay connected to the audience and show some clear visuals for those points that need them.

Your most important tool for keeping connected is the *remote control,* which allows you to move freely. Many presenters make the mistake here of facing the screen for their entire talk while they punch buttons on their remote. Others stay in front, rigidly facing the infrared "eye" of the remote receiver, because they are afraid that otherwise the remote control won't work. In truth, the remote will work just as well if you aim it at the back of the receiver or even at an angle.

If you don't have a remote, you'll have to accept a somewhat clumsier delivery, since you have to return to the computer for each slide change or other operation. However, it's no clumsier than operating an overhead projector, and it still allows you to exploit most of the advanced features of electronic slide shows.

In every other respect, delivering electronic slide shows should follow the same sound principles we discussed in Part 2 of this book. Some things are so good, they just don't change!

EXERCISE AND DISCUSSION

Exercise 20-1. Build a slide show with transitions, hidden slides, an embedded presentation, and simple embedded video and audio clips (see Chapter 19 for guidance). Then practice delivering it, as described in this chapter. If you have access to an LCD projector, practice complete setup and troubleshooting; otherwise, practice only the slide show controls and the computer-related setup and troubleshooting, including changing the screen resolution and activating the external VGA video out port.

Discussion 20-1. Think back over electronic slide shows that you have observed. How common were technical and delivery problems? Of those problems, how many could have been avoided by practicing in the way described in this chapter, even if the presenter had no access to an LCD projector before the presentation?

21

Web Presentations and Web Meetings

In this age of the incredible shrinking budget, it seems certain that electronic meetings will take over, given the savings they promise over traditional meetings. Whether you like it or not, you need to get ready for this new form of communication.

WHAT IS AN E-MEETING?

An E-meeting is a conference held over the Internet or your organization's intranet. Unlike a video conference, it requires no expensive hardware and facilities or even software but only ordinary telephones and Internet or intranet access.

The on-line documentation for Microsoft's NetMeeting program (usually included in Windows) gives a flavor of what you can do, in principle:

- Share work and programs with meeting participants
- Work on documents simultaneously
- Send and receive files
- See and hear other people
- Exchange Chat messages with several people simultaneously (messages are displayed in the Chat window)
- Explain concepts on the Whiteboard, which can also be used to copy areas of your desktop

Tip

E-meetings can save time, money, and effort — and you may be able to try them without charge through an on-line meeting service. To find information, try keywords such as *e-meeting* or *on-line meeting service* on your Internet browser.

Unfortunately, this doesn't mean you can just pick up the phone, call a few people, and "meet" — although in time, it may involve not much more than that. For now, some or all of these features are most easily available to you through *on-line meeting room services* found on the Internet, such as WebEx, iMeet, PlaceWare, and Genesys Conferencing.

WHY MEET THIS WAY?

There is no doubt that electronic or virtual meetings, no matter how sophisticated, cannot match the power of face-to-face communication, especially when you need to persuade people or break down emotional barriers. It's good to remember that, and not act as if the new millennium had produced a new kind of human being. However, even when the subject matter or the people are difficult, you may often have to settle for an E-meeting because travel is impossible or too expensive.

Web-based E-meetings have a number of obvious advantages. First, you can hold a meeting on very short notice, since people do not have to travel to a common place. In today's fast-moving world, this is a great plus. Second, you can save yourself the work of faxing or e-mailing notes and presentation slides to 20 participants in a conference call. Third, you can collaborate directly with others during the meeting — for instance, everybody can add notes to a word processing document or annotate slides. Yet, all this can be cheaper and more flexible than videoconferencing, which is typically tied to elaborate company facilities.

GETTING STARTED

The best way to get experience in this area — if your organization is not already set up for it — is to try some of the *free services* and compare them. When connected to the Web, type in key words such as *web meeting service* and check the offerings. As of this writing, for instance, PlaceWare (my.placeware.com) offered a free trial, as did SneakerLabs iMeet (imeet.com). Typically, these free trials are limited in the number of participants and the features offered — for instance, only up to four people may be able to participate, and only the presenter can put documents on the screen; however, others are probably able to annotate, point, and type text, as well as send "chat" messages in parallel with the presentation. Once you find a service that appeals to you, you can scale up to more powerful versions as needed.

Remember that all these services are still developing: there is not much standardization, and new features are continuously added. However, for now they may prove more reliable and powerful than what you or your organization could put together.

The point is: this form of communication is here to stay, and grow. In the long term, you can expect it to become as easy and streamlined as ordinary Internet access is today. *Your* job is to become used to the idea of "showing" and "participating" electronically, on multiple windows appearing on the computer screen — and to compensate for the loss of personal contact by making your contributions as positive and enthusiastic as possible.

PRESENTATIONS, THE WEB, AND MULTIMEDIA

Integration of our work with the Web and with multimedia seems to be our inevitable lot in the future. Nowhere is this more obvious than in presentations. The more companies struggle to contain travel costs, the more they look to the Web for solutions. And to serve as an effective substitute for live talks, Web presentations will often need the help of sound, animation, and video.

Let's look at some of the tasks involved in managing such new-age presentations. As you will see, good software makes the basic stuff a breeze, but multimedia can still be a challenge.

Visiting the Web During a Presentation

Suppose you want your presentation to include an optional visit to our web site. This is a simple matter in PowerPoint: create a text box, then pick "Hyperlink" from the "Insert" menu, then type the Internet address — in our case, www.allaboutcommunication.com. When you click on this hyperlink during the presentation, your browser should start your Internet service program and then go to our web site. Done! (Need we say that you must be connected to a phone line?)

Saving a Presentation for Web Delivery

Unless you use an online meeting service that does the file conversions, you cannot just save your presentation and broadcast it over the Web — usually, you need to convert to Web format first. This is easy in most programs. Typically, you need to check under the *File* menu, which should offer such options as *Save as Web Page, Internet Publisher,* etc. Your software will save your Web presentation as a bunch of web pages and graphics files, grouped under a folder that has a name based on the name of the original presentation. (For instance, if your presentation was called *TechStrategy*, then the web presentation might be stored as a number of files in a folder called *TechStrategy_files.*)

To check how the finished Web presentation looks, start your browser (such as Internet Explorer) and try opening some file in this folder, such as *frame.htm, slide*n.*htm, master*n.*htm,* or *outline.htm.* This should display either the first or some subsequent slide of your show in a window that looks similar to the one in Figure 21-1.

If everything looks right, you are ready to upload the presentation to a web site or online meeting service. However, everything may not look right. For instance, embedded presentations you included may be inaccessible, slide transitions and animations may not show, and video clips may not play. This is where you need more advanced skills (see below).

Adding Animation, Transitions, and Video or Audio Clips

Text and graphics animation and slide transitions usually are set from a menu entitled *Slide Show, Presentation,* or *Format.* (We've discussed the general subject in detail in Chapter 19.) To insert a video clip or other multimedia file, you typically choose *Object* from the *Insert* menu, then specify your file and the activation options. (Again, see Chapter 19 for details.)

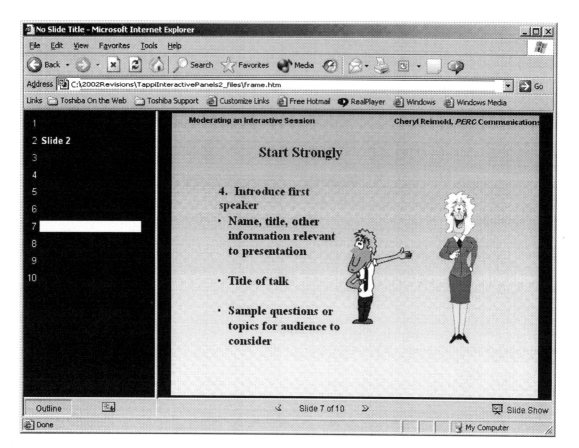

Figure 21-1. Typical look of a web presentation. To jump directly to different slides, click on the slide number in the outline on the left side; to move forward or back by one slide, click on the right or left arrow beneath the current slide. To run a full-screen slide show, click on the "Slide Show" button at bottom right.

In an ordinary live slide show, your animations, transitions, and video or audio clips should now work as intended. For instance, clicking on the link to a video clip will play the video. Not so in a Web presentation: if you use the default options in the *Save as Web Page* or *Publish to the Internet* menu, none of these features may work, or they may produce unexpected results!

The solution is threefold:

1. For a Web presentation, *keep things as simple as possible:*
   - Don't use embedded presentations — they may not play at all.
   - Use only basic transitions and animation schemes.
   - Consider dropping bullet animation altogether; it's of limited value in a Web presentation.
   - Don't overload pages with graphics.
2. Check the Help section under *Web* or *Publish a presentation to the Web* for up-to-date restrictions and solutions to problems.
3. Test your web presentation thoroughly before uploading it to a meeting service or web site.

Here are some tips that may save you time and trouble:

- If a graphic doesn't display, try grouping or ungrouping it; this often fixes the problem.
- If text bullets appear in the wrong sequence or all at once, you may have typed them with the text tool instead of using a bullet-list template in a predefined layout. Only bullets typed into a template will follow the overall bullet animation scheme you set for the slide show.
- If sound, video, or a graphic doesn't play or appear, check if you chose to "link" it to the presentation rather than save it as an integral part of it. Linked files are often not transferred to a web presentation and thus don't work.
- If you can expect your audience to have recent versions of Internet Explorer or other browsers, consider saving your web presentation as *web archive* file type rather than simple html. This puts all information conveniently into a single file with *.mht* extension rather than into lots of files grouped in a special folder.
- If animations don't work, check the options under the *Save as Web Page* or *Publish as Web Page* menu. You may have to enable an option to *show slide animations*. Also, you may have to specify *Internet Explorer 4 or later* (or an equivalent vintage of your browser) as target format. Earlier versions do not support animation.

Narrated Presentations

When you can't deliver a presentation in person, or key people can't attend, you might consider distributing a ***narrated electronic slide show.*** When people play the file as a slide show, they hear the narration you recorded with each slide. The show may advance either manually or automatically when the narration for the current slide is complete.

The Cost of Good Sound

Sound files can grow large very quickly, especially if you opt for good sound quality. Here are some examples.

- Low-quality 8-bit sound with cut-off at 11,000 kHz takes up **10 kb/sec., or about 10 MB for a 15-minute talk.**
- High-quality 8-bit sound with cut-off at 48,000 kHz takes up **46 kb/sec., or ca. 46 MB for a 15-minute talk**

Will people really download a presentation file of such a size? Perhaps yes, but it would have to be really important information.

    More than anything, what this illustrates is that progress in multimedia Web communication continues to depend on (1) fast, cheap *storage* and (2) fast, cheap means of *transmission.*

To produce a narrated show, first fix your slide show to your satisfaction, then record the narration:

- Plug a decent-quality microphone into the microphone port of your computer.
- From the *Slide Show* or other appropriate menu, select the *Record Narration* or equivalent command. This should allow you to test your microphone and adjust the sound level as well as the sound quality. (Remember, the higher the sound quality, the greater the storage requirements!)
- When you are satisfied with the settings, press *OK* or a similar option in the dialogue box. Typically, the program will switch to Slide Show mode and let you record your narration with each slide.
- To record narration for the next slide, change to that slide, then continue your narration.
- When finished, save the recording with the appropriate settings. ***Note that if you want to deliver the show over the Web, you must save the sound file with the show rather than as a "linked" file, or the sound will not play.***

You (or others) can of course also run the presentation without the narration by choosing that option under the *Set Up Show* submenu, of the *Slide Show* menu, or similar menus. Finally, you can turn off the timings by choosing "Click Manually."

EXERCISES

Exercise 21-1. Take a presentation you have prepared previously and turn it into a web presentation ready for uploading to a web site.

1. Make a copy of your presentation and save it under a new name.
2. Adjust all features, such as transitions, animations, and embedded presentations, so they fit the restrictions of web presentations as outlined in the Help section of your software.
3. Save your presentation as a web page or web archive. (Web archive produces a single file; web page produces many files under a common file folder based on the name of your presentation.) From "Publish" or other suitable commands, set the proper web options, such as "show animations."
4. Test the presentation by starting Internet Explorer or another browser, then opening an appropriate file to activate your presentation. View the presentation both in normal mode and in slide show mode.
5. Fix any parts that did not work, such as transitions or animations that did not display. Then resave and retest your presentation.

Exercise 21-2. Take the web presentation you prepared in Exercise 21-1 and add video clips (such as the ones that come with Windows, if you don't have your own) and audio clips to it. Make the audio clips yourself by using a microphone and suitable recording software, such as Sound Recorder (an accessory that is part of Windows). Test and troubleshoot the presentation.

APPENDIXES

Appendix A   Sample Annotated Presentation Structure 285

Appendix B   Procedure and Worksheet for Analyzing Audience and Purpose 287

Appendix C   General Presentation Outline Form 291

Appendix D   Specific Outlines for Common Presentation Types 293

Appendix E   Checklist for Presentations 305

Appendix A

Sample Annotated Presentation Structure

Rapport

Good afternoon. I'm delighted to have this chance to talk to you about something that has interested me greatly for a long time, and that I believe can make a big difference in anybody's career: namely, how to give a powerful, persuasive presentation.

*Introduction follows the **RAMP** formula*

Attention getter

Not too long ago, I *fell asleep* during a presentation one manager was giving. Unfortunately, I happened to be videotaping that presentation. I almost crashed to the floor with my camera. **[Briefly, some details]** Now, *why* did this happen? Because this manager committed *three deadly sins* — all in the same presentation: (1) he used a *weak start with a "pseudo message,"* (2) he overused *abstract ideas* without examples, and (3) his visuals were all boring *word charts and tables* with lots of numbers.

Main message

To give a powerful presentation, you need only avoid those three sins. This will turn even a "dry" or "technical" presentation into an exciting event. In the next fifteen minutes, I'll show you why and how you should do this.

Key point #1

Plan *(here simplified, because attention getter already mentioned all three key points)*

First, stay away from *weak starts*. Most presentations start lamely with a pseudo-message such as: *"This morning, I'd like to update you on the progress of the Super Chip project. First, I'll review our major objectives. Then, I'll discuss progress over the last six months. Finally, I'll outline the revised schedule and requirements."* Why do I say this is a pseudo message? Because it *says nothing* about the topic. It just *announces* it. You can't really agree or disagree with it—and you sure can't get excited about it. By contrast, a *real message* makes a proper statement about the subject. **[Example of real message]** After you hear a real message, you're not tempted to ask, "What *about* it?" as you are after a pseudo message. **[More examples of pseudo and real messages]**

Example

Explanation

Examples

Subpoint to key point #1

Why do so many speakers gravitate toward a weak start? There are two main reasons:

(1) They are exposed to plenty of *bad examples* in the workplace. It takes *courage* to be "different." **[Example of young engineer losing his nerve and abandoning a planned strong start—and never getting to give his main message at all]**

Example to back it up

285

Sample Annotated Presentation Structure, *Continued*

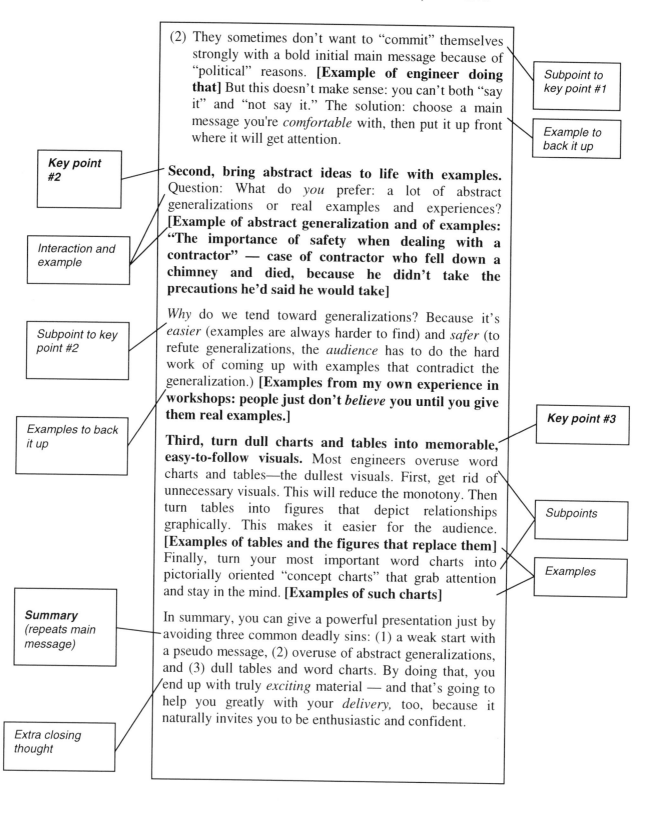

(2) They sometimes don't want to "commit" themselves strongly with a bold initial main message because of "political" reasons. **[Example of engineer doing that]** But this doesn't make sense: you can't both "say it" and "not say it." The solution: choose a main message you're *comfortable* with, then put it up front where it will get attention.

> Subpoint to key point #1

> Example to back it up

> *Key point #2*

Second, bring abstract ideas to life with examples. Question: What do *you* prefer: a lot of abstract generalizations or real examples and experiences? **[Example of abstract generalization and of examples: "The importance of safety when dealing with a contractor" — case of contractor who fell down a chimney and died, because he didn't take the precautions he'd said he would take]**

> Interaction and example

> Subpoint to key point #2

Why do we tend toward generalizations? Because it's *easier* (examples are always harder to find) and *safer* (to refute generalizations, the *audience* has to do the hard work of coming up with examples that contradict the generalization.) **[Examples from my own experience in workshops: people just don't *believe* you until you give them real examples.]**

> Examples to back it up

Third, turn dull charts and tables into memorable, easy-to-follow visuals. Most engineers overuse word charts and tables—the dullest visuals. First, get rid of unnecessary visuals. This will reduce the monotony. Then turn tables into figures that depict relationships graphically. This makes it easier for the audience. **[Examples of tables and the figures that replace them]** Finally, turn your most important word charts into pictorially oriented "concept charts" that grab attention and stay in the mind. **[Examples of such charts]**

> Key point #3

> Subpoints

> Examples

> *Summary* (repeats main message)

In summary, you can give a powerful presentation just by avoiding three common deadly sins: (1) a weak start with a pseudo message, (2) overuse of abstract generalizations, and (3) dull tables and word charts. By doing that, you end up with truly *exciting* material — and that's going to help you greatly with your *delivery*, too, because it naturally invites you to be enthusiastic and confident.

> Extra closing thought

Appendix B

Procedure and Worksheet for Analyzing Audience and Purpose

DEVELOPING MESSAGE AND KEY POINTS: GENERAL PROCEDURE

Here is an effective approach to developing your message and key points in an audience-focused way. It will not only give you high-quality material but also save you time by avoiding useless details.

1. Write down your presentation *purpose.*
2. Translate it into a tentative *main message.*
3. Write down *audience questions and objections.* Make them
   - *Tough and specific*
   - *Complete* (aim at 20 questions — don't give up before 10).
4. Revise your trial message to make it *persuasive,* given the audience questions.
5. Formulate 3-5 *key points* that answer audience questions and objections.
6. Decide on the basic presentation *format* (interactive vs. formal).

The following two-part form gives more detailed guidance on analyzing your audience and purpose.

AUDIENCE/PURPOSE ANALYSIS: WORKSHEET, PART 1

PURPOSE
What do I want to tell them?
What do I want them to DO as a result of this talk? • Immediately: • In the long term:
What do I want them to BELIEVE as a result of this talk?
What can I realistically achieve in this presentation? • What can they take in?   • What can they remember?   • What can best be clarified through discussion?
Other ways to achieve those things I can't do with the presentation: • Handout: • Follow-up memos/report: • Follow-up actions:

AUDIENCE/PURPOSE ANALYSIS: WORKSHEET, PART 2

AUDIENCE NEEDS AND QUESTIONS
Who are they? (List individuals/groups)
What do they want to know? (List all questions different people or groups might have.)
What do they hate or fear? Why might they not accept what I am saying? (List all objections and emotional comments.)
What do they like or need?
What benefits could outweigh objections?
What do they already know? • Things not to belabor: • Things to review briefly:
What's unfamiliar to them? What might they have trouble understanding? • Difficult details to skip: • Familiar concepts to use to explain unfamiliar ones:
Main message: **Three to five key points:**
Extra questions to prepare for:

Appendix C

General Presentation Outline Form

INTRODUCTION (__R__apport - __A__ttention - __M__essage - __P__lan):
Rapport Builder:

Attention Getter:

Main Message:

Presentation Plan (usually, preview of key points):

- -

BODY:
(Note: Repeat main message __somewhere__ — e.g., as transition between key points)

Key Point #1:

Backup/Examples/Explanations/Visuals etc.:

Key Point #2:

Backup/Examples/Explanations/Visuals etc.:

Key Point #3:

Backup/Examples/Explanations/Visuals etc.:

- -

SUMMARY:
Main message & key points restated:

Action close (related to what audience should DO), or final attention getter:

Appendix D

Specific Outlines for Common Presentation Types

GENERAL NOTES

- Use the structures presented here with caution — they are only broad suggestions.
- Consider your specific purpose and your audience — they may dictate a very different structure.

The best use of these common structures is as a completeness check for your own original outline based on your own audience analysis. However, if you are stuck for ideas, the suggested sections may spark some useful thoughts.

NOTES ON USING PREDEFINED PRESENTATION OUTLINES PROVIDED BY YOUR PRESENTATION SOFTWARE

Using model outlines provided by your presentation software, such as Microsoft PowerPoint (Auto Content Wizard) or Lotus Freelance (SmartMaster), has some value but also many dangers.

Advantages

- Usually produces a professional, consistent look.
- Gives you some starting ideas.
- Can save quite a bit of time if you do it right and use it flexibly.
- Can serve as a completeness check.

Disadvantages

- Encourages you to omit the essential step of audience and purpose analysis.
- If people know the models, they'll recognize your presentation immediately as "canned" and may tune out much of what you're saying, assuming that you didn't put much original thought into it.
- Fixing up the bad parts of the outline often takes longer than starting from scratch.

One solution is to take some of these outlines, adjust them to fit your needs, and then *save them as templates.* In the future, you can then use your templates rather than the original "Wizard" or "SmartMaster" models as your starting outline.

An example of this approach is the Basic Presentation Structure shown below, which uses the formatting of PowerPoint's "Generic Presentation" but imposes a new outline plus content advice. We saved this as a PowerPoint template which we will be happy to send you by e-mail.

1. BASIC PRESENTATION STRUCTURE

Introduction: R-A-M-P (Rapport – Attention getter – Main message – Plan)
Title Slide/Establish Rapport
- Title of your presentation
- Author
- Affiliation, how to contact, etc. (as appropriate)
- **Don't omit first step: R = Rapport.** Make real human contact; express pleasure at the opportunity to present to this audience.

Attention Getter
- Example or anecdote; relevant quote; interaction with audience; demo object; simple chart illustrating your main point; dramatization of the problem, opportunity, or main benefit; etc.

Message Preview
- State your main message in briefest form
- Make it a strong statement rather than a "pseudo message" (pseudo message = a promise that you'll say something later)
- Add preview of major benefits and other essential information (for a management audience, this may include costs)

Plan
- State the key points you'll be talking about
- Establish rules for Q&A

Body
Key Point 1
- Your point in **simple terms**, followed by no more detail than useful to the audience
- Supporting examples, visuals, and information
- How it relates to your audience
- Time-limited Q&A session on Key Point 1 if you choose intermittent Q&A

Key Point 2
- Your point in **simple terms**, followed by no more detail than useful to the audience
- Supporting information and examples
- How it relates to your audience
- Time-limited Q&A session on Key Point 2 if you choose intermittent Q&A

Key Point 3
- Your point in **simple terms**, followed by no more detail than useful to the audience
- Supporting information and examples
- How it relates to your audience
- Time-limited Q&A session on Key Point 3 if you choose intermittent Q&A

Summary
Main Message & Key Points Restated
- Add a strong statement that summarizes how you feel or think about this topic
- Summarize key points you want your audience to remember

Next Steps & Closing
- Summarize any actions required of your audience and of you
- Finish on a forward-looking thought or appropriate quote **[Caution: Keep it brief!]**
- Lead enthusiastically into question-and-answer

2. PRESENTATIONS AIMED AT PERSUADING OR MOTIVATING THE AUDIENCE

Follow the guidelines for Basic Presentation Structure (#1 above), unless one of the more specific outlines seems more useful.

3. OVERVIEW OF A SYSTEM, PROCESS, FIELD, AREA, ETC.

Introduction: R-A-M-P (Rapport – Attention getter – Main message – Plan)
Possible attention getter:
- Audience interaction (question)
- Demo object related to the field or area
- Interesting statistic related to the topic
- Personal incident illustrating your relation (or a change in your relation) to the field — leading over to an indication of the importance of the area to the audience

Possible main message (preview):
- What the audience can **gain** from learning about this area (e.g., apply some of the principles or tools of this area to their own work or personal life)
- What the audience should **do** or **understand** after or as a result of the presentation (e.g., interact differently with the system, have more realistic expectations, etc.)
- The most interesting, most challenging, or most promising aspect of this field or area

Body: Follow the Basic Presentation Structure (#1 above), with these cautions:

- Guard against **"complete coverage"** or excessive detail, especially if the audience is not actively involved in this area.
    - Cover only a few points; leave others to the question period.
    - Even on those points, go into detail only where you judge it to be of interest to this audience (e.g., an area that illustrates the greatest challenge, or the greatest potential for future development)
- Periodically return to the restricting theme set in your main message in order to keep the discussion interesting to the audience.

Summary: Follow the Basic Presentation Structure (#1 above).

4. EVALUATION OF ALTERNATIVE SOLUTIONS

Introduction: R-A-M-P (Rapport – Attention getter – Main message – Plan)
Possible attention getter:

- Recent incident or personal experience highlighting the problem/opportunity that called for the evaluation
- Interesting statistic related to the topic
- Relevant quote from a respected source
- Simplified chart illustrating the problem/solution
- Demo object
- Thought-provoking question
- Brief "what if" scenario that shows the importance of solving the problem or seizing the opportunity

Possible main message (preview):

- Main result of the evaluation and main benefits of the solution
- For a management audience, rough cost figure, set off by ROI or similar measure if appropriate
- What audience should **do** (e.g., implement the proposed solution, or make a choice among the alternatives on the basis of the evaluation)

Body
Background:

- Objectives of the evaluation
- What led to it
- Urgency of finding a solution

Criteria for evaluation:

- How to choose among alternatives
- Why those criteria were chosen *(be prepared for disagreement)*

Evaluation: Details of your analysis

- Description of alternative ideas
- Evaluation of each idea against the criteria

Conclusion/Recommendation:
- Outcome of your evaluation:
  - Solution or alternative to be adopted *or*
  - Ranking of alternatives, with choice left to audience or others
- Main benefits of the chosen or top-ranked alternative(s)
- Issues to be resolved before or during implementation

Summary
- Ideas to be evaluated
- Purpose of evaluation
- Main recommendations
- Next actions

Handout: Supporting data and attachments

5. TRIP SUMMARY
Introduction: R-A-M-P (Rapport – Attention getter – Main message – Plan)
Possible attention getter:
- Incident, simple chart, or demo object illustrating the reason for the trip
- Interesting statistic related to the purpose of the trip

Possible main message (preview):
- What the trip was all about and what came out of it
- In what way the trip result is important or useful to the audience
- What main follow-up actions you recommend

Body
What & Who:
- Who went where
- Who else was involved
- Use slide listing participants if there were more than three

Activities & Problems:
- What you did (avoid excessive details; put them in a handout or reserve them for Q&A)
- Planned work completed
- Other achievements
- Problems (such as planned work *not* completed) and their significance

Outcome:
- Results of the trip in more detail
- Suggested follow-up actions (in more detail than in the introduction)

Summary
- Main results of the trip and their significance
- Main recommendations
- Next actions

Handout: Supporting data and attachments

6. PROJECT UPDATE/PROGRESS REPORT

Introduction: R-A-M-P (Rapport – Attention getter – Main message – Plan)

Possible attention getter: Hand out deserved compliments (also serves purposes of rapport). *(Note: An attention getter for such an update presentation is often not appropriate unless something unusual has happened or you need to shake up the audience to re-commit to the project. The same holds true for regular team meetings.)*

Possible main message (preview): The shortest possible answer to any of the obvious audience questions about an ongoing project:

- Where do we stand, in general terms?
- Are we on schedule, or what is the final completion date?
- Are we on budget, or what is the new estimated cost?
- Are there any major technology, marketing, personnel, or other issues?
- Do we need to discuss changes in scope? Should we carry on as planned, scale down, scale up, or stop the project?

Body

Background: If audience needs the reminder, brief background on the project, its purpose, and how it fits in with other projects or the overall system

Progress: Achievements since the last update

Issues:
- Problems and delays
- Actions taken to correct problems
- Resulting changes in overall schedule or budget
- Reasons issues were not anticipated in initial project plan

Schedule/Future work: In more detail, work planned for the next step:
- Work being done now, but not completed
- Problems that will be solved
- Completion dates
- Date of next update

Costs:
- New estimates
- Explanations of deviations from earlier estimates
- Actions taken to correct or contain cost overruns

Summary
- General progress
- Major issues
- Main actions to be taken

Handout: Supporting data and attachments

7. PROJECT COMPLETION

Introduction: R-A-M-P (Rapport – Attention getter – Main message – Plan)
   Possible attention getter:
   - Incident or simple chart illustrating the original problem addressed by the project
   - Demo object illustrating the problem or the success of the project
   - Any standard attention getter illustrating the urgency of implementing the project recommendations

   Possible main message: brief overview of the project purpose, the main findings, and the outcome (major conclusions and recommendations)

Body
   Background:
   - Larger context of the project (where it fits in with other, higher-level projects)
   - More detailed explanation of purpose and scope, if necessary

   Project details:
   - How the project was tackled (only insofar as relevant to the audience — avoid excessive detail)
   - Guidelines established for the project
   - Results

   Outcome:
   - Conclusions (what the results mean)
   - Recommendations

   Implementation (if applicable):
   - Benefits and urgency
   - Issues to be resolved
   - Costs
   - Schedule

Summary
   - Review of project result and main recommendations
   - Next actions

Handout: Supporting data: charts, cost analyses, computer printouts, etc.

8. PROPOSAL

Introduction: R-A-M-P (Rapport – Attention getter – Main message – Plan)
   Possible attention getter:
   - Incident, simple chart, or demo object illustrating the problem or opportunity that led to the proposal
   - Relevant quote or statistic
   - Interaction with audience (question)
   - A challenging "what if" scenario that dramatizes the problem or opportunity

Possible main message (preview): Synopsis of the project's most striking benefits and features, including costs if they are important to audience members

Body

Background:
- The circumstances leading to the proposal
- Problems to be addressed/opportunities to be exploited

Proposal in detail:
- Description of the proposal in nontechnical terms
- Benefits
- Goals

Plan:
- Exactly what will be done
- How it will be done (method and standards; team; resources)
- Costs
- Timing
- Conditions: contractual details, etc.

Alternatives to the proposal, including "do nothing":
- Discuss advantages and disadvantages of each alternative

Issues to be resolved:
- Discuss problems
- Indicate solutions and confidence of success
- If applicable, give dates and people responsible for solving problem

Summary
- Main benefits vs. costs
- Features that make the proposal attractive
- Next actions

Handout: Supporting data and attachments

9. MAJOR CAPITAL INVESTMENT PROPOSALS (CIPs)

9.1. General Notes

To increase your chances of approval, *imagine the approval process as concretely as you can.* Remember, above all, that upper management

- Needs sound reasons for spending the requested money
- May get distracted by inessential technical detail

Here are some specific ways to make approval easy:

1. Make the product and the process *visible* if they are unfamiliar. Simple figures and flow diagrams help. Avoid architectural or engineering drawings.
2. Include only information and numbers that are needed to justify the request. Cut anything that doesn't pass this test.
3. Address all questions and concerns top management would have about major capital requests:
   - *What is the problem or opportunity?*
   - *What is the proposed solution?*
   - *How much will it cost?*
   - *What exactly are the benefits of the solution?*
   - *How sure can we be of these benefits?*
   - *What alternatives have you considered, and why did you eliminate them?*
   - *How can we be sure that the solution will not introduce new problems?*
   - *How and when will the solution be implemented?*
   - *Can we be confident that you will manage costs, schedules, and quality in the best way possible?*
4. Be specific about benefits, costs, items included or not included in cost estimates, and implementation schedules.
5. Give the presentation a *professional look* that inspires confidence. Use a master page for consistent layout and pay attention to detail.
6. When including process figures, clearly mark the places where you propose to introduce changes. Adding big text that names the change may help.
7. Use nontechnical language where possible. Where you need technical terms for equipment and processes, define them as simply as possible and then be *consistent* in using them.
8. Use clear, simple words and sentence constructions.

9.2. Typical Sections for a CIP Presentation

Introduction: R-A-M-P (Rapport – Attention getter – Main message – Plan)
Title Slide/Establish Rapport
- Title of your presentation; author, Division and Group; required project/ proposal numbers
- **Don't omit first step: R = Rapport.** Make real human contact; express pleasure at the opportunity to present to this audience on an important subject.

Attention Getter
- Stay with a highly professional approach, such as a simplified trend line or bar chart illustrating the problem you're trying to solve, or a *very brief* illustration of the main problem or opportunity.

Message Preview
- State the proposed solution in briefest form
- State only the biggest benefit, described in simplest terms.
- State the cost

Plan
- State items to be covered
- Establish rules for Q&A

Body
- Section titles are flexible. They may mirror sections of a written CIP (problem/current situation, proposed solution, benefits, alternatives, investment required, schedule) or go along more with the specific questions you expect from your audience.
- Even if you decide on more formal, generic section/slide titles, make sure you address the questions listed above under General Notes for this presentation type, as well as more specific questions related to your proposal.

Summary
- Repeat the main problem or opportunity and the proposed solution.
- Summarize main benefits vs. costs
- State next actions

Handout: Supporting data and attachments

10. PROBLEM INVESTIGATION

Introduction: R-A-M-P (Rapport – Attention getter – Main message – Plan)
Possible attention getter:
- Incident or simple chart illustrating the problem
- Demo object illustrating the problem
- Any standard attention getter illustrating the urgency of implementing the proposed solution

Possible main message (preview):
- Short definition of the problem and the best way to overcome it

Body
Background: Description of the problem and the circumstances leading to it
Investigation:
- Approach (what you did)
- Findings (what you found out)
- Ideas (how the problem can be overcome)
- Criteria for evaluating ideas (how to choose among alternative solutions)
- Evaluation (how effective each method would be)

Recommendations: Exactly what should be done about the problem

Summary
- Restatement of problem, findings, and recommendations
- Next actions

Handout: Evidence and other supporting information

11. "HOW TO" PRESENTATIONS

Introduction: R-A-M-P (Rapport – Attention getter – Main message – Plan)
Possible attention getter:
- Audience interaction (question)
- Demo object related to the activity
- An interesting or humorous visual illustrating the activity
- A brief dramatic demonstration of some aspect of the activity
- Interesting statistic related to the topic
- Personal incident illustrating something interesting or important about the activity

Possible main message (preview):
- What the audience can **gain** from learning this
- For those who would *not* actually do the the activity you're explaining: how they can benefit from understanding this (e.g., can they transfer some of the methods, skills, or principles to their work or personal life?)
- The most interesting, most challenging, or most promising aspect of this activity
- What the audience should **do** after learning about this

Body and Summary: See "Overview of a System, Area, Field, etc." (Outline #3 above)

12. FACILITATING A PROBLEM-SOLVING MEETING

Introduction: R-A-M-P (Rapport – Attention getter – Main message – Plan)
Possible attention getter:
- Recent incident or personal experience highlighting the problem
- Interesting statistic related to the problem
- Relevant quote from a respected source
- Simplified chart illustrating the problem/solution
- Demo object
- Thought-provoking question
- Brief "what if" scenario that shows the importance of solving the problem or seizing the opportunity

Possible main message (preview):
- What you hope to achieve with the meeting and why it is important

Body
Problem/Opportunity Definition
- Spell out importance in more detail
- Give starting definition
- Take comments and ideas on problem definition
- Record ideas and get agreement on a working definition

Goals

- Suggest starting definition of goals
- Take alternative ideas and record them
- Get agreement on goals

Problems To Be Overcome

- Get ideas on issues to address in order to achieve goals
- Get agreement on priorities for issues

Solutions

- Get ideas on solutions to problems, in order of agreed-upon priorities of the problems
- Rank solutions by cost, feasibility, and other criteria chosen by the group
- Get agreement on best solution(s)
- Get agreement on actions, schedule, and responsibilities (who does what)

Summary

- Summarize achievements
- Describe next steps
- End on a high note of appreciation

Appendix E

Checklist for Presentations

Content and Approach

Audience needs and interests addressed?
Level and tone right?

Introduction

R	apport established?
A	ttention-getting beginning?
M	ain message stated clearly and simply up front?
P	lan of presentation given?

Body

Does the talk follow the plan given in the Introduction?
Main message restated clearly?
Significance of main message made clear?
Are there 3-4 (at most 5) clear **key points**? _____WHAT ARE THEY?

Is each assertion **backed up** or reinforced with data, illustrations, examples, or anecdotes?

Summary:

Main message and key points reviewed succinctly?
Appropriate **action** requested?
Memorable ending (e.g., story or quote)?

Delivery:

Clear, simple, personal language?
Spoken from notes (or freely) rather than read or memorized?
Loud voice?
Clear articulation?
Pace not too fast, not too slow?
Enthusiastic delivery?
Eye contact with audience?
Generally, focused on message rather than on self?

Visuals:

Clearly related to the main message and key points?
Effective choice for getting the message across?
Properly introduced?
Legible?
One major point per visual?
Speaker facing the audience while discussing visuals?

Solutions to Exercises

Chapter 1

Exercise 1-1. Audience and Purpose Analysis for one topic:

Topic	Audience
d. The urgent need to deliver more to the customer, at lower cost, in order to stay competitive (You are the manager of a production facility)	Employees who already feel stretched to the limit and are afraid to lose vacation time, travel budgets, etc.

The following real-world case illustrates an initial faulty approach and a revised better one. The manager used a free-form approach to Audience and Purpose Analysis, so this is what is recorded. Here is the case:

A mill manager wants to tell employees that competition is fierce and times are tough. To survive, they will have to *increase* customer satisfaction while at the same time *decreasing* costs. This is the planned main message of his presentation.

His initial plan: to tell them that they have to do this — increase customer satisfaction while spending less money. He will suggest ways to do both (pay more attention to quality, work extra hours if necessary to produce something good at less cost, etc.)

When he looks at the audience analysis, his approach changes. His purpose — what he wants to happen as a result of his talk — is to get them to think of creative ways to do this seemingly impossible task.

His trial message is still the same: To survive, we must *increase* customer satisfaction while *decreasing* costs.

When he looks at the probable audience questions and objections following his message, however, he finds they will focus on *fear:*

> *Does this mean my job is in danger?*
> *Will I then lose the raise I was hoping for?*
> *Are they going to cut travel because of the crunch?*
> *Is he telling us this because negotiations are coming up?*
> *This is impossible – the one half of the message cancels out the other.*

Clearly, his plan of delineating ways to increase customer satisfaction and decrease costs will not answer their questions. That's not what they are focused on.

So, he decides to modify the main message to focus more on *us*—you, the employees, and me, the mill manager. We're all facing a tough situation, and it has as much effect on my job as it does on yours. But we can meet it and win, together, if we all put our minds to the task of coming up with creative, painless ways to do what seems at first impossible.

To get them to see that his concern is based on reality, he gives an attention getter that is a story of an actual competitor in another country. This competitor recently made a comparable product for less money and got it to the customer more quickly. The reality is severe competition.

Then, his key points will be the following.

Key Point #1: I know this may seem threatening to you. You may be worrying about how this may affect your job, vacation time, and travel opportunities. These are understandable worries, but they don't have to come true if we come up with some good solutions together. And this can be done. Harley Davidson did exactly that when it faced the same situation.

Key Point #2: It may seem impossible. How can we do more for our customers on less capital without killing ourselves? Not impossible — one employee here came up with a way to do exactly that. She used less packaging material but applied it more effectively. Result: less material cost for us and greater satisfaction for the customer, who was happy to have less garbage to dispose of.

Interlude: Question. How about the rest of you? Any ideas about how we could make similar improvements? Open up to the floor.

Key Point #3: The negotiations. Some of you may think I'm raising this because of the upcoming negotiations. Nothing could be further from the truth. I just want you to know that. The reason for raising it is that we have to act now to survive and thrive.

Summary: We must beat the competition to survive. We don't have to lose jobs, raises, or travel. We can do what appears impossible — others already have. Now is the time to start. Let's meet in small groups and brainstorm on ideas. In a month, bring your group's ideas to the Lead Team Meeting. I can't wait for that meeting — I know we'll have ideas for ways to knock the socks off the other guys!

Chapter 2

Discussion 2-1. Many presentations start by wasting time on boring preliminaries or general background, then develop details, finally work toward some main message, and then fizzle out with a lame remark such as "I guess that's all." The faulty view of the audience's natural attention curve this implies is something like this:

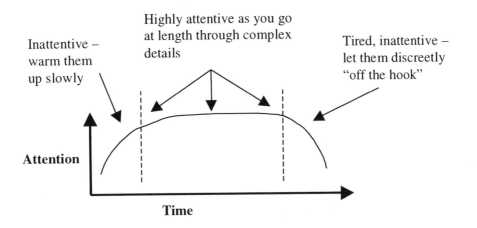

Compare this to the correct view of the audience's natural attention curve in Figure 2-1.

Chapter 3

Exercise 3-1. Critique and revise the following presentation openers.

> **Note:** The following revised openers are written out rather than outlined. This is only to give a better flavor of the approach — it does not mean you should write your opener out as a script. On the other hand, as explained in Chapter 7, you may want to rehearse the introduction thoroughly several times from key-word notes, and even record some of your wording loosely once you are satisfied with the way it sounds. The purpose of this is to get you over the first awkward minute in good style.

(a) ORIGINAL: "Good afternoon. I'm glad to have this opportunity to talk to you, even though our topic today doesn't seem very pleasant. **[Comment: Don't dwell on negatives of your topic — it adds nothing to your rapport but takes away from it.]** Because what I'm going to be talking about is *compliance* — what it means to the *company* and what it can mean to *you* personally. Briefly, I'm going to bring you up on some new developments in this whole compliance issue and give you some examples of recent experiences we had at some of our mills." **[Comment: All this just announces that you will say something about the topic LATER – it states nothing useful or important NOW. Also, the attention getter is missing.]**

Audience: Mill or facility managers, business managers, environmental personnel, and some technology managers

Purpose: Convince them that compliance has become a much more urgent issue that should be given top priority. For instance, negligence is no longer just a company problem, but people are personally liable. To make matters worse, the government doesn't have to prove that you were negligent — *you* must prove that you were *not*. Some people at two facilities are in the middle of such legal problems.

(a) REVISED: "Good afternoon. I'm glad to have this chance to talk to you about something that is important not just to the company but to you personally – namely, compliance. Let me ask you a question: How would you like to spend some time – maybe a *long* time – in jail?" **VISUAL:**

"Well, that's a real possibility for some of our managers right now, all because they took compliance lightly. Briefly, compliance with environmental laws has become an urgent issue of *personal liability* as well as survival of the company. And the worst is that the government doesn't even have to prove you were negligent — *you* have to prove that you were *not*.

"My first task, then, will be to show you how you — and the company — can stay out of trouble by understanding recent legal developments in the compliance area. Second, I'll explain the repercussions of any negligent mistakes or willful violations. And finally, I'll give you some examples of recent experiences we had at some of our mills."

(b) ORIGINAL: "Good morning. I'm Jim Beam, and I will be presenting on the pellet classifier evaluation. **[Comment: This lacks the friendly touch.]** We looked at several plastic-pellet classifiers, and my objective today is to report on that evaluation. **[Comment: This gives not a hint of the result of the evaluation; like the opener in (a), it contains no real main message but just a pseudo message, or a *promise* of some future substantive statement. There is also no *attention getter*.]** To begin with, I'll take you through the main criteria that governed our evaluation, such as accuracy, testing speed, operator time involvement, and availability of automatic data storage. Then we'll see how five major pellet classifiers stacked up against these criteria." **[Comment: This may be an acceptable statement of your presentation plan, but a more strongly worded preview of your key points would support your main message better and show the audience right away where your talk is headed.]**

(Assume the following: Speaker is suggesting that all production facilities switch to a more expensive plastic-pellet classifier than they're using now. This classifier costs 20% more than the cheapest of the five models evaluated, but it offers extensive automation, high testing speed, and the second-best accuracy. The plastic pellets are

used as raw material for various plastic products; they must be a mixture of different sizes, with the specific mix depending on the product produced. Testing is done continuously to ensure that the pellet mix falls within the specified size ranges. The audience for the presentation consists of technical and management people from various facilities, plus some managers from Technology.)

(b) REVISED: "Good morning. I'm Jim Beam from the XYZ Dept., and I am delighted to report on our project to identify the best pellet classifier for our mills. First of all, I'd like to direct your attention to the screen. There's a big number there: 4%. Do you happen to know what that stands for? ... Well, it's our current **reject rate** for final product – and it's due mostly to an out-of-range mix of plastic pellets. What that translates into is a yearly waste of **$1.2 million**.

"The simple solution to this problem is to install better pellet classifiers throughout our mills. We've compared the five top models and identified the ABC Classifier as the most effective solution. It offers extensive automation, high testing speed to minimize off-spec production, and very good accuracy. Although it's not the cheapest choice, it delivers the best return on investment for us.

"I'll now take you through our evaluation criteria in more detail and show you how the five classifiers stacked up against them. Then I'll describe our suggested plan for installing our choice, the ABC Classifier."

Chapter 4

Exercise 4-1. Presentation outline for the following theme and background:

Topic: Recommendation to install a security system using miniature closed-circuit TV cameras.
Audience: Management and employees.
Background: See Chapter 4, Exercise 4-1.

Purpose:
1. Persuade management to buy and install this system.
2. Get employees' cooperation in making this a successful implementation.

Audience questions and objections (some to be covered in the body; others reserved for Q&A):
Management:
- Will it work?
- How do we know?
- Won't employees object?
- Sounds expensive — affordable only for big companies.
- Who is going to do it? We don't have time.
- Who'll fix it when it doesn't work?
- Who is going to do the extra daily work? Are we going to hire extra people for this?

- Are there guarantees?
- What's the reputation of the seller (manufacturer and retailer)?
- How much are we actually losing each year through theft?
- How much real risk of violence is there?
- How much have we suffered through security breaches — outsiders getting access to privileged info? Aren't we being a bit paranoid?
- What's the time table if we accept this idea?

Employees:
- Sounds like Big Brother — we don't like the idea of being videotaped.
- Who's going to be hit with the extra work — the receptionists?
- This will just be abused by management to spy on employees in ways that have nothing to do with security!
- Having the TV screens in the reception area will make it look like a cheap liquor store or supermarket — a real step down in the quality of life around here.

Main message: The proposed security system will remove big financial risks for the company and safety risks for all of us.

Key points:
1. It's proved itself to be very effective in many businesses.
2. It's inexpensive and quick and easy to install.
3. It's simple and inexpensive to operate and will save money by reducing the need for guards.

STRUCTURE:

Introduction:

Rapport: I appreciate the opportunity to present a proposal that will reduce serious risks for the company and for all employees.

Attention getter: Sketch scenario of a mugger attacking a woman in the company's parking lot. The woman is seriously injured; her lawyer sues the company for negligence (i.e., for not providing easily available security for the premises and parking lot). The woman has lost her health and ability to work; the company, money and reputation, and a valuable employee.

Main message: The proposed security system will remove big financial risks for the company and safety risks for all of us.

Plan (= key points):
1. It's proved to be very effective in many businesses.
2. It's inexpensive and quick and easy to install.
3. It's simple and inexpensive to operate and will save by reducing the need for guards.

Body:

Key Point #1: The system has proved to be very effective in many businesses.
Backup:
- Statistics on *violent crimes* in parking areas and on business premises
- Statistics on violent crimes in businesses that have such security systems: a dramatic reduction
- Example: restaurants

Subpoint: Is it *distasteful* to people to have CCTV screens in the reception hall? Not at all!
- Example: restaurant. **VISUAL:** newspaper photo showing customers in the bar having fun watching the parking-area video.
- Restaurant customers became unpaid part of the security force; employees do the same for businesses

Subpoint: Will people resent being "spied on" by the cameras? Not if they think about it clearly!
- **Audience interaction:** "Who here is planning on some security violations or theft?" Obviously, nobody. Then it's in *our interest* to have a system that proves that we were not the ones causing some damage.
- **Video:** Showing a visitor sneaking into a restricted area. "Something proprietary has been removed from your top-secret lab. Aren't you glad this video establishes that an *outsider,* rather than you, took this thing?"
- **Example:** Return to the initial attention getter (scenario of attack). "Weigh the irrational discomfort with being taped against the real improvement in your *personal safety:* With the system, your chances of becoming a victim of violent crime will be sharply reduced."

Key Point #2: The system is inexpensive and quick and easy to install.
Backup:
- Demo objects: a sample camera and monitor, with "price tags" attached. Read out the price on each.
- **Visual** showing layout of premises, with location of cameras.
- **Visual** listing cost of hardware, installation, and total.
- Visual comparing cost of just one lawsuit, or one theft of high-level intellectual property, with cost of system installation.
- Visual comparing the proposed system with a more costly alternative considered: VideoEye, $6,000 for equipment.

Key Point #3: The system is simple and inexpensive to operate and will save money by reducing the need for guards.
Backup:
- Photos of reception areas with such systems, with close-ups of monitor and VCR for continuous recording

Subpoint: We will save on security guards.
- **Visual** using graphic symbolization (see Chapter 6): Current 3-guard operation vs. 2-guard operation with new system, with yearly cost for each. *Proposed system pays for itself in first year.*
- Explain *how* the two guards will provide effective security: one watches the screens, radios the other as needed.

Subpoint: Alternative considered (VideoEye) but not recommended would cost additional $300/month for monitoring 24 hrs/day from central station — still less than an extra guard.

(**Visual** showing part of VideoEye brochure that advertises the central monitoring service graphically.)

Summary:
Main message and key points: Repeat them.
Next steps: Order the system and have it installed; entire process can be completed within 1 week after order is placed. Reap the benefits of improved security.

Chapter 5

Exercise 5-1. Critique and revise the following summary and closing:
"So, I hope you can see the benefits of this project — the impact on the product line for the next two years and the lower production costs by 3 percent — which more than pay for the costs of $420,000. Questions?"

Critique and Revision:
1. "So" is not strong enough as a signal that you are moving into the summary; many listeners will not wake up from their body-section semi-snooze through the details but mishear it as a mini-summary of body subpoint #14. Use a clear signal such as "In summary, then..." or "In closing."
2. "I hope" is superfluous and unnecessarily weak — use strong, positive language for your closing: "In summary, this project has impressive benefits..."
3. Benefits are stated weakly as phrases instead of in proper sentences. Revise along these lines: "First, it will enrich our product line over the next two years in crucial ways that tie in with the company's overall strategic plan. Second, it will lower our production cost by 3 percent, or $800,00, per year. This saving alone pays almost twice for the project cost in the first year. In sum, we have nothing to lose and a lot to gain."
4. "Questions?" is a lame drop-off and not a good way to invite or direct responses. Keep your eye on what you want and encourage questions with enthusiastic and targeted wording. Here is one possibility: "And now I'd be delighted to answer any further questions you have. We already discussed many issues you raised. I hope that we can use the remaining time to answer all your concerns and come to a decision on a firm schedule. You'll find details of the costs, projected savings, and implementation plan in the handout which I'm distributing right now."

Chapter 6

Exercise 6-4. Critique and revise bar chart entitled *Average satisfaction of internal clients with services performed during years 1999-2002 by corporate research and development teams, as determined by after-service surveys.*

Critique:
- Title is wordy.
- Grid is unnecessary, especially since the data values are shown for each bar.
- Entire Y axis is also superfluous. Relative size of the bars, plus the data labels, tells the whole story.
- Extra tick marks between years on x axis are superfluous and distracting – the audience may wonder if some intermediate data have been omitted.

Revised Visual:

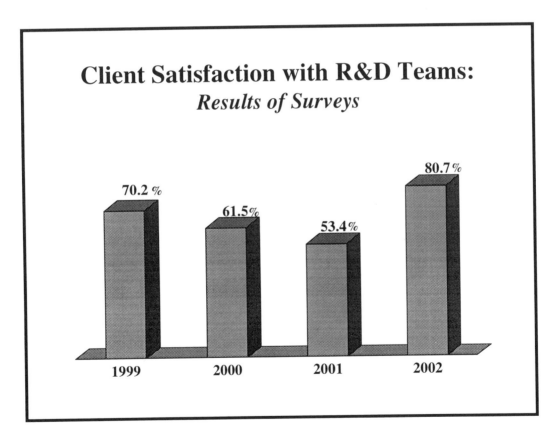

Exercise 6-5. Critique and revise double pie chart entitled *Contribution of various factors to overall satisfaction with service from research and development teams, as determined by after-service surveys: year 1999 vs. 2002. Note the shift in priorities, from "understanding of needs" and "cost-effectiveness" to "timeliness" as the most important factor.*

Critique:

- Title is wordy. Its second sentence ("Note the shift in priorities, from 'understanding of needs' and 'cost-effectiveness' to 'timeliness' as the most important factor") is superfluous — this is information you should just give in your talk. Having it on the slide as well, in sentence form, interferes with your saying it.
- Legend is double and hard to process — label the slices directly instead.
- Because of the space taken up by the legend, the pies and the numbers are too small.
- If the focus is on the shift to timeliness as the most important factor, then a chart that emphasizes that slice in each pie (by taking it half way out of the pie) would be more helpful.

Revised Chart:

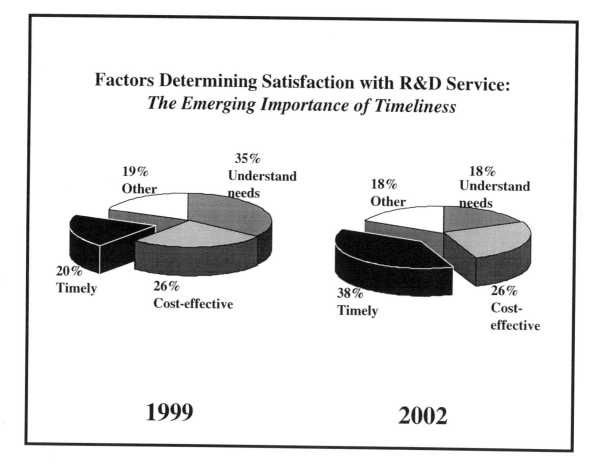

Exercise 6-6. Critique and revise word chart with little graphic images, entitled *Client Satisfaction with Research & Development Service: Problems Related to Timeliness.*

- Avoid whole sentences. The audience will get lost reading so much verbiage. Instead, use only short phrases.
- The key ideas in each bullet item are buried — make each item start with the idea.
- Too many ideas are mixed into the slides, without separation. A better solution would be to divide between problems and solutions or challenges.
- Some of the ideas don't belong in the slide at all — just discuss them if appropriate. Examples:

    (1) This is an issue of honesty (on the client's side) as well as diplomacy (on the provider's side).
    (2) Realism in this instance means expecting more of the same for the next years.

- Graphic embellishments are useless and distracting. Graphics can help people remember key ideas — but if you put too many graphics into a slide, then *nothing* will be remembered. Use graphics sparingly so they can have a strong effect.
- 12-point text for bullet items is too small — minimum size is 18 points.
- The title does not get to the main idea (timeliness) quickly enough. Instead, it emphasizes a higher-level idea, client satisfaction.

Revised Visual:
Two word charts, to divide the amount of information into half-size chunks.

Chart 1:

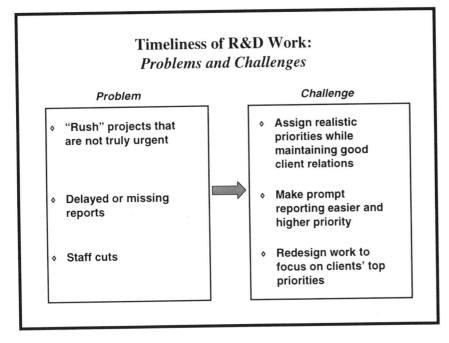

Chart 2:

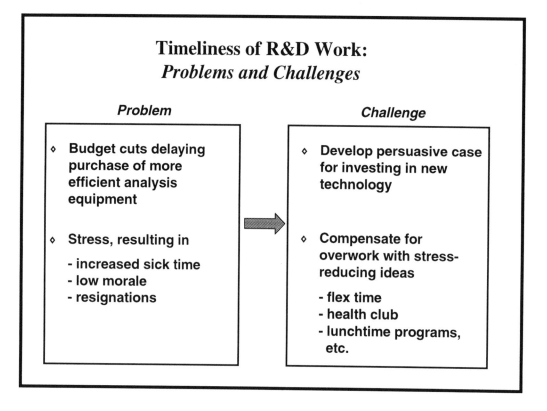

Exercise 6-7. Critique and revise the line chart entitled *Frequency of reportable safety incidents at company locations A, B, and C over the last four years.*

- Extra tick marks on x axis are confusing.
- Markers are faint and indistinct.
- Legend is dispensable — it demands time-consuming cross-referencing. Label curves directly instead.
- Lines are too thin.

Revised Visual:
(Note direct data labels for maximum and minimum value for Location C; these highlight the focal point and at the same time serve as your notes.)

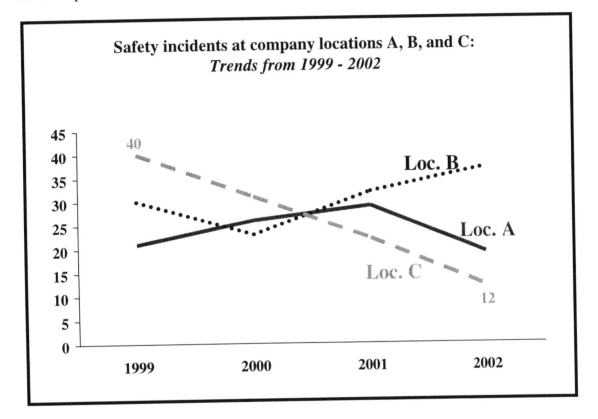

Chapter 10

Exercise 10-1. Understanding and Controlling Body Language: Answer Sheet

Note that the meaning and importance of most body language signals depend on **context** — in particular, facial expression and tone of voice.

Signal	Likely Meanings	Importance*
Constantly clearing throat, without sign of a cold or cough	Nervous; disagreeing; resentful	2
Crossing arms over chest	Defensive; negative; possibly just trying to relax	0-1; 2 if facial expression agrees
Tightly crossing legs	Nervous; intimidated	1-2
Stroking chin while looking intently at the other	Interested; thinking	1
Avoiding eye contact	Insincere; disagreeing; afraid; lack of interest; etc.	2
Very long eye contact (steady stare)	Trying to control or dominate	2
Looking at other person's forehead rather than eyes	Attempt to dominate by "depersonalizing"; may also mean same as avoiding eye contact	1-2
Slowly removing eyeglasses, then cleaning them (although they don t seem dirty)	Thinking	1
Abruptly taking glasses off and putting them on the table	Annoyed; disagreeing sharply	2
Peering over top of eyeglasses	Doubtful; evaluating	2
Partially covering mouth with one hand while speaking	"Shielding the truth"; nervous	2
Rubbing eyes, ears, or side of nose	Doubtful	2
Leaning forward while sitting on the edge of the chair	Attentive, interested; possibly impatient	1-2
Folding hands on top of table, rubbing thumbs together	Distracted; thinking; nervous	1
Leaning back, putting hands behind head, stretching	Relaxed; may be an attempt to dominate or intimidate (e.g., in interview situation)	2
Sucking on a pen	Distracted; thinking; may be attempt to unsettle or dominate if done aggressively	1-2
Tapping, jiggling, fiddling with objects	Impatient; possibly disagreeing	2
Yawning	Bored; nervous	2
Wringing hands	Very anxious	2
Raising eyebrows	Surprised; disagreeing	2
Rubbing back of head	Doubtful; insecure	2
Biting lower lip	Anxious	1-2
Narrowing eyes	Disagreeing; angry; resentful	2

* Relative importance of signal: 0=unimportant; 1=moderately important; 2=very important (avoid it yourself; watch carefully if others do it)

Exercise 10-4. Stand in front of a mirror (or, in a group setting, get up and observe one another as you do the exercise). Now use energetic upper-body gestures that support the following words or phrases:

Compress	Put hands together as if compressing something
Tease apart, disentangle	Show teasing-apart motion with several fingers of both hands
Down	Thumb(s) or hand(s) down
Bottom	Flat hand low
Up	Raise flat hand
Wide	Hold two hands wide apart
Narrow	Move two hands close together
Circular	Describe circle in air with index finger or hand
Evolving	Move open hand outward slowly
Interwoven	Interweave fingers
Erratic	Describe erratic up-and-down motion with hand
Smooth	Describe even sideways movement with hand
Two	Two fingers up
Backward	Move hand toward chest
Comes back	Describe circle ending up at your chest
It makes you think	Index finger to temple
Spread out	Two hands, fingers spread out, moving apart, palms facing outward
Concentrated in one spot/area	Two hands, each forming half circle, moving together
Stay	Point down energetically
Move	Move a hand outward quickly
The center	Same as "concentrated in one spot" above
At the periphery	Make large circle with two index fingers or hands
Isolated instances	Poke "here & there" in the air
Over here ... over there	Point to opposite areas in space
Segment	Make cutting motion with one hand
Stack	With one or two hands, show two layers (with one hand, make the second "layer" movement higher than the first)

Chapter 14

Exercise 14-1. Is there some spot, *other* than next to the projection screen, where you can stay **throughout your presentation** without blocking somebody's view of the visuals?

Answer: There is no such spot. Therefore, you need to move frequently to give everybody a chance to see what is on the screen.

Exercise 14-2. Suppose you are pointing at sections of a flow diagram directly on an overhead transparency. Can you do this without blocking a single person's view of the visual? How? If not, does it matter that just one person cannot see the visual you are discussing, as long as you make sure it's not always the *same* person?

Answer: When you're standing next to the projector, you're always blocking somebody's view (unless nobody happens to be sitting in the position being blocked). Since it is **essential** that everybody see the visual when you are discussing it in detail, you need to be next to the screen, where you are not blocking anybody. An alternative is to work with a remote pointer (e.g., laser pointer); however, even with that solution you need to make sure you don't stand in one spot, blocking somebody's view.

Discussion 14-1. How many people in the group dislike "stepwise revelation" of a transparency (placing a piece of paper over the transparency and sliding it down a step at a time to reveal the next points on the slide)? Why? How many dislike the equivalent approach in a computer slide show: a "build" slide with bullets appearing one at a time, and old bullet points perhaps dimming? What practical consequences does this have, in your view?

Notes:
1. In our experience, there are always quite a few people in any group who dislike stepwise revelation with a transparency. Some dislike it *intensely*. Therefore, this is generally not a good technique. Instead, prepare several slides showing just what you want the audience to see.
2. "Build" slides that add one bullet point at a time are generally not disliked in the same way. The only cautions here are (a) not to overuse this device and (b) to decide in each case whether the audience would be better served with a complete view of your points before you go into details.

Chapter 15

Exercise 15-1. Handling Tough Questions

Note: As the instructions stated, all the questions are of the kind that are predictable in a business presentation. Therefore, you should be fully prepared to answer them effectively, or your presentation preparation was faulty.

Caustic Question	Question Rephrased in a Neutral Way To Allow Effective Answer	Outline a Brief Possible Answer
Attack on PRACTICALITY or COST: "Let's just suppose everything you say is true. Now, if we tried to actually put this thing you're proposing into our mills, do you have any idea what it would *cost?* It would blow us right out of the water!"	"O.K. You're understandably concerned about costs of implementing these proposals."	Contrast costs with benefits; show that benefits outweigh the costs.
Attack on EXPERIMENTAL METHOD: "I have no doubt you got the data you say you did. The problem is, those data all result from a totally inappropriate methodology. The proper method you should have used for such an experiment is..."	"I see. You're wondering about our experimental method."	Explain in the briefest terms why your method is appropriate for the problem. If you can, explain why the other method was not or should not be used.
Attack on INTERPRETATION METHOD: "I've been looking at those data you presented, and I don't think they show anything like what you claim. With the kinds of variables you were studying, the only statistical method that would give you meaningful results would be the Mandelbrot two-tailed beta-square chaos test."	"O.K. The question is, what is the best statistical interpretation method to apply to our data?"	State the main reasons your method gives valid results. If you know the method he is proposing, state why it is less appropriate, if that is so; otherwise, ignore this part (it may well be wrong or irrelevant) or postpone discussion until after the talk.
Attack on GOALS: "I'm sure we all enjoyed your little presentation. But I don't see how it relates to the *real problem* we set out to tackle. If you remember, we were trying to ... But you only told us how to..."	"All right. How do these ideas apply to the problem we set out to solve, namely *X?*"	Summarize how the ideas help solve the main problem.

Exercise 15-1. Handling Tough Questions *(continued)*

Caustic Question	Question Rephrased in a Neutral Way To Allow Effective Answer	Outline a Brief Possible Answer
Attack on *PERSUASIVENESS*: "You say X is Y. But why should we *believe* you? Can you *prove* it? I may have missed something, but I don't recall hearing any *evidence*."	"Yes, of course. What's the evidence that X is Y?"	Summarize why X is Y — even if you said it clearly in your talk and this person just slept through that portion!
Attack on *RESULTS*: "I'm sorry, but I just can't believe those data. I remember two recent studies that showed that the trend is just the other way round. How do you explain *that*?"	"All right, how credible or reliable are our data?"	Summarize why the data are solid (presumably, you used solid methods). Only then explain why results from the other studies might differ (if you know about that — otherwise postpone discussion until after the talk).
Attack on your *AUTHORITY*: "You talked at great length about XYZ. I just wonder: Have you ever actually been *involved* in a real XYZ? [Then, when speaker admits he hasn't : "So it's all just a *theory* you've been presenting. Thanks. That's all I wanted to know." [Audience laughs]	On a corporate project, anticipate this and *avoid* it: take a *team* approach, with experienced members on board so you can invoke that practical experience.	Otherwise defend the importance and relevance of good theory: "Yes, this is theory — based on a broad body of practical research. Good theories are a powerful way to avoid costly practical mistakes. I think it would be in our interest to take it very seriously."
Attack on *RELEVANCE*: "This is all very interesting. But what's it got to do with our operational realities? Our proc-esses are totally different from the one you discussed. They don't even use the same *chemistry!*"	"O.K. How can these processes be applied to our current operations?"	Outline how they apply. Only then take up the specific objection about difference in chemistry, if you can.

Exercise 15-2. Handling Negative Comments

Suggested Solution:

As indicated at the end of the instructions, this is an extreme situation (imminent customer loss) calling for a *radical response,* not for a bit of rephrasing and clever answering.

The new *goals* in this situation are to (1) get information about the causes of dissatisfaction and (2) reestablish trust.

An *initial response* might be something like: "Thank you for your honesty. Let me stop right here. What you are saying comes as a total surprise to me, and I'd be grateful if you could help me get to the bottom of the problem. I assure you, we are really serious about Total Customer Satisfaction — but obviously, that's not the message you are getting. There is something severely wrong if you, and perhaps others, are considering switching suppliers. Whatever it is, I promise to look into it immediately and thoroughly, and get back to you with solutions. So, could you tell me in a little more detail what are the things that have been bothering you about our attitude or performance?"

The *strategy* would simply be to abandon the presentation, which would fall on deaf ears anyhow, and have an honest discussion session. Obviously, the presenter should take thorough *notes,* do the promised *research,* and *follow up* with these customers.

The general point is this: a bit of political glossing over won't always do. You need to be flexible in any situation and see if a radical change in approach is called for. This is a case in point.

A *closing statement* would clearly be useful: it gives the presenter another chance to summarize the problems and any solutions that were already offered, and repeat the promise of follow-up.

Should the presenter have been *prepared* for such an attack? Absolutely. When you get up to paint a rosy picture of company policies and strategies, you must expect that half the audience takes a cynical view.

The *traits* and *skills* required to handle such a situation include *honesty, flexibility, and goal-oriented thinking*. Anybody can develop greater honesty simply by learning to appreciate the advantages it offers, such as dramatically improved response from the people you are dealing with. Similarly, you can improve your flexibility and goal-oriented thinking by doing exercises such as the ones in Chapter 15 and Chapter 17.

Chapter 17

Exercise 17-1. Controlling Inappropriate Questions: Solutions and Notes

Inappropriate Question	How To Control/Redirect/Rephrase
"I'm sick and tired of all these academics coming along and telling us what to do. Obviously, you've never seen the inside of a factory, or you wouldn't be telling us this stuff about all this fancy new chemistry. Do you have any *idea* what's involved in changing basic chemistry between production runs?"	*Humorous moderation:* "Well, John, you've obviously stirred up some emotions with your ideas. So, the question is: Do you have some thoughts on the costs and other difficulties involved in changing basic chemistry when shifting from one production run to another? Perhaps you also have some ideas on how to minimize the costs and physical work. For instance, do you see any easy ways to automate the changes?"
"I don't know what the *point* of all this is. Who cares if the bonds between those fibers are because of hydrogen or Van der Waltz or whatever you call him, or subatomic forces, or gravity, or the moon, or whatever! We all know they stick together, or we wouldn't have paper. Why don't you start telling us how to *make better paper* – that's all we care about! We don't want to hear about these age-old theoretical battles between structuralists and hydrogenists and all the rest of you!"	"OK, the question is: why should we care about hydrogen bonding? In what ways can knowledge of this theory help us make better paper? For instance, you talked about some of the factors that can *interfere* with hydrogen bonding. Can you go into more depth on those? I think that would be very relevant to this practical question."
"This is all very interesting. But what's it got to do with our operational realities? Our processes are totally different from the one you discussed. They don't even use the same *chemistry!*"	"OK … can you elaborate on the practical applications of this theoretical work? What kinds of processes would it be applicable to?"
"I think this whole thing was totally biased. You obviously have some special interest that leads you to choose or twist your data and interpretations. I don't trust any of it."	"Let me rephrase that. Obviously, you're an interested party in this debate, but we're not going to say you twisted your data. However, can you give our audience some reassuring information about the objectivity of your data and interpretation methods? Do you want to say anything about that?"
"I have no doubt you got the data you say you did. The problem is, those data all result from a totally inappropriate methodology. The proper experimental method you should have used for this is a double-blind randomized noise-controlled XYZ method…"	"Essentially, can you say anything in support of the specific experimental method you used for your study?"

Exercise 17-1. Controlling Inappropriate Questions: Solutions and Notes *(continued)*

Inappropriate Question	**How To Control/Redirect/Rephrase**
"I don't know about anybody else, but I find all this incredibly boring. What's the point of it?"	[Moderator: "Well, it certainly wasn't boring to me, but obviously your perspective is different. [*To speaker:*] You don't need to answer that. But is there anything you'd *like* to say?"
"I'm sorry, but I just can't believe those data. I remember some recent studies that showed that the trend was just the other way round."	*To speaker*: "Are you aware of such data?" If not, challenge questioner to say *where*. If he can't, treat the comment as "off the record" – nonverified reference to opposing data. *(This is important, because a speaker can be discredited by a nasty trick like that, even when there is no real evidence contradicting him!)*
Question that goes on for more than 3 minutes and really is a show-off mini-lecture.	Cut it off: "Excuse me, can you shorten this and formulate it as a direct question? We need to keep questions short to stay on track."
"I'm sorry, I just can't believe any of this. It all seems totally far-fetched."	"Well, it certainly didn't seem far-fetched to me. But do you want to briefly summarize your main evidence for your position, or add anything to make your case?"
Question that shows that person slept through part of the presentation	State that you think it was answered in XYZ way – but again give speaker *option* to add to that.
Question that is clearly *off the subject*	"That seems to go somewhat beyond what we're discussing here. I suggest that we take other questions first. Perhaps we can discuss it at the end or you can take it up after the session."
Persistent question	Remind them: "Only one question." "We'd like to hear from other people, too. I suggest you continue the discussion in the break."
No questions	Suggest rough ranges of questions (falling back on your notes from the preparation and initial discussion with the panelists); call on people you know, who have an interest or specialized knowledge in key areas covered; ask a specific focused question yourself.

Chapter 19

General Note on Exercises 19-1 – 19-4:

All the outlines in these exercises share two major faults: (1) they have *too many key points,* with no clear indication of which are more important; and (2) they do not pull the main message to the front so the audience absorbs it while still fully attentive. If you want to take advantage of the templates or wizards that are the basis for these outlines, restrict their use to *checking your ideas for completeness.*

Appendix D in this book has some outlines for specific presentation tasks that are based on sound presentation theory and encourage you to put information where it belongs. However, even these sample outlines cannot substitute for thoughtful analysis of your audience and their needs and interests, as explained in Part 1 of this book.

Exercise 19-1. Jam-Free Multipurpose Paper: Project Status

Detailed Comments and Suggestions:

1. In general, see Appendix D, outline #6 (Project Update) for a more effective outline scheme for this type of presentation.

2. The initial lengthy Agenda makes for a slow, boring start.

3. If no "wake-up call" is involved, then an attention getter may not be appropriate for such a "working discussion" (see the discussion in Appendix D, Outline #6). However, if you think there is a great danger that funding will be cut off simply by management's indecision, then an attention getter *is* in order. For instance, you might use a visual with just one large number: the *yearly market potential* that would be missed if the project were dropped because it ran over time and budget. Point: "We should keep this in mind as we review the project." This attention getter could incorporate the points under "Benefits of the project." Follow the attention getter with a preview of your main message, along the lines of the current Summary. Close the Introduction with your Plan for the presentation – e.g., (1) Brief review of project, (2) Current status, (3) Going forward.

4. The many "review" points after the Agenda slow down the presentation — in all likelihood, this audience will break in with questions on current status very soon. Restrict the review to essentials, namely "Technological and Financial Challenges of the Project." Keep these major review points *brief* and relate them to the main message (the need to make a decision on possible budget overrun if the technical obstacles persist longer than envisaged).

5. In key point #2, Current Status, consolidate schedule and budget, then focus on technical issues. Leave the discussion of "Action Items" for the third key point, Going Forward.

6. In key point #3, Going Forward, move from "Opportunities" to "Risks," then to a discussion of "Next Steps" which includes the current first subitem, "Milestones & Completion Dates," as well as the budget forecast now under "Current Status." Note that the "Action Items" mentioned under "Current Status" duplicate or overlap the "Milestones."

7. The Summary can remain essentially unchanged.

Exercise 19-2. Outline for a Project Proposal – Expanding Into Distance Learning

Detailed Comments and Suggestions:

1. Generally, for a more effective outline scheme for proposals, see Appendix D, outline #8.

2. There are too many key points, with no indication of relative importance. Omit points not crucial for this audience (they may be taken up in the question-and-answer session); consolidate others.

3. The material is not focused on the most important aspects of this audience: resistance to technology and fear of repeating past failures.

4. Presenting an Agenda slows things down and invites the audience to tune out from the very start. Instead, begin with an **attention getter** that emphasizes the opportunity or competitive threat. For instance, show a simple line chart of the number of companies looking into distance learning for their employees — say, as an accelerating trend over the last five years. Then lead to the **main message** — say, a recommendation to go after this rapidly expanding market and avoid being seen as out of touch with modern training technology.

5. In the current outline, the main message is buried and distributed over many sections. Presumably, it will re-emerge in the Summary (usually, that is where presenters remember that they ought to say something definite). However, to take advantage of the audience's natural attention curve, it must be delivered strongly in the first two minutes and restated somewhere in the body.

6. The key points that must be emphasized are (1) why it is urgent to invest substantially in a high-quality effort in this area, Distance Learning, and (2) why management should be confident that the company will not face a repeat of past technology failure. Most of the current key points can be subsumed under these two. The rest forms a third complex: implementation details.

Exercise 19-3. Presentation to Potential Recruits at a Top-Notch College or University — Two General Outline Schemes

Detailed Comments and Suggestions:

1. In looking for a model outline, it's tempting to go for the *most specific* you can find. The two examples in this exercise illustrate that this can be a mistake. As a recruiter, you are not so much giving a *company overview* as you are *persuading, motivating,* and *challenging* candidates. The PowerPoint scheme contains nothing useful for this. The Lotus Freelance model might invite you to put the right kind of material toward the end, under "Strengths and Weaknesses" and "Corporate Outlook."

2. With eight key points or top-level sections, the PowerPoint template is too long. The Lotus Freelance model is more than three times as long (26 points); however, you are obviously meant to pick out a few points that matter most to you. Unfortunately, there is nothing to guide your choice, and as we noted in comment #1, there are no sections that really fit your needs properly.

3. The best scheme to follow is simply the basic presentation structure discussed throughout this book, and reproduced as outline #1 in Appendix D.

4. The **key points** that matter most in this situation are (1) who we are — what we produce or do and whom we serve, (2) what kinds of people we are looking for — their skills and attitudes, and (3) what we offer (e.g., fast career advancement for good performers, stability, exciting responsibilities, good financial package, etc.)

5. The talk needs an introduction with a strong **attention getter** to set it off from all the other recruitment presentations. This might be a brief story of an exceptional employee, a recent technological breakthrough that illustrates the company's commitment to innovation, an excerpt from a recent news story, etc.

6. The attention getter must lead straight to a strong **main message** — say, the most outstanding thing you can expect when you join this organization.

7. The summary must bring together the main message and the key points, probably followed by an **action step:** the next thing a candidate should do if he or she is interested in joining the company.

Exercise 19-4. Critique of an Outline for "Company Meeting"

Here are the assumptions for this exercise:
- You are a mill manager addressing employees at the yearly meeting.
- Competition and markets are tough.
- Downsizing is overloading employees and making them fearful and resentful; morale is low.
- The company needs technological breakthroughs and 10% gains in productivity to get out of profit/stock decline and avoid further layoffs.

Detailed Comments and Suggestions:

1. As in Exercise 19-3, going for a *specific* outline scheme — here, "Company Meeting" — produces poor results. It's more important to reflect *what you want to achieve* in the meeting. This will give you better criteria for choosing an outline scheme — even if you want to use that scheme only to double-check your points for completeness.

2. Here, the main purpose of the presentation is to *motivate* stressed-out employees to excel in innovation and productivity in order to save their own jobs and the future of the company. The appropriate scheme for this is again the basic structure covered in this book (outline #1 in Appendix D).

3. The presentation needs a strong attention getter that sets a *positive* tone. These employees already know that there is trouble; they need *hope* and a *challenge*. A brief story of an employee who achieved a breakthrough or improved productivity works best. Even if nothing dramatic is available, reflect that at least in the area of productivity improvement, *small gains add up!* Therefore, you usually do have some success stories to tell.

4. The main message ideally is a positive statement, such as "I believe in your ability to propel this company to a great future, and I will unleash your potential by removing every barrier I can." It must be delivered right after the attention getter.

5. The key points in this situation might be (1) the kinds of innovations we need, with examples of successes, (2) the kinds of productivity improvements needed, again with examples of successes, (3) why all this is more urgent now than before, and (4) how barriers will be removed to make successes easier (e.g., open doors, financial rewards, no red tape, etc.).

6. The Summary should be followed by a "next action" step in order to set the whole process immediately in motion.

Index

35mm slides, 223

Abstract, of conference speech, 206
Accessories, for dealing with presentation
    problems, 102
Accidents, avoiding, 259
Action items
    Recording, in slide show, 256, 266
Active voice, 146
Adjectives, 146
    Overcoming overuse of, 148
Agenda-style beginning
    vs. strong presentation start, 47
Aggressiveness, 178, 203
    And questions, 185
Aloofness
    And eye contact, 152
    Expressions of, 124
Animation
    Of curves in chart, 243
    Of graphic, 243
    Of slide, 222, 224, 225, 241, 242, 243,
        277, 278, 279, 280
Annotating, projected slide, 256, 266
Annotation tool. *See* Pen tool
Answering questions, 203, 215
    "Simple answer", 175, 179, 181, 183, 192
Arms, 128, 178, 192
    And athletic stance, 125
Arrogance
    And eye contact, 152
    Toward audience, 115
Arrow key, 263
Arrow tool. *See* Pointer tool
Articulation, 139, 140, 142, 149
    And questions, 182
Athletic stance, 123, 124, 125, 126, 128, 138
    And questions, 178
Attention curve, audience's natural, 24 1, 54
Attention getter, 29, 33, 34, 35, 36, 39, 40,
    41, 47, 48, 50, 51, 52, 53
    Anecdote as, 37
    Delaying, 35

Attention getter, *ctd.*
    Demo object as, 43
    Demonstration as, 43
    Joke as, 44
    Problem or benefit as, 35
    Question as, 38
    Quote as, 37
    Reasons for, 34
    Relating directly to main message, 33
    Statistic as, 41
    Visual as, 39
Attitude toward audience, 110, 113, 117,
    121, 137
    And questions, 175, 178, 185, 186
    Expressing, 113
Audience
    Fear of, 115
    Liking, 115
Audience & Purpose Analysis, 12, 16, 20
    Example, 12, 16
Audience analysis, 7, 13, 21, 22
Audience connection, 109, 110, 111, 161,
    167, 168, 170, 267
    And visuals, 167
    Four elements of, 110, 111
    Magic triangle, 109, 110
    Persuasion and, 113
    Trust and, 113
Audience focus, 161
Audience limitations, 23
Audience questions, considering, 7
    Being specific in, 8
    Tough questions, 11
Audience resistance
    Handling, 197
Audio, 219, 225, 226, 239, 245, 246, 259,
    277, 279, 280
    Activating, 256
    Problems, 259
Authority, 181
    And handling questions, 177
Axes, in chart, 230

Back, showing to audience, 122, 128, 162, 164

Background knowledge of audience
    And presentation detail, 53

Background, slide, 233, 234, 246, 249

BACKSPACE key, 263, 264, 265

Backup transparencies, 255, 267, 268, 269
    As remedy for equipment problems, 101

Battery, computer
    vs. AC power, 261, 262, 268, 271

Biographical information, 203, 205, 206

Black slide, 245

Blocking, view of visuals, 225

Boardroom-style room arrangement, 162, 163, 258

Body, 51

Body language, 121, 135, 137
    And context, 135
    And questions, 178, 192, 193
    Exercise, 135
    Listeners' signals, 135

Bored audience
    Handling, 197

Boredom, 152

Brightness, of projector, 225

Browser, Internet, 277, 279, 280

Build-up slide, 239, 241

Bullet chart, 142, 174, 219, 234, 235, 241, 242, 243, 278, 279
    And pointing, 168
    Stepwise display of, 224

Cables, 220, 221, 224, 226, 258, 268, 270
    Connecting, 256

Cartoon
    Use of, in visuals, 84

Change
    As tool for maintaining attention, 55

Chart options, 229, 232

Chart types, 70, 71, 92
    And best uses, 70, 71

Charts
    3-D, 219
    Ensuring readability of, 72
    Minimum text size in, 72

Chat message, in E-meeting, 275, 276

Civil tone, enforcing, 208, 211, 212

Clarity. *See* Articulation

Classroom-style table arrangement, 164, 165, 166

Clichés, in visuals, 85, 86

Clicking, mouse, 227, 228, 229, 230, 231, 241, 244

Clip art, electronic, 84, 85, 86, 236, 247, 248, 254

Close to audience. *See* Distance

Closing
    Conference session, 209, 215

Cluster bar chart, 78

Clutter, in visuals, 74, 76, 78, 79, 81

Coins, jingling, 135

Color scheme, 233, 234

Compatibility
    Of computer and projector resolution, 256

Computer. *See* Laptop computer

Conference, 165, 166

Connecting, computer and projector, 258, 259, 268

Connection. *See* Audience connection

Consistency
    Of slides, 227, 233, 242

Consonants
    Pronouncing clearly, 139, 140

Conversational style of delivery, 142, 145, 151, 153, 154, 155

Color in visuals, 87, 88, 89, 91, 219, 220, 221, 223
    Analogous scheme, 90
    And moods, 91
    Background, 221, 223
    Balanced palette, 88
    Complementary colors, 88
    Contrasting, 223
    Monochromatic scheme, 89
    Perfected Harmony, 90
    Primary colors, 88
    Psychology of colors, 91
    Restricting number of colors, 88
    Secondary colors, 88
    Triad Harmony, 91
    Using different shades of same color, 88, 223

Color scheme, 223

Color wheel, 87, 88, 89, 90, 91, 92

Complexity
    vs. simplicity of structure, 24

Compression, of sound files, 226

Conference, 203, 204, 205, 206, 207, 209, 215, 219, 221

Confused audience, 151, 152
    Handling, 197

Consistency, of visuals, 223

Corel Presentations, 228, 233, 234, 244
Coughing, interpretation of, 136
Credibility, 181
    And handling questions, 175
Criticism, 177
    And eye contact, 152
Cropping, image, 223, 236
Crossing arms, 136
    And questions, 178
Cross-referencing, in visuals, 74, 78
    Minimizing the problem through helpful
        delivery, 78

Data labels, 228, 230, 232, 243
Data series, in chart, 229, 230, 231, 232
Data sheet, of chart, 228, 229, 230
Defensiveness, 178
Delivery
    Conversational style, 142
    Low-key, 144
    vs. material and value, 4
Demonstration
    As attention getter, 43
Demonstration objects, 162, 170, 171
    As attention getter, 43
    Avoiding distraction when using, 70
    Showing vs. passing around, 171
Details, 175, 176, 178, 180, 181, 183, 185,
    192
    Avoiding unnecessary or overly complex,
        53
    Supporting, 220, 223
Digital camera, 224
Digressions, 176, 184
    Anticipating, 176
Dimming, lights, 220, 267
Disagreement, and eye contact, 152
Disapproval
    And eye contact, 152
    Expressing, 135
Discomfort. *See* Nervousness
Discussion, 175, 176, 177, 183, 187, 192,
    203, 207, 208, 209, 210, 211, 215
    Controlling, 175
    Dominating, 203, 208
    Postponing, 177
    Reviving stalled, 210
    Stimulating, 175
"Display Properties" menu, in Windows,
    260, 261

Distance
    Of projector from screen, 257
    Of speaker to audience, 121, 122
Distracting verbal habits, 139
Distraction, 134, 161, 166, 167, 170, 240,
    241
    And visual, 240, 245
Dominating. *See* Discussion, dominating
Drawing
    Engineering, 223
    Graphic images, 233, 236, 238
    On projected slide, 219, 224, 256, 272
    On transparency, 225
Duct tape, 259, 268

Editing, chart, 228, 229, 230, 236, 238, 239,
    243
Electronic meeting, 275
E-meeting. *See* Electronic meeting
Electronic slide show, 220, 223, 224, 227,
    245, 256, 257, 262, 263, 264, 265, 266,
    267, 273, 278, 279, 280
Embedded presentation, 244, 245, 256, 262,
    264, 266, 273, 277, 278, 280
    Exiting, 256
    Skipping, 256
Emotions, and voice, 139, 142-145
Energy, and body language, 123-124, 126-
    129
Engineering drawing, 223
ENTER key, 263-266
Enthusiasm, 139, 142, 167, 170
    Lack of, 124
Equipment, 219, 220, 222, 223, 224, 225,
    245, 255, 258, 259, 267, 268
    Problems with, anticipating, 101
    Problems with, handling, 195
    Problems with, in conference, 208
    Setup, 161
ESC key
    Exiting slide show via, 256, 264, 266
Exiting
    From embedded application, 266
    Slide show, 256
Expression, facial, 178
Extension cord, 259, 268
Eye contact, 121, 136, 151-155
    And distance from audience, 122
    And questions, 178, 182, 188, 192, 193
    And visuals, 163, 167, 168
    Faking, 152

Eye contatc, *ctd.*
  Shifting, 152
  Straight vs. sideways, 153, 154
Eyebrows, 135, 136, 178, 192
Eyeglasses. *See* glasses
Examples
  And preparing for questions, 175
  As tool for engaging audience, 56, 57

F1 key, 264, 266, 271
Far away. *See* Distance
Fear
  And eye contact, 152, 153
Feedback
  And eye contact, 152
  From colleagues, 175
Feet
  And athletic stance, 125
  Crossing, 126
Fidgeting, 124, 178
File conversion, 277
Filler words, avoiding, 142
Flip chart, 115, 170
  Switching to, 196
Flow diagram, 168, 174
Focused question, 210, 211
Focusing, projector, 220
Follow-up, written, 196
Formatting, slide, 227, 231
Freezing, of program, 270

Gestures, 125, 126, 127, 128, 129, 130, 131, 133, 134, 135, 137, 138
  And action verbs, 131
  And contrast words, 132
  And direction & limit words, 132
  And "good/bad" adjectives, 132
  And pronouns *I, we, you,* etc., 132
  And quantity or count words, 132
  For abstract concepts, 133
  For processes, 133
  For systems, 134
  Practicing, 130
  Repetitive, 135
  Whole-body, 128
Glasses, 178
  Distractions caused by, 135
Graphics, 233, 234, 242
Grid, 227, 228, 229, 230, 231, 236
  And clutter in visuals, 74, 76

Grinning, 178, 192
  Interpretations of, 135
Grouping, parts of graphic, 236, 239, 242, 243, 279

Handouts, 97, 103, 105
  And preparing for questions, 175
  Avoiding distraction when using, 70
  Uses of, 103
  When to distribute, 103
Hands, 127, 128, 129, 130, 131, 132, 133, 136, 178, 192
  And athletic stance, 125
  In pockets, 129
  Wringing, 128, 129
Header, of slide, 223
Help menu, key, 264, 266
Help menu, software, 271, 278, 280
Hidden slide, 221, 227, 239, 243, 244, 256, 258, 262, 264, 265, 273
  Exiting, from series of, 256
  Skipping, 256
html file, 279
Humor
  In correcting mistakes, 204
  In moderating questions, 212
  In visuals, 84, 239
Hyperlink, 277

Image, projected, 171
Image problems, 259
Image size, 257, 258
Impersonal style, 146
Impromptu talks, 179, 199
  Structured approach to, 199
Inconsistency
  Of voice and message, 145
Interaction with audience, 176, 203, 204, 207
  And eye contact, 152
  Using transparencies for, 170
Internet, 275, 276, 277, 278, 279, 280
Interruptions, 176, 177, 184, 192
  Handling, 199
  Prompted by falling pitch, 145
Introducing speakers, 204, 206, 209
Introduction, 27, 28, 35, 44, 46, 47, 49, 55
  Four functions of, 27
  Two-minute time limit for, 28

Joke
As attention getter, 44
Jumping, to slide, in electronic slide show, 258, 264, 278

Keyboard, 256, 258, 262, 263, 266
Key words, in notes, 157
Keystone effect, of projectors, 172, 268, 269

Labeling, curves, 223
Labeling, lines in charts, 74, 77, 78, 79, 86
Limits of, 78
Labels, for data points in chart, 227, 230
Language, 139, 145, 146, 147, 149
Bureaucratic, 146
Flowery, 146
Formal, 146
Impersonal style, 146
Passive voice, 146
Technical, 146
Laptop computer, 161, 162, 219, 220, 221, 223, 224, 225, 226, 255, 256, 258, 259, 260, 261, 262, 263, 267, 268, 269, 270, 271, 272, 273
Laser pointer, 219
Layout of visuals, 82, 83, 233, 243
LCD projector, 219, 220, 221, 222, 223, 224, 225
Learning styles, 147
And variety of material, 55, 56, 57, 64
Lecture, vs. interaction, 207
Legend, 227, 228, 229, 230, 231, 243
Avoiding when possible, 74, 76, 77, 78, 79
Lens cap, 269, 270
Lighting, 255
Adjusting, 115
Line chart, 74, 76, 88, 92, 221, 227, 228, 229, 243
Line markers, 74, 76, 227
Line of terror, 121, 122
As obstacle to connection, 121
Crossing, 121
Line styles, in charts, 74, 230, 231, 232
Linking, graphic to presentation file, 278, 279
Listening, 178, 179, 192
Lotus Freelance, 233, 234, 235, 244, 246, 249, 252
Low-key delivery style, 144

Main message
And content templates, 234
First, 51
In the Introduction, 27, 28, 34-36, 39, 43-49, 53
Keeping positive, 114
Pseudo message, vs. complete message in the Introduction, 45, 47
Masking tape, 172, 173
Meeting Minder, in PowerPoint, 266
Memorable visuals, producing, 84
Memorization
vs. conversational style, 146
vs. speaking from notes, 101
Menu, in software, 227, 228, 229, 230, 231, 232, 233, 236, 237, 243, 244, 245, 260, 261, 262, 263, 264, 266, 270, 271, 277, 278, 279, 280
Message, 269, 271, 272
And audience questions, 175
Enthusiasm for, 170
Focusing on, in handling surprises, 195
Focusing on, to beat stage fright, 118
vs. topic, 51
mht file. See Web archive file
Microphone, 219, 280, 281
Mistake, simulating, in practice, 257
Moderator, 115, 203, 204, 205, 211, 212, 215
Monopolizing the discussion
Preventing, 176
Stopping people from, 184
Monotony
Of content, 53
Of gestures, 129
Of speed, 142
Of voice, 142, 143, 145
Mouse, computer, 256, 261, 263, 264, 266, 270, 272
Movement
And eye contact, 123
Reasons for, 123
Senseless, 123
To keep visuals visible, 123
Movie, 220, 245, 246
Moving, 236, 241, 249
And questions, 178
Into audience, 121, 128, 162
Multimedia, 219, 222-224, 255, 276, 277
"Mute" setting, of computer, 271
Checking, 262

Narrated presentations, 246, 279, 280
Nervous energy
    Expressions of, 124
Nervousness, 152
    And pause, 142
    Showing with hands, 130
NetMeeting program, Microsoft, 275
Nontechnical audience, 223
Notes, 97, 98, 99, 100, 101, 103, 104, 105,
    121, 128, 129, 157, 158, 159, 160
    And audience connection, 97
    And eye contact, 152, 156
    And visuals, 162, 163, 168, 169
    Common questions about, 99
    Content of, 98
    Index cards for, 97, 98, 100
    Keeping short, 98
    Key words vs. sentences, 157, 159
    Moderator's, 209
    On transparency frames, 100
    Parking, 157, 158, 160
    Practicing from, 97
    Recording, in slide show, 256
    Right type, 97
    Using key words in, 97
    Visuals as, 98
    vs. memorizing, 101
    vs. written-out speeches, 99
    Weaning yourself from, 97, 99
Numbers, 141, 142, 146
    To support answers, 175

Object, embedded in slide, 244, 245
Objections, by audience, 175, 192
On-line meeting. See Electronic meeting
On-line meeting service, 277
Outline, presentation, 235
Overhead projector, 171
    Limitations of, 171
    vs. computer slide shows, 171, 174
    Setting up, 115
Overview
    Of conference session, 206, 207, 208, 215
Overview presentation
    Of process, area, or discipline, 50

Panelists, 203, 206
Passive voice, 146
Pause, 142, 147, 149, 179, 181
Pen tool, software, 256, 264, 266

Personal style of delivery, 151
Persuasion, and notes, 158
Photograph, 222, 223, 236
    vs. demo object, 171
Pie chart, 221, 227, 254
Pitch, 139, 145, 149
Plan of presentation, in the Introduction, 27,
    36, 37, 39, 44, 46, 47, 48, 176
Poems
    As voice practice, 143
Pointer, 170
    Fiddling with, 170
Pointer tool, software, 256, 264, 266
Posture, 182
Power, electric, 255, 259, 260, 261, 262,
    263, 268, 270, 271
PowerPoint, 228, 233, 234, 235, 236, 243,
    244, 245, 251, 252, 263, 264, 265, 266,
    271, 277
Power saving mode
    Deactivating, 260
Power strip, 259
Practicing, 222, 223, 225, 243, 244, 245,
    246, 255, 257, 258, 260, 262, 263, 264,
    266, 267, 268, 270, 271, 272, 273
    From notes, 98, 99
Preparation, 203, 204, 205, 209
    For questions, 175, 179, 181, 186, 191
Presentation format
    Interactive vs. formal, 8
"Presentation mode," of computer's power-
    management program, 261
Presentation openers, exercise, 54
Presentation plan
    In the introduction, 46
    Supporting visual for, 47
Presentation problems
    Audience resistance, 103
    Time shortened, 103
Presentation purpose. See purpose of
    presentation
Presentation room
    Arranging for, 102
Presentation software, 222, 223, 224, 225,
    227, 228, 239, 243, 245, 250, 251
Presentation structure, 23, 24, 25
    Example, 58
    Need for simplicity of, 51
    Universal, 23
Printer, color, 222
Project update, presentation, 52, 144

Projector, 161, 162, 163, 164, 165, 166, 167, 170, 173, 219, 220, 221, 223, 224, 225, 226, 255, 256, 257, 258, 259, 260, 262, 267, 268, 269, 270, 271, 272, 273
  Beam, 161, 162, 163, 165, 166
  Bulb, 270
    Burned-out, 195
  Brightness, 225
  Contrast, 269
  Focus, 255
  Focusing, 269
  Position, 257, 268
  Sound, 271
  Standby button, 271
  Sync, adjusting, 271
  Table for, 219, 220
  Tracking, adjusting, 271
Pronunciation, 140
Props, 162
Purpose of presentation, 109, 272

Question
  As attention getter, 38
  Qestion-and-answer rules, 176, 177, 183, 185, 187, 192, 208
  Question-and-answer session, 175, 176, 177, 185, 206, 207, 211, 245
    Closing, 185
    Format, 176
    To bridge technical problem, 270
Questioning skills
  Moderator's, 204
Questions, 203, 204, 206, 207, 208, 209, 210, 212, 214, 215
  Acknowledging, 181
  Closed, vs. open or focused, 210, 211
  Complex, 176, 183, 184, 185, 193
  Cutting off, 184
  Cutting short, 177
  Encouraging, 203
  Focused, 208
  Focused, vs. open or closed, 210
  Handling uncivilized, in conference, 208
  Hearing, 203, 208
  Holding or postponing, 176
  Hostile, 178, 185, 186, 187, 193, 212
  Inviting, 177
  Inviting at end of summary, 66
  Lengthy, 176, 183
  Not knowing answer to, 181
  Off-track, 212

Questions, *ctd.*
  Open, vs. closed or focused, 210, 211
  Persistent, 184, 187, 193, 212
  Preparing for, 8, 175
  Postponing, 183, 184, 192
  Repetitive, 176
  Rephrasing, 181, 208, 212
  Rephrasing hostile, 179, 186, 191
  Rephrasing hostile, exercise, 188
  Timing for, 176, 177, 179, 192
  Tough, 175, 186, 188, 192
  Uncivil, 209, 211
  vs. statements, 146

Quote, 146

RAMP formula for introduction, 27, 28, 29, 33, 35, 47, 51, 60
Rapport builder in Introduction, 29, 31, 32
Recovering, from mistakes, 257
Rehearsing, 97, 243, 257
  And checking timing, 97
Remote control, 219, 220, 221, 222, 224, 225, 245, 256, 258, 262, 263, 266, 267, 269, 270, 271, 272
Repetition, 52
  Need for, 24
Rephrasing questions, 212
Resizing, image, 236, 245
Resolution
  Of computer or projector, 219, 224, 225, 260, 261, 267, 270, 273
  Video, of computer, 256
Respect for audience, 115
Responsibility
  Moderator taking, 204
Rocking
  vs. athletic stance, 125
Room, 219, 220, 222, 225, 255, 257, 258, 267, 268
Room setup, 115
  Classroom style, 115
Rules
  Setting, in conference session, 204
  Time-keeping, in conference, 207
Rushing
  In answering questions, 179, 186

Safety talks, 12
Sarcasm, 187
Scanner, 223, 224

Screen, projection, 161, 162, 163, 164, 165, 166, 167, 168, 169, 170, 171, 172, 173, 174, 219, 220, 221, 225, 256, 257, 258, 259, 260, 261, 262, 264, 265, 266, 268, 269, 270, 271, 272, 273
   Blank, 245, 256, 260, 262, 268, 271, 272
   Facing, 169
   Position, 257
   Setting up, 257
   Table-top, 258
   Tilt, improvising, 268
Screen saver, computer, 260, 261, 268, 271
   Deactivating, 260
Screen, tilt. See Tilt screen
Selecting, image parts, 228, 229, 231, 232, 233, 236, 237, 238, 240, 243, 250
Self-assessment of presentation skills, exercise, 21
Sentence structure, 145, 146, 149
Seriousness, interpreted as unfriendliness or negativity, 116
Setup, 119, 161, 162, 163, 164, 165, 166, 167, 170, 219, 221, 225, 255, 257, 258, 267, 268, 273
   Adjusting, in conference, 114
   And conference, 208
   Checking, 114
   Checklist, 114
   Examples of mistakes, 165
Shadows, avoiding, 165, 167, 170
Shuffling feet
   vs. athletic stance, 125
Simplification
   vs. overly complex details, 53
Size, of image. See Image size
Skepticism, 151
   Expressing, 135
"Sleep" mode, of computer, 261
Sleepers, handling, 198
Slide
   Jumping to, in electronic slide show, 256
Slide master, 233, 234
Slides, 227, 228, 233, 234, 237, 239, 240, 241, 242, 244, 245, 247, 248
   Black, 256, 264, 266
   Build-up, 222
   Changing, 162, 163, 165, 166, 167, 174, 224, 256
   Templates, 227, 234, 235
Slide show. See Electronic slide show

Slouching, 178
   vs. athletic stance, 125
Smiling, 115, 116, 117
   And questions, 178, 182, 186, 192
Snap-to, grid
   Overriding, 236
Software, presentation, 227, 230, 232, 233, 234, 245, 249, 256, 262, 263, 264, 265, 266. Also see Presentation software
Sound. See Audio
Sound file, 226, 280
Sound, of projector, adjusting, 262
Speed, 139, 142, 149
Spreadsheet, 245
Stage fright, 118
   Beating by focusing on audience and message, 118
   Cure for, 118
Stance. See athletic stance
Starting strongly
   Obstacles to, 47, 48, 49, 50
Statistic
   As attention getter, 41
Stepwise revelation, 170, 174
"Stream of consciousness" organization
   vs. message first, 52
Subconscious
   And gestures, 128
Summarizing, reasons for, 65
Summarizing skills, of moderator, 204
Summary, 65, 66, 67, 68
   Examples, 66
   Final thought or call to action, 65
   How to construct, 65
   Of conference session, 204, 206, 209, 215
   Time limit for, 65, 67
   Words to use in, 65
Surprises, handling, 186, 195
Suspense
   vs. main message first, 50

Talking, interruptive, during presentation, 198
Technical presentations, 134, 142, 143, 176
Template, for slide, 233, 235, 243
Tension, 124
Testing, 225, 255, 267, 278, 280, 281
   Slide show, 242, 247, 248
"That's a good question"
   Avoiding overuse of, 179

Theme, of conference session, 203, 204, 205, 206, 207, 208, 215
Tilt screen, 171, 172
Time, for presentation
  Handling shortening of, 196
Time limit, 203
  Enforcing, 209, 215
Timing
  Checking, 257
Title slide, 31
  vs. rapport builder, 31
Title, of chart, 230, 235
  As aid in delivery, 148
Topic
  Announced wrongly, 204
  vs. message, 51
Touch-Turn-Talk formula for handling
  visuals, 167, 168
Transition, slide, 222, 224, 225, 239, 240, 277, 278, 280
Transition words, 148, 149
Transitions, 158
  And visuals, 168
  Summaries in, 52
Transparencies, 161, 162, 163, 164, 165, 166, 173, 220, 221, 222, 223, 224, 225, 227, 239, 240, 241, 243, 267, 268, 269
  Backup, 221, 222, 223, 225
  Covering up, 170
  Curling, 171, 173
  Pointing at, 170
  Sliding or falling off, 171, 173, 174
  Writing on, 170
Troubleshooting, 255, 257, 259, 260, 265, 267, 273
Tuning out, 128, 133, 166
  Gestures preventing, 128, 133

U-shaped room, 161, 162, 163, 164
"Uhm", 187
  Avoiding, 142, 147
Ungrouping, chart or graphic, 228, 230, 232, 234, 236, 237, 242, 243, 279
Uploading, presentation to Internet, 278, 280
Upper body
  And energy, 126, 128, 129
  And gestures, 126, 127, 128, 138
USB port, computer, 224, 256
U-shaped room arrangement, 258

Variety
  In the presentation body, 54
  Of speed, 142
  Of volume, 142
VCR, 219, 220, 224-226, 258, 268, 270
Verbal habits, distracting, 147
VGA port, computer, 256, 258ff, 268, 273
Video, 222-226, 239, 245ff, 250, 256, 258-260, 266, 268, 270, 272ff, 275, 277-279, 281
  Activating, 256
Video conference, vs. E-meeting, 275
Video editing hardware, 224
Video file, 226
Video frame grabber, 223, 224
Video out port, computer, 256, 259, 268, 273
  Activating, 256, 260
Videotape, of presentation, 143
Videotaping, 223, 245
Visual, 221, 222, 224, 227, 243
  As attention getter, 39
  Black-and-white, 220, 222, 223
  Clutter, avoiding, 227
  Type size, 227
  Unreadable, 227
Visuals, 161, 162, 163, 164, 167, 168, 169, 170, 173, 174
  And eye contact, 152
  And notes, 157, 158, 159, 160
  And preparing for questions, 175
  Avoiding clutter in, 74
  Blocking view of, 163, 172, 174
  Considering purpose of, 69
  Creating memorable, 69, 81, 87
  Effective use of color in, 74, 87-92
  Ensuring easy processing of, 73
  How to produce memorable, 84
  Humor in, 84
  Key attributes, 69
  Main purposes, 69
  Optimum number, 69
  Symbolic images in, 82, 85
  Three-Second Rule for, 73, 74, 76, 79, 80
Voice, 139, 142, 144, 146, 149
  Volume, 139, 142, 149
  Volume, and questions, 182
Volume. *See* Voice, volume
Volume, of projector, adjusting, 262, 271

Web. *See* Internet
Web archive file, 279, 280
Web meeting. *See* Electronic meeting
Web page, 277, 278, 279
Web presentation, 277-281
Weight, distributing, 126
   And athletic stance, 125
"Well", 180, 185, 187

Whisper
   As articulation exercise, 140
Whiteboard, in E-meeting, 275
Wizards, software, 234
Word charts, 79, 241
Word choice, 139, 144-149

Zoom control, of projector, 257, 269